D0408510

What the Experts Are Saying About . . .
THE MUTUAL FUND MASTERS

66*Bill Griffeth's* The Mutual Fund Masters *is a true delight and an invaluable addition to any investor's library. There is no wiser or surer way to become a successful investor than to learn from the masters themselves. As the diversity of styles and philosophies represented in this book demonstrates, there are many different ways to win in the investment markets. The trick is to match properly the right approach to the right investor. By learning the disciplines that have worked for these masters, individual investors may better forge their own path to investment success.*99

Don Phillips, Publisher
Morningstar Mutual Funds

66*Bill Griffeth's* The Mutual Fund Masters *should be required reading for all those who serve mutual fund shareholders. He has caught the essence of key fund personalities. His color gives depth to our numbers.*99

A. Michael Lipper, CFA, President
Lipper Analytical Services, Inc.

66*Bill Griffeth has assembled a collection of mutual fund experts that may well be unprecedented in any one book. The all-time top mutual fund masters share their collective wisdom and experience in enlivening and enlightening fashion.*99

Carl Surran, Editor
Personal Investing News

66*Although their individual strategies cover the full spectrum of investing philosophies, the all-stars gathered in this book share a common talent for making money. Bill Griffeth's skillful probing unveils the secrets to their investing success. Whether you're a novice investor or an old pro, you'll find scores of valuable insights in this work.*99

Gordon T. Anderson, Editor
Individual Investor magazine

"Bill Griffeth, an excellent financial commentator for CNBC, has delivered an exceptional book on mutual fund investing. The Mutual Fund Masters is entertaining and is a must read for individuals who own or are contemplating the purchase of mutual funds.**"**

> **Stephen Leeb, Ph.D.**, President
> *Leeb Investment Advisors* and
> Editor, *Personal Finance*

"In a financial world filled with puffery, snake oil and sinkholes, Bill Griffeth has distilled some wisdom from true modern alchemists.**"**

> **John F. Wasik**, Senior Editor, *Consumers Digest*
> and author of *The Investment Club Book*

"These are most astute 'market master' interviews since Jack Schwager's The New Market Wizards. *Even people who invest in stocks directly will find* The Mutual Fund Masters *enlightening.***"**

> **Michael Pellecchia**
> Syndicated Business Book Columnist

"Anyone interested in learning how top mutual fund managers win on Wall Street should read The Mutual Fund Masters. *By questioning some of the most successful portfolio managers of the modern era, Bill Griffeth provides readers with valuable insight into the investing process.***"**

> **James Picerno**, Associate Editor
> *Investment Advisor* magazine

"Bill Griffeth's interviews are a symposium on investing. They're also an entertaining personal look at the best investors—and money managers— ever.**"**

> **Tom Siedell**, Senior Editor
> *Your Money*

Bill Griffeth Interviews

THE MUTUAL FUND MASTERS

A Revealing Look Into the Minds & Strategies
of Wall Street's Best & Brightest

Bill Griffeth

Host of *CNBC's Mutual Fund Investor* and
Author of *10 Steps to Financial Prosperity*

PROBUS
PUBLISHING

Chicago, Illinois
Cambridge, England

© 1995, William C. Griffeth

ALL RIGHTS RESERVED. No part of this publication may be reproduced, stored in a retrieval system, or transmitted, in any form or by any means, electronic, mechanical, photocopying, recording, or otherwise, without the prior written permission of the publisher and the author.

This publication is designed to provide accurate and authoritative information in regard to the subject matter covered. It is sold with the understanding that the author and the publisher are not engaged in rendering legal, accounting, or other professional advice.

Authorization to photocopy items for internal or personal use, or the internal or personal use of specific clients, is granted by PROBUS PUBLISHING COMPANY, provided that the U.S. $7.00 per page fee is paid directly to Copyright Clearance Center, 222 Rosewood Drive, Danvers, MA 01923, USA; Phone: 1-508-750 8400. For those organizations that have been granted a photocopy license by CCC, a separate system of payment has been arranged. The fee code for users of the Transactional Reporting Service is 1-55738-582-3/94/$00.00+$7.00.

ISBN 1-55738-582-3

Printed in the United States of America

RRD

1   2   3   4   5   6   7   8   9   10

ZGraphics

Probus books are available at quantity discounts when purchased for business, educational, or sales promotional use. For more information, please call the Director, Corporate/ Institutional Sales at (800) 998-4644, or write:

Director Corporate/Institutional Sales
Probus Publishing Company
1925 N. Clybourn Avenue
Chicago, IL 60614

PHONE (800) 998-4644   FAX (312) 868-6250

I dedicate this book to mutual fund shareholders everywhere. I hope it encourages them to learn more about how their money is being managed, and by whom.

TABLE OF CONTENTS

ACKNOWLEDGMENTS

F irst of all, I have to acknowledge that this book was my publisher's idea. It was a terrific idea, and I hope I did it justice.

Second, I have to comment on how this book was put together. I recorded each interview onto audiocassette. I then sent each cassette to the publisher, and the publisher transcribed each interview onto a computer disk. I then edited each interview on my computer and sent the disk back to the publisher. Even though we printed copies of each chapter on paper, if we had chosen to, this could have been a completely paperless process. I am not the most computer-literate person on the face of the earth (yet), so I was impressed with the whole procedure, and I thank the talented staff people at Probus Publishing for their encouragement and patience. And I must also thank two of my CNBC colleagues, coordinating producer Alex Crippen and my co-anchor Neil Cavuto, both of whom are light years ahead of me when it comes to computers. They both provided valuable assistance and advice along the way.

I must thank the staff people who work for the fund managers profiled in this book for providing whatever information I needed and for finding the tiny holes in their boss's schedules necessary for our interviews. I especially want to thank John Reilly at MFS for all the historical data and photos he provided for chapter one, Betty Williams in Grace Pineda's office at Merrill Lynch Asset Management for her extra help, Robin Tyce at Fidelity for finding time for me in Peter Lynch's schedule, and most especially Zita Ng at the Templeton office in Singapore for wedging me into Mark Mobius's insanely hectic life.

I also must thank the very talented producer of CNBC's "Mutual Fund Investor," Lidj Lewis, for his support, researcher/booker Berlinda Garnett for cheerfully finding the files I needed, and summer intern

Gerelyn Terzo for handling some important correspondence for me. Thanks also to Jason Zweig of *Forbes* magazine for his helpful suggestions.

I also want to thank my wife, Cindy, and our children, Chad and Carlee, for their love and understanding while this book was in production. Tight deadlines caused me to edit several chapters on my notebook computer during our "vacations" on the beaches of Massachusetts and North Carolina and during plane rides to and from Los Angeles.

Finally, I must thank the Mutual Fund Masters themselves for taking time out of their incredibly busy schedules to talk to me. Each of them brought enthusiasm and creativity to the interviews, and for that I am grateful.

INTRODUCTION

*I*f you could pick up the phone and talk directly to the people who manage your mutual funds, what would you ask them?

That's what this book is about. It is a series of interviews I conducted in the summer of 1994 with 20 of the best known and/or most successful fund managers in the country. And during the interviews, I tried to ask the questions I thought you would want answers to.

You will find very few specific buy or sell recommendations here, because I wanted the interviews to be timeless conversations about how these people do what they do and about what makes them tick.

But getting to know a fund's manager is only part of the homework you need to do before you purchase shares in any mutual fund. Before we talk about who the Mutual Fund Masters are, and how I chose the people profiled in this book, let's briefly go over the steps you must take before you invest in a mutual fund.

How to Choose a Mutual Fund

Before you invest in a mutual fund, you should have a pretty thorough understanding of three things:

1) Yourself,

2) The mutual fund you have your eye on, and

3) The person who manages that fund.

1) UNDERSTANDING YOURSELF

Before you invest in a mutual fund (or any investment, for that matter) you need to understand why you are investing. That means understanding:

- *Your investment goals,*
- *Your investment objectives,*
- *Your risk tolerance, and*
- *Your time horizon.*

Your Investment Goals: Why are you investing your money? Answering that question will help you decide how and where to invest.

Are your goals short term in nature? In other words, are you putting away money in order to buy a house in a few years? If so, you probably don't want to take too much risk. A money market mutual fund, for example, which invests in safe, low-risk Treasury securities might be appropriate.

What about your long-term goals, like retirement or your child's college education? In order to meet those goals, you would probably be wise to look for equity mutual funds. If you still have 10 to 20 years to go, you might consider aggressive growth funds. If your time horizon is something like 5 to 10 years, you might think about more conservative growth and income, or balanced funds, which invest in both stocks and bonds.

Your Investment Objectives: What do you want the money you're investing to do for you? Do you, for example, simply want it to continue to grow over time, or do you want it to provide you with some income right now? If you want growth, look for growth or capital appreciation funds. If you want income, look for funds in that category.

Your Risk Tolerance: Understanding your level of risk tolerance is very important. If you can't sleep at night because you're worried about your investments, you may have taken on too much risk. On the other hand, if your investments haven't grown fast enough over time to suit you, you may not have taken on enough risk.

In my first book, *Ten Steps To Financial Prosperity*, I divided risk takers into three categories: 1) Speculators, who fully understand the nature of investment risk and are willing to assume as much as possible, 2) Investors, who understand risk and are willing to take on a modest amount, and 3) Savers, who understand what risk is all about but would just as soon avoid it as much as possible.

You must also understand the potential consequences of your own risk tolerance. If you're a speculator, for example, your investments have the potential for either better than average returns or worse than average losses. On the other hand, if you're a Saver, your money may be safer, but chances are it will not grow as fast as a Speculator's or an Investor's.

Your Time Horizon: How long do you have before you will actually need the money you are investing? The answer will tell you how much patience to exercise with your investments. If, for example, you have a 10- or 20-year time horizon, you shouldn't worry too much about how your investments are performing in years one or two (or perhaps even in years five or six!). On the other hand, if you will need the money soon, pay close attention.

2) UNDERSTANDING THE MUTUAL FUND

Before you invest in a mutual fund, you should first learn all you can about:

- *Its investment objective,*
- *Its past performance,*
- *Its fee schedule, and*
- *Its shareholder services.*

The Fund's Investment Objective: What kind of mutual fund is it? Aggressive Growth? Growth and Income? Capital Appreciation? Capital Preservation? Mutual fund services like Morningstar or Lipper Analytical assign a category to each fund to help you better understand its objective.

You should also understand how a fund tries to meet its objective. Does it invest only in stocks, only in bonds, or in a combination of both? What percentage does it invest in foreign securities? Does it use futures or options contracts to hedge or speculate? And does it have a high or low turnover? In other words, does it frequently buy and sell securities, or does it tend to employ more of a buy and hold strategy?

It's also a good idea to understand how much risk a fund assumes. That is sometimes difficult to quantify, but Morningstar and Lipper try to do that for you. Both services, by the way, are available in public libraries.

The Fund's Past Performance: Even though a fund's past performance doesn't guarantee its future performance, it is still a good idea to find out what its track record is. If the fund is old enough, find out, for example, how it performs when the market is going up and when it is going down. Sometimes funds that tend to do very well when the market is going up also do poorly when it is going down. Conversely, a fund that provides only average returns in up markets sometimes will not lose as much as other funds in down markets.

The Fund's Fee Schedule: How much are you going to pay for a fund's services? And how will you pay for it?

If you purchase shares in a fund through a broker, chances are you will pay a commission, also known as a load, up front.

No-load funds don't charge commissions when you purchase shares, but that doesn't mean you'll get a free ride. All funds charge periodic management fees, and some charge a commission when you sell your shares. That is known as a Contingent Deferred Sales Charge. Often, if you hold your shares long enough (say, up to eight years) you won't be charged anything when you sell.

Some funds also charge what is known in the business as a 12(b)1 fee. Fund companies use that to pay for distribution and/or marketing costs.

The Fund's Shareholder Services: Once you have purchased shares in a fund, what kind of services does it provide? Does it, for example, allow you to continue to invest by automatically deducting money from your bank account? Does it allow you to automatically reinvest any dividends? If your fund is part of a family of funds, can you switch money from one fund to another over the telephone without being charged a fee? And if you're invested in a money market fund, does it offer check writing privileges? (If it does, make sure the fund maintains a net asset value, or price per share, of $1. If it doesn't, and the NAV fluctuates, you could be assessed a capital gains tax on every check you write!)

3) UNDERSTANDING THE FUND MANAGER

This is the toughest part of the whole process of investing in a mutual fund, because the reality is that government and industry regulators only require fund companies to publicly disclose the name of a fund's manager.

But a shareholder should know more. You should know the manager's:

- *Background,*
- *Experience,*
- *Investment philosophy and methodology, and*
- *Investment track record.*

Background: What is the manager's educational background? Are his degrees in economics or finance, or something else? (Be careful with this, though. One of the most successful managers profiled in this book has a bachelor's degree in secondary education and no formal training in security analysis.)

Experience: How long has the manager been managing money? And what did she do before that? And did that past experience enhance her current position? For example, if someone is managing a fund that invests money in small foreign countries, has she visited those countries? Can she speak the language? Or if someone is investing in municipal bonds, does she have prior experience working for a municipality?

Philosophy and Methodology: Try to find managers who invest money the way you would. As you will see in this book, there are a vast number of ways to invest money.

How does your manager invest money? Does he take a so-called top down approach and start with big-picture themes? Or does he take a bottom up approach and build a portfolio one stock at a time? Is he a growth investor looking for companies with good earnings momentum? Or is he a value investor looking for cheaply priced companies everyone else has overlooked?

Track Record: You can forget education, experience, even philosophy. The bottom line is: does the manager deliver the goods? Are her funds consistently top performers? And how do they perform in up markets and down markets?

Some professionals in the mutual fund industry argue that you don't need to know as much about a fund manager who works for a big fund company like Fidelity or Vanguard or T. Rowe Price, because those companies have stringent hiring practices. That may be true, but I think you should still find out as much about a manager as you can. I'm not all that comfortable having a total stranger managing my money.

It's easy finding information on a high-profile manager who frequently talks to the media. But it is obviously more difficult if your fund manager is a recluse. And if that is the case, call the fund company and ask them to send you a copy of your manager's biography. If they are reluctant to do it, then you have to decide whether or not you're comfortable staying with the fund.

Who Are the Mutual Fund Masters?

When I was a junior in college, for a period of about two weeks I wanted to be a movie critic. Not the kind who awards motion pictures a thumbs up or five stars. I wanted to be a real critic in the tradition of James Agee or Pauline Kael. (Then I found out how much money real movie critics make, and I decided I wanted to be the next Tom Snyder. But that's another story.)

It was during my movie critic period that I studied the *auteur theory*, which was first developed by French movie critics in the late 1950s. I won't bore you with all the minutiae, but the premise was that certain directors who had distinctive styles and visions were, in the final analysis, the authors of their movies, instead of the producers, the stars, or even the writers. Alfred Hitchcock, Frank Capra, and even Jerry Lewis (who was the French critics' favorite) are good examples of famous motion picture *auteurs*. (Woody Allen or Oliver Stone—who directed movies like *Platoon* and *JFK*—are more recent examples.)

This book is about mutual fund *auteurs* who do more than just oversee a portfolio of stocks and bonds. As Bill Berger of the Berger Funds told me, "All of us who manage money are reading the same music, it's just that some of us conduct the orchestra differently. There is a very fine line that separates the good conductor from all the directors of high school bands across the country who are just waving a baton." Indeed, when you understand that investing is more art than science, you realize how important a thoughtful, creative manager is to the long-term success of a mutual fund.

Mutual fund masters build cohesive portfolios that make sense. Some, like John Neff of the Vanguard/Windsor fund, build them stock by stock, while others, like Gary Shilling of the Thematic Investment Partners hedge fund, use sweeping sociological or economic themes to find profitable investments. All of them are constantly revising their portfolios, looking for new companies the way writers search for just the right word to express their meaning.

How did I choose the people profiled in this book? My criteria were quite simple. First, I wanted people who had at least ten years' experience in the finance business, although I should point out that not all of them had actually been managing money that long when I interviewed them for this book. Grace Pineda, for example, has only been managing emerging market funds since the late 1980s, but she has been travelling around the world visiting hundreds of companies for more than a decade. Today she manages the largest emerging markets fund in the U.S, the Merrill Lynch Developing Capital Markets Fund. But you will also meet Phil Carret who, in 1928, founded a small mutual fund that today is the cornerstone of the Pioneer Group of funds.

Second, I wanted people with better than average investment records. All fund managers measure their success against the performance of some index of stocks or bonds. All of the managers in this book have consistently beaten the indices. But that is not to suggest that none has ever had a dry spell. Actually, all but a few have experienced down years.

All of the people profiled in this book are highly intelligent, very competitive, and they all live, eat, and breathe investing.

And the fruits of their labors run the risk spectrum, from Jim Benham's safe Capital Preservation money market fund to Heiko Thieme's very risky (and very controversial) American Heritage Fund.

Some of them are pioneers. (The first interview, for example, is devoted to America's first open-end mutual fund and the men who created and developed it.) And some are legends. (The final conversation is with Peter Lynch.)

There are over 5,000 mutual funds in the U.S., and the odds are that not all of those funds will still be around in five or ten years. Some, for example, will go out of business during the next bear market, and others will be purchased by larger companies. Still others will fail because the people managing them were simply not cut out for the job. The aim of this book is to acquaint you with a small group of people who, for the most part, were born to be mutual fund managers.

But I want to make something very clear: I am not suggesting that these people are perfect. They are, after all, only human, and they make mistakes. And even though they all had better than average track records at the time I interviewed them, there is absolutely no guarantee that their investment success will continue. In fact, there is no guarantee that they will all still be in business five or ten years from now. Such is the nature of the markets.

My interviews with the people profiled in this book took place between June and September of 1994. During that period, the stock and bond markets had been disrupted by two things: 1) the Federal Reserve was in the process of raising short-term interest rates, and 2) a number of supposedly safe money market funds had to be bailed out because of the excessive use of risky derivatives (another word for things like futures and options contracts, which are used to either hedge a portfolio against excessive volatility or to enhance the portfolio's yield. Because they involve leverage, they are generally riskier than stocks and bonds). You will discover that both issues were very much on the minds of the mutual fund managers in this book.

Many of the managers also spoke out about the very strong growth the mutual fund industry had experienced in the early 1990s, when roughly $1 trillion poured into funds over a three-year period. Some of the managers were encouraged by it while others were concerned about it. Almost all of them voiced their opinions here.

My hope is that you will come away from *The Mutual Fund Masters* with a greater understanding of the investment process and the risks involved, and that you will find a way to fit that process into your life so that you can achieve a greater level of prosperity.

THE ORIGINAL
MUTUAL FUND MASTERS

O n March 21, 1924, the first open-end mutual fund in America
was offered to the public. The Massachusetts Investors
Trust, as it was called, was unique in the investment world
in four ways: First, at a time when most prudent investors
put their money in bonds, MIT chose to devote its portfolio
exclusively to common stocks. Second, it adopted a conservative
approach to investing in equities, unlike most of the more speculative
and highly leveraged closed-end trusts that met their doom in October
of 1929. Third, the fund chose to publicly disclose what was in its portfolio, which was unusual for the time. Now, of course, all funds must
by law disclose what they are invested in. Fourth, and perhaps most
important, MIT introduced the mutual fund world to the concept of
redeemable shares. Investors could view the fund the way they did a
deposit account at the bank.

Today, Massachusetts Financial Services (MFS, the restructured MIT) is a subsidiary of Sun Life Assurance Company of Canada.
In 1994 it managed more than $34 billion in assets in 49 different
mutual funds, including the original Massachusetts Investors Trust and
the Massachusetts Investors Growth Stock Fund.

This chapter is not about a single mutual fund master. It is
about four of them. Each of them pioneered concepts that helped build
MIT and shape the entire mutual fund industry.

1) L. Sherman Adams

Adams is arguably the father of the
modern mutual fund, but that is the
result of timing as much as anything.
There were actually a handful of
investment professionals in Boston
working on the redeemable share
concept at about the same time,
including Paul Cabot's State Street
Investment Corporation, which was
founded in the fall of 1924 and first
offered shares to the public in 1926. But
it was Sherman Adams, who along
with fellow stock broker Charles Learoyd and banker Ashton Carr, put

together a portfolio of 45 common stocks worth $50,000 and allowed shareholders to redeem their shares at will.

Prior to his death, Adams retired as Fund trustee in 1952, at the age of 65.

2) Merrill Griswold

Griswold was a partner in the law firm of Gaston, Snow, Saltonstall, Hunt & Rice when, in 1925, he was asked by MIT's trustees if he would like to invest any money in the fund. Griswold provided legal counsel to a number of private estates at the time, and he saw the new fund as a way to more efficiently invest his clients' money. So he put up an initial $50,000, and then in order to keep an eye on his stake he became a trustee.

But Griswold also saw the potential the redeemable share concept held for all investors. So he became more involved in the management of the fund, eventually becoming its full-time chairman in 1932.

Griswold oversaw the development of the entire mutual fund industry during the 1930s and 1940s. During that time, he made two major contributions: First, he helped win congressional approval of the so-called "conduit" tax treatment for all mutual funds. This kept investors from being taxed twice on their capital gains and income by requiring mutual funds to distribute all capital gains and income, thereby passing the original tax liability to shareholders. That rule, more than anything, made mutual funds more marketable for the industry and more desirable for small investors.

Griswold's second great contribution to the fund industry was in helping to draft the landmark Investment Company Act of 1940, the industry's self-governing body of regulations which are still in effect today. The trustees at MIT liked to boast that much of the Act was patterned after their own bylaws, including the requirement that all funds publicly disclose to shareholders what they are holding in their portfolios.

Merrill Griswold retired as chairman of MIT in 1954. He died in 1962 at the age of 75.

3) Dwight P. Robinson Jr.

Between the stock market crash of 1929 and 1932 when the market hit its lowest level to date, Massachusetts Investors Trust lost 83 percent of its value. Merrill Griswold knew that if the fund were to have a long-term future, it had to become a full-time operation. For eight years, the fund's trustees had met in each other's offices to decide which stocks should be bought and sold. But the fund didn't have an office of its own. So on January 1, 1932, MIT opened its own office on the ninth floor of 19 Congress Street in Boston. On that day, Griswold became the fund's full-time chairman, and Dwight Robinson became its first, and the industry's first, director of research. MIT was growing up.

Robinson was a quiet, methodical Harvard man who brought structure to MIT's investment style. Prior to 1932, mutual funds simply invested in brand name blue chip companies most people had heard of. This served two purposes: It provided a measure of stability to the portfolio, and it made it easier for the brokers selling the fund to convince potential shareholders to invest.

But under Robinson's leadership, the fund began to more carefully scrutinize the balance sheets of each of the companies it invested in. And eventually, Robinson had members of his growing research staff visit the management of each company and prepare standardized research reports for the fund's trustees.

Robinson succeeded Griswold as MIT's chairman in 1954. In 1959, Time magazine put him on its cover when it wrote about the burgeoning $14 billion mutual fund industry. At that time, MIT was the industry's largest fund with $1.5 billion in assets and 203,000 shareholders.

Time's profile of Robinson portrayed him as someone the public could trust their money with, "mild in manner, mellow in voice, retiring with all but his closest friends." At that time, he earned over $400,000 a year, but lived in a modest home and drove a four-year-old Oldsmobile.

As for his legendary methodical nature, Time wrote:

"Robinson runs his life on a prearranged schedule as exact as a balance sheet. In his 15 room stucco home in Brookline, he rises at precisely 7:05 each morning, hops onto his exercycle for a 15-minute ride. He breakfasts alone over the Boston Herald, drives himself to work. At 9:30 he enters MIT's modern offices on the 25th floor of Boston's John Hancock building, the city's highest . .

"All day Robinson pores over financial statements, reads market letters and industry reports, tries to keep a knowing eye on the management of dozens of corporations . . .

"Robinson is out of the office by 4:30, dines at 7 with his wife, a Boston girl (Mary Helen Gass) whom he married in 1943 at 43. The Robinson house is so well ordered—Mrs. Robinson keeps two maids—that guests may be asked in advance at what time they would like a drink."

Just the kind of guy you would want managing your money.

Robinson retired in 1965. He died in 1989 at the age of 89.

4) John L. Cooper

Cooper could be called the father of the modern growth stock fund. He was working for Dwight Robinson in MIT's research department when he was called upon in the early 1950s to do something with another fund the company had acquired in 1934. As Cooper tells it in the interview you are about to read, his job was to figure out exactly what a "growth stock" was and which ones to put in this other fund.

Cooper was elected a trustee at MIT in 1954, and he became president of the growth fund in 1965. In 1969, Cooper and then-chairman William Moses (who, by the way, replaced Sherman Adams as an MIT trustee when Adams retired in 1952) oversaw the modernization of the company when it was restructured into Massachusetts Financial Services (MFS). Cooper was named president of the new company, and he retired as company chairman in 1978.

Jack Cooper is a congenial man with a terrific sense of humor and a great memory. I called him at his summer home in Rhode Island, and we talked about his memories of Sherman Adams, Merrill Griswold, and Dwight Robinson, about how MIT used to pick stocks, about the evolution of the mutual fund business, and about the monster it has become today.

AUGUST 16, 1994

What's a Growth Stock?

Bill Griffeth: When did you first join Massachusetts Investors?

Jack Cooper: I started to work there in August 1947. Gosh, that's a long time! [Laughing]

Griffeth: [Also laughing] It impresses even you!

Cooper: I guess that's 47 years ago!

Griffeth: What had you done before that?

Cooper: I was at the Bankers Trust Company from 1935, when I graduated from college, until 1947, except for the five years I was gone during the war.

Griffeth: What did you do there?

Cooper: I was in the investment research department. That's why when I was offered a job at Mass Investors Trust in the investment research department, it seemed like a good thing to do.

Griffeth: So you worked in research to begin with?

Cooper: Yes. When I first started at Bankers Trust we did a little of everything. We were in the bond department and stamped confirmations and tried to sell bonds to ladies in the branch offices, and so on. Those were pretty trivial jobs, but when I got into a serious job which was sort of permanent I was in the investment research department.

Griffeth: And when did you start managing the growth fund at MIT?

Cooper: When I went to work there in August of 1947, there were only two funds in the office. Mass Investors Trust was the biggest fund in the business at $200 million. It was thought to be too big to be manageable. $200 million!

Griffeth: Now that's considered small, of course.

Cooper: That hardly qualifies you as a fund now!

And then the growth fund was only $20 million, and it had no real character of its own. It had simply been taken over during the early 1930s by the trustees of MIT. Brown Brothers Harriman had a fund which they had started just before the Depression and stock market decline, and it hadn't amounted to anything. Also, there was the Glass Stegall Act, which suggested that a bank which took deposits, like Brown Brothers Harriman, shouldn't be in the investment banking business, which the mutual fund business was considered to be. So they were kind of wondering what to do with this fund.

Now Brown Brothers Harriman had a fine, fine salesman whom MIT needed at the time. So the trustees of MIT made a deal with Brown Brothers to take over this little tiny fund if they could take over the salesman, too. And that's what happened. [*NOTE: The super salesman Mr. Cooper is talking about was Mahlon Traylor, who was president of Massachusetts Distributors, the sales and marketing unit of MIT, until his death in 1942.*] What is now Mass Investors Growth Stock Fund was called Supervised Shares in those days. It simply was carried along as kind of a tiny duplicate of MIT until sometime after the war when a fellow named Bill Shelly at Vance, Sanders, who were our distributors, thought there ought to be some kind of separate character to this other fund. See, they couldn't sell it because it was just a tiny duplicate [of MIT].

And so they decided in the late 1940s to see if they couldn't establish a separate character for this Supervised Shares Fund. So they decided they would make it a fund of growth stocks. The only trouble was nobody quite knew what a growth stock was in those days. They just assumed you meant a stock whose price went up all the time! [Laughing] They changed the name at one point to Mass Investors Second Fund, and that was sort of a nothing name, you know, because people thought, "Why buy something that is just the second?"

At some point I guess after I'd been at the company for a few years they assigned me and another fellow to sit down and try and figure out what growth stocks were. We looked at IBM and DuPont and all the things that were considered growth stocks at that time, and we asked, "What distinguishes them from General Motors or U.S. Steel?" The major thing, of course, was they spent a fair percentage of their revenues, maybe 5 or 6 percent, on research.

So we tried to designate some things that seemed to characterize growth stocks, and we got up a kind of matrix of things. And from that I became more associated with the growth stock fund than anything else, although officially that wasn't my job. I was no more the manager of the growth stock fund than the other four trustees were.

Everything was done by a vote of five people both at MIT and with the growth stock fund. Incidentally, I guess it was in the early 1950s that they changed the name from Second Fund to Massachusetts Investors Growth Stock Fund.

Management by Committee

Griffeth: So MIT and the growth fund were managed by committee to begin with.

Cooper: Exactly, yes. Everything from the time MIT was founded in 1924 until 1969 was done by majority vote of the people who happened to be the trustees at the time. And then we formed a management company in the latter part of 1969, and we began to divide up the responsibilities so that one or perhaps two or three individuals had responsibility for each fund. That is to say they had the daily investment responsibility for the funds instead of all the trustees being involved.

Griffeth: So let me be clear. Before 1969, a particular stock or a group of stocks would bubble up from research, and it would be left to the five of you to decide whether these stocks belonged in the fund?

Cooper: Yes, that's exactly right. Our research fellows would do a job on some companies they thought ought to be bought or sold, and they would write a memo to the trustees. The five trustees, in due course, would sit down and consider the memo and then take a vote. And if three or more of the five decided that a stock should be bought, why, we bought it. And if only two decided that we should buy it, that was the end of that.

Now, the buy and sell ideas didn't have to come from a research fellow. One of the trustees could have the idea, instead. The investment spectrum was divided up among the research people so that a given individual had, say, the chemical industry and the insurance industry and the business equipment industry to follow. And that individual would normally call on a company, come back, write a summary and say, "I think this stuff ought to be sold. It's not what we had thought it to be for a long time, and it's time to sell it." And then the trustees would consider that.

◆

"I would think if you had to characterize it in today's terms, you would certainly call MIT a value fund."

◆

Griffeth: There are a number of investment disciplines that can be quantified by various names. I mean, there are the value investors, there are growth investors, some use a top down approach, some a bottom up approach. How would you describe the way you managed MIT and the growth fund in those early days?

Cooper: I would think if you had to characterize it in today's terms, you would certainly call MIT a value fund. We tried to establish whether a company seemed to have a good position in its industry, and whether it had a well regarded management, a good financial condition, reasonable prospects for growth, and a decent dividend. To me that's what value investing is about.

Griffeth: How did the committee of trustees decide whether a particular stock belonged in MIT or the growth fund?

Cooper: The growth fund was driven primarily by a record of continued per share growth of earnings with the prospect that that growth would continue over the visible future. MIT, on the other hand, might allow a company's earnings growth to be a bit irregular, but its price-to-earnings ratio had to be low and it had to pay a decent dividend.

General Motors was a great stock for MIT, for example. Everybody knew it would have good years and bad years, but by and large over the years you'd be glad to own General Motors. And you knew the dividend would grow over time.

On the other hand, we wouldn't have owned General Motors in the growth fund, because its objective was to have companies like IBM in those days. In those days you could look at IBM and see that its per share earnings had grown since the dawn of time, and the way things were going then there was every reason to believe that the per share earnings would continue to grow. That's what the objective was in the growth fund.

Griffeth: These days a fund manager's success is measured against a corresponding average or index of stocks, and as long as they can beat that average they are considered a success. How did you measure success then?

Cooper: Pretty much the same way. In the days when I first began, it was a matter of where you stood in the whole spectrum of comparable funds. If you wound up in, say, the top quartile of funds that were comparable to MIT, what they now call value funds, you felt that was pretty good. Some years you'd be closer to the top than others but you wanted not to be in the last quartile, that's for sure. So it was much more a matter of what I'd call relative performance to your comparable group.

Griswold and Adams

Griffeth: Let's talk for a moment about Merrill Griswold and Sherman Adams.

Cooper: Sure. Merrill made the place. Merrill *was* MIT, and he was the [mutual fund] industry in some respects for a long period of time.

Merrill was a lawyer, and he was quite familiar with the problem of providing investment management for an estate account. You know, that's where an estate was passed on to the second or third or fourth generation so that each little segment had become smaller and smaller.

Let's say somebody leaves a million-dollar estate (and remember, this was back when a million dollars was a heck of a lot of money) by the time it got to his grandchildren each kid might have, who knows, $50,000 or $15,000. And Merrill was very familiar with the problem of trying to have some kind of diversified investment portfolio for what were relatively small accounts.

Along came a man named Sherman Adams. Sherman was a stock broker/entrepreneur in Boston, kind of a small-time fellow. But he had a fantastic idea: a security portfolio where you had the presumed advantage of growth of equity value combined with this savings bank advantage of being able to get money out any time. That was really what Sherman's idea was.

Now, as I say, he was kind of a small-time broker. I think he was a member of the Boston Stock Exchange, but he wasn't a member of the New York Stock Exchange. But he got this idea, and shortly thereafter he and some other people started the fund.

He went around to see Merrill Griswold one day in 1925, about a year after they started. And Merrill, from his probate law experience, apparently thought to himself, "Holy smoke, this is the answer to my small account investment problem," So he said something like, "I'll buy $50,000 worth of this thing. But I don't know anything about you and your fellow trustees, so I'll do it if you make me a trustee so I can keep an eye on this." So that's about how Merrill became a trustee of the fund.

> "... he [Merrill] was a guy with the mental discipline of a lawyer, a good streak of PR, and a realization that there was a real place for this funny thing in the investment world and in the probate world."

Merrill was a brilliant man with no pretense of being an investment guy. But he was a guy with the mental discipline of a lawyer, a good streak of PR, and a realization that there was a real place for this funny thing in the investment world and in the probate world. I think in the early days there were three trustees, if I remember correctly.

Sherman was a brilliant guy, very controversial around town. He was brilliant in that he had this one perfectly magnificent idea along with a lot of half-baked ideas. [Laughing]

He was still a trustee when I went to work there in 1947. His method of operation with the research department was to tell you that you were wrong about everything. And then after you had argued a point so vigorously you decided that maybe he was right! [Laughing] It was very difficult to deal with him.

But you can't get away from the fact that he had a hell of an idea.

First MIT Portfolio

Griffeth: I have here a copy of the fund's first quarterly report, dated July 15, 1924 (See pp. 22,23). It lists the fund's first trustees, and there were indeed three. They were Charles H. Learoyd, L. Sherman Adams, and Ashton L. Carr.

Cooper: Yes, Ashton Carr was an officer of the State Street Bank which from the very beginning was the custodian of the assets of the fund. He lent some credibility to the list of trustees because he was the guy in charge of the custodian department at the bank. In other words, people knew he was a man of substance. Charlie and Sherman were sales types.

When they got started in 1924, the three of them just met in each other's offices. They didn't have any kind of office or staff or anything of that kind. Sherman would go over to Ashton Carr's office, I suppose, and they would have called Charlie Learoyd and said, "Come on over. We've got $10,000; let's figure out what to do with it."

Griffeth: A bit more casual than it is now.

Cooper: Yes, exactly. And there wasn't much money involved for a long, long time.

Griffeth: Have you ever taken a moment to study this first portfolio they put together?

Cooper: Yes, we used to talk about it a lot when we had various celebrations, like the 25th and 50th anniversaries of the fund. I guess it was at the 50th that we noted we still had a couple of stocks from the original portfolio.

Griffeth: [Looking at the original portfolio] Let's see, you had a couple of banks and insurance companies, and you had several railroad companies obviously.

Cooper: Yes, railroads were very big.

Securities Owned by the Massachusetts Investors Trust

As of July 15, 1924

Company	Shares	Cost
Bank & Insurance		
Boston Insurance Company	3	682-1/4
Springfield Fire & Marine Insurance Co.	5	325
Industrial & Miscellaneous		
American Radiator Co.	10	102-1/8
American Tobacco Co.	5	145-1/4
Bates Manufacturing Co.	10	200
Eastman Kodak Co. of New Jersey	10	107-5/8
Farr Alpaca Co.	5	172-3/4
General Electric Co.	5	232-1/4
General Motors Co.	50	13-1/4
Island Creek Coal Co.	10	102-1/2
Lowell Bleachery Co.	10	120
Nash Motors Co.	10	109-5/8
National Lead Co.	5	145-5/8
Naumkeag Steam Cotton Co.	10	176-1/4
Punta Alegre Sugar Co.	20	50-3/4
Standard Oil of Indiana	20	57
Standard Oil of New York	20	40-1/4
Texas Company	20	38-7/8
United Fruit Co.	5	195-1/4
U.S. Steel Co.	10	97
West Point Manufacturing Co.	15	135
Railroad & Equipment		
American Car Foundry Co.	5	160-1/4
American Locomotive Co.	15	73-1/2
Atlantic Coast Line Railroad Co.	10	120-5/8
Atchison, Topeka & Santa Fe Rail Co.	10	104
Baldwin Locomotive Co.	10	112-3/8
Baltimore & Ohio R.R. Co.	20	57-1/4
Canadian Pacific Railway	5	147-3/8

SECURITIES OWNED BY THE MASSACHUSETTS INVESTORS TRUST

As of July 15, 1924

Company	Shares	Cost
Railroad & Equipment (continued)		
Illinois Central Railroad Co.	10	106-3/8
New York Central Railroad Co.	10	104-3/4
Northern Pacific Railway Co.	20	56
Pullman Co.	10	125-1/4
Southern Pacific Co.	10	93-5/8
Southern Railway Co.	20	60-3/4
Union Pacific Railroad Co.	10	135
Public Utilities		
American Gas & Electric Co.	5	70-1/2
American Power & Light Co.	5	261
American Telephone & Telegraph Co.	10	121-1/4
Brooklyn Edison Co.	10	111-3/8
Consolidated Gas of New York	15	68-1/4
Edison Electric of Boston	10	175
Massachusetts Gas Companies	15	71-1/2
North American Co.	40	26-3/4
Southern California Edison Co.	10	101-1/4
Western Union Telegraph Co.	10	109-5/8

Griffeth: There were a number of public utilities and then a number of stocks that came under the heading *Industrial & Miscellaneous*. I see General Electric and General Motors.

Cooper: Yes, those were the two which were in there from the very beginning and stayed.

Griffeth: Do you have any idea how they put this original portfolio together? What their thinking was?

Cooper: I can't tell you what their decision was in each instance. None of them was a great investment genius, but they had a good vehicle for people to save a little bit of money when they didn't know how to invest it.

I think at that time they were probably looking for brand names that people would have some confidence in. I think if you'd come out with a portfolio of 25 stocks with names that didn't mean anything in terms of consumer trademarks and so on, you probably would have had trouble. Remember this was a whole new idea, and they were sort of feeling their way into what made sense.

After the decline in the stock market in late 1929, three to six months later, the demand for mutual fund shares rose and an increasing number of people must have said to themselves—having lost money in the stock market—"Well, I hear there's this thing that sort of diversifies a portfolio for you. I obviously don't know what to do with my own money. I haven't been a very successful common stock investor, and I think I'll fall for this line some salesman is giving me about a mutual fund."

If I had been doing it, I'm sure that when I had this new idea I would have thought to myself, "When I'm talking to a doctor or a service station owner who's got $5,000 burning a hole in his pocket, I had better talk to him about this fund that has some names that mean something to him." That must have been the idea.

Cooper on Dwight Robinson

Griffeth: When did Dwight Robinson enter the picture?

Cooper: Around 1931–1932, the trustees decided it was time to have an office and hire somebody to keep the files and answer the telephone. (Now remember this was eight years after they started.) So they hired Dwight Robinson and a fellow named Henry Sawyer, and they opened an office on the first business day of 1932. And they began to do some in-house research as well as keeping the files and doing stuff like that.

This was kind of an innovation, apparently, to have a staff where people sat down and read Moody's manual and kept investment research files on companies. By this time it was still primarily a business that was in the minds of individuals like Paul Cabot and his partners at State Street and Tudor Gardner and his partners at Incorporated Investors, which is now part of Putnam Investors.

Griffeth: Tell me something about Dwight Robinson. Do you remember the first time you met him?

Cooper: Yes, I met him when I went up to Boston to be interviewed for a job. It was on a Saturday morning. That was in the days when we worked a half-day on Saturday. And he was obviously the person who had been assigned to come in and see this neophyte from New York and take him in and introduce him to the great man, Mr. Griswold, who was also there that day.

Dwight was quiet and thorough, and that's the way he was the entire time that I knew him. He was also a somewhat shy individual. But when he became chairman he made himself take an active part in industry public relations, just as Merrill Griswold had, even though it wasn't his natural inclination. He was a thoughtful person, and he was the right person to succeed Merrill as chairman of the company. Then he retired early in 1965, so I knew him from 1947 until 1965 and thereafter too, but he was in the office every day until 1965.

MIT Grows Up

Griffeth: Talk about how the company grew under Griswold and Robinson through the 1940s and 1950s.

Cooper: Merrill was not an investment guy. But from the point of view of a person who went to work there as an investment research guy that was a great thing, because if you wrote a learned memo and thought you knew everything there was to know about a company and your recommendation was unassailable you then had to go before these five people and demonstrate some reason they should believe you were right. The great thing about Merrill not being an investment guy was he always voted with the recommendation of the research guy. [Laughing] You could go into the meeting and know that you had one vote. And, by the way, there was a pretty good chance that Sherman Adams would vote against you. [Laughing]

Merrill was sort of brilliant and public relations minded and not terribly given to precisely following an agenda. For instance, he would just grab anybody who came by, or whom he thought would be appropriate to do some job. For instance, when we had the wage controls reinstituted in 1949 when we got into the Korean War, Merrill just grabbed some member of the research department and said, "Find out all about wage controls and what we're going to have to do about it." Well, that outraged the office manager and the treasurer and all the administrative people. But Merrill was just that way. He didn't follow some table of organization very well. He was what was needed in those early days when his vision of what this industry could become was evolving.

Now Dwight, on the other hand, when he became chairman he immediately began to be much more organized about what he expected each person to do. And it was time for us to get into that mode. I can't remember what the total size of the two funds was when he took over on January 1, 1954. It was nothing like what it is now, but it was still pretty big compared to this industry, which was still small.

Dwight was not the kind of a manager who ever said, "I've been up all night thinking about this portfolio, and I think we ought to have more oil stocks. I want you fellas to go out and study the oil industry." He didn't do that. But he did try to bring a reasonable organization to the approach of the research guys and an orderly processing of their recommendations. That was what Dwight was good at.

Griffeth: Talk more about his contribution of applying research to the investment process of filling a mutual fund portfolio.

Cooper: Well, his mind worked in such a way that we divided the portfolio up into all these industrial categories, unlike that early portfolio we talked about where it was railroads and utilities and industrials, and so on. Under Dwight, we divided the portfolio into categories like oil and business equipment and chemicals, and so forth. And he was very meticulous about making sure each industry was covered by a specific member of the research department. That didn't mean an individual had only one industry. Each person would have three, four, or five, depending on the size of the industry, and he was careful about making sure that we called on all the companies that were of any interest in the business a couple of times a year at least, whether we owned them or not. And he followed up on that kind of thing. He'd want to know when you last went down to

DuPont, when the last time was that you wrote a memo on it, and why didn't you write more.

Mutual Fund Industry Today

Griffeth: I guess neither Griswold nor Robinson could foresee the size of the industry today.

Cooper: Oh, no. I just can't believe it. [Laughing]

Griffeth: Is that good? I mean, have mutual funds become tulips?

Cooper: Well, I would say this. I think there is a sales problem. The business has become so successful and so well-known and so highly publicized and so commented on on TV and in the papers and everything else that almost everybody who has any contact with the news at all knows something about mutual funds. And like anything, I suppose it can be overdone. You inevitably attract into the management some people who probably shouldn't be there, you know. You get people who sell a fund any way they can. It is too bad, for instance, that as interest rates came down [in the early 1990s] sales of high income mutual funds skyrocketed, because I dare say it's true that many shareholders didn't realize that they were buying a far more risky thing if they bought a long-term bond than if they bought a six-month CD.

"I think there is a sales problem. The business has become . . . so highly publicized. . . that almost everybody who has any contact with the news at all knows something about mutual funds."

So, as I said, I'm sure there is a sales problem. But you know, there always have been some sales problems. There are, unhappily, in the human race, people who do things wrong.

Griffeth: To be fair, though, there is certainly a lot more competition today in the mutual fund business than there was when Dwight Robinson was overseeing MIT I wonder if you— the trustees—would have found yourself taking a little more risk to try to improve the performance of the fund in order to meet the competition just as some managers find themselves doing today.

Cooper: Well, I suppose so, yes. With the growth stock fund there was a tendency to be a little bit more risky because we became aware of the fact that there were no longer just MIT and State Street and Incorporated Investors and Affiliated Fund and you know, a couple of hundred funds like that. There were beginning to be funds of all kinds and some of them did better at times and therefore we had better be a little bit more adventurous.

Griffeth: I guess if you are going to do that you need to educate the investor at the same time.

Cooper: Yes. Not everyone in the world understands the different categories of risk in the investment business, and too many salesman don't find it advantageous, shall we say, to tell them.

Griffeth: And it all started with Sherman Adams. He would love to see $2 trillion in the business now, wouldn't he?

Cooper: Oh, God yes. He'd be looking for his share of the compensation on the first day of the quarter! [Laughing]

JAMES M. BENHAM

Birth Date: November 24, 1935

Education: Michigan State University: B.A. in Finance, M.A. in Economics

Hobbies: Trumpet, Golf

Alternate Career: Musician

*J*im Benham is the founder and chairman of the Benham Group of mutual funds in Mountain View, California, right in the middle of Silicon Valley, which is known for innovation in technology.

Benham's legacy to the mutual fund world is an investment innovation: the money market fund that invests solely in Treasury bills. Prior to 1972, the only way individual investors could buy T-Bills was to purchase them directly from the Treasury Department. But the rather high minimum investment required and the cumbersome process involved in buying them tended to discourage the little guy from direct participation in that market.

With bank savings accounts paying next to nothing, Benham saw a need to provide people with a vehicle that would pay a higher return without added risk. When he couldn't convince his employer at the time, Merrill Lynch, to start such a fund, he struck out on his own and in October of 1972 founded the Capital Preservation Fund (CPF). It floundered for a few years until the mid-1970s when two things happened: 1) interest rates started to rise, making the fund's yield more attractive, and 2) the federal government's borrowing needs increased as the budget deficit grew, and that provided a great deal of liquidity for the fund.

Today, CPF is the cornerstone of Benham's company, which as of 1994 managed $10 billion through 33 no-load equity and fixed income funds.

I interviewed Benham in a New York City hotel where he was preparing to speak to one of the many shareholder seminars his company holds during the year. Over lunch, we talked about the economic and political climate that led to the founding of the Capital Preservation Fund, about derivatives, and about the future of the mutual fund industry.

June 9, 1994

Growing Up

Bill Griffeth: You were born at the height of the Depression, and I understand that you are one of 10 children.

Jim Benham: I'm the sixth child out of 10. There were five boys and five girls, and my father was a minister so we had limited financial means. Fortunately for me, my father also played the coronet. During services, he would hold it in his right hand and finger the valves and lead the congregation with his left hand as though he were an orchestra leader.

And after years of seeing that I started playing when I was 12 years old, and I got a scholarship to Michigan State playing the trumpet. I didn't have to major in music. I majored in business, but I probably never would have gone to college without a trumpet in my hands. I didn't have the money, and my parents didn't have the money to send me. I did bus tables and do other things to earn money, but I never would have gone to college without the trumpet scholarship.

Griffeth: Did you realize you didn't have money? Was that an issue when you were growing up?

Benham: Yes. Absolutely. All the time. There was hardly a day that we didn't know that we didn't have much money.

Griffeth: You're a pretty conservative fellow. Is that because of the circumstances under which you grew up? Did that color the rest of your career?

Benham: Absolutely, yes it did. I am very competitive because of it as well. And very guarded in some ways. Survival was the number one issue for me much of my life. It has only been in recent years that I found out there are other things to think about besides survival, and it actually frees your mind up to a variety of different things. Unfortunately, numerous people on the globe—most people by far—are still fighting that number one battle: survival. And in our business, you know, if you don't get past survival, you never have money for investment and discretionary spending.

I used to feel guilty when I didn't buy the lowest costing this or that. Even now that I have a lot of money in my pocket, I still find myself trying to save money when I don't have to. It's old baggage that still comes up for me.

Banking Problems

Griffeth: Is that where the germ for Capital Preservation Fund came from? It just seems to me to be poetic justice that the thing that you made your name and reputation on would be a very, very conservative investment for people.

Benham: That vehicle was more the outgrowth of my impressions of having been a bank examiner with the Federal Reserve. It was my first job out of college. I had driven a brand new car from Detroit to California to deliver it to a dentist who had just bought it. And two weeks after I arrived, I landed a job as a bank examiner.

Griffeth: What year was that?

Benham: That was March of 1961. I joined Merrill Lynch in 1963, so I was a bank examiner for two years. And in that job I learned a lot about *the lack* of FDIC coverage, how it really was a joke. I saw how bankers tried to finesse regulators.

Griffeth: Do you have an example?

Benham: Bankers would oblige over-leveraged borrowers by telling them that the bank examiners were coming in next week and that they (the borrowers) should either get the loan current in order to get it past the examiners, or they should take the bad loan to another bank (at least while the examiners were around) in order to make the banker look good. The same loan would move from bank to bank to stay ahead of the examiners.

I remember a fellow who had $11 million in assets, $10 million in liabilities, and he paid a million dollars a year in interest. He was a bad loan. He was a highly leveraged builder-type. And his loan portfolio moved from bank to bank in order to stay ahead of examiners.

Griffeth: So you developed a distrust of the banking industry.

Benham: I thought that the FDIC insurance coverage was inadequate and that if interest rates moved substantially higher than Regulation Q allowed, the banks would be *disintermediated*. In other words, people would take their money out of banks and put it directly in money market funds or T-Bills.

————— ◆ —————
"There was a huge reservoir of money in America that was running dead. It wasn't sensitive to market changes because of the herd instinct."
————— ◆ —————

Then, at the peak in 1980 we had a prime rate of 21-1/2 percent, we had T-Bills at 16 percent, and because of Reg Q limits banks could only offer to pay depositors 5 percent. And yet the banks didn't close. Why didn't everybody who was earning 5 percent go out and buy T-Bills at 16 percent? There was a huge reservoir of money in America that was running dead. It wasn't sensitive to market changes because of the herd instinct. People figured, "If anything drastic ever happens, the banks will be saved and the money market funds won't be." I didn't know the American public would be that slow to catch on and learn.

Starting Capital Preservation

Griffeth: You wanted to develop the fund within the confines of Merrill Lynch, as I understand it.

Benham: Yes, I did. And they said it was a lousy idea, and it'll never work.

Griffeth: Why?

Benham: They didn't feel there was a problem with the banking system.

Griffeth: In other words . . .

Benham: There wouldn't be any inflation, there wouldn't be high money rates.

Griffeth: Their thinking was you either save your money in a bank or you invest it through a brokerage firm. There was no need for an intermediary.

Benham: That's right. They didn't have room for the money market component. Later on, interestingly, they started the RAT

Fund. The Ready Asset Trust. It turned out to be the largest money fund. They thought they might gather $4 or $5 million, and of course they gathered $25 billion. And they were very surprised about that phenomenon.

Griffeth: So you decided to go out on your own. Tell me about that.

Benham: I was called crazy. I was called stupid to leave Merrill Lynch where I was on a track to become a branch manager some day. I owned stock in the firm before the public did, I was the number one producer in the San Jose office when they opened it in 1963. I was one of seven people selected to be a broker there, and for the seven subsequent years I was the number one broker each year. But I kind of lost faith in the system in the late 1960s. I was having difficulties with myself personally. I drank my lunch each day in order to stay comatose, just so I could do the party line and try to sell the offerings that Merrill Lynch research tried to get us to sell.

Griffeth: You felt guilt . . .

Benham: I felt a lot of guilt. I felt like I was lying to people.

Griffeth: Because you couldn't get behind the stock market at that time? Was that also the problem you had?

Benham: Right. I had these fears about what was coming down. And particularly after what Nixon did on August 15, 1971. I remember very vividly that I was on vacation, and I listened to his speech on this crackling little radio. I couldn't get a good signal, because I was up in the mountains of northern California at Lake Tahoe with my family. And I listened to his speech on that Sunday when he took the country off the gold standard immediately, and he imposed the wage and price controls. Both of these maneuvers were designed to rev up the economy and inflate the system before the election the following year.

It was at that moment that I decided I had to leave Merrill, and I left the next month.

Now in this period, we also had some help from the oil embargo [of 1973], and we had a crop failure in soybeans when the El Niño [weather system over the Pacific Ocean] caused the jet streams to change, all of which caused inflation. We also had a government that was revving up inflation. This was the excitement that gave rise to the inflationary pressures Paul Volcker faced when he became chairman of the Federal Reserve late in October of 1979. He pushed the Fed Funds rate up enough and eventually broke the back of inflation.

Griffeth: And these higher interest rates made your money market fund more attractive.

Benham: Yes, the money market reflects these inflationary anxieties I'm talking about.

In the 1970s, things you could touch like tables and chairs and buildings and gold went to the sky in price, and people borrowed money in order to buy these things. They leveraged themselves.

People who owned homes in the 1970s typically would refinance every second or third year, take out a lot of equity, and go buy a new car, or go on a vacation, or get a new wardrobe. Of course, we found out later that leverage works the other way. In the late 1980s of course, a lot of these people went bankrupt.

So that was the period in the late 1970s when money market funds began to flourish. Then, when money market rates began to decline, the bond fund phenomenon swept Wall Street. Money rates came down, and these providers of mutual funds who had money funds began to offer bond funds. And that was the next huge area of growth in the mutual fund area.

Today, the three pieces of the [mutual fund] pie are almost the same size. The industry is about a third cash, or money markets, bonds are about a third, and equities are about a third. But it was the phenomenon of the money market that revolutionized the mutual fund industry.

Griffeth: Do you remember the highest rate you ever offered at the Capital Preservation Fund?

Benham: Yes, we paid 16 percent one month.

Griffeth: That's astounding to think about a money market fund paying 16 percent!

Benham: We had a repo fund that paid 19 percent. We were earning 20 percent and paying 19 percent. Incredible. Those were really strange times.

Growing the Business

Griffeth: I keep hearing from people that part of the success of your fund was also your prodigious marketing efforts. I mean, you had to convince people that they needed this kind of fund.

Benham: We got a lot of help in that respect, Bill. I'll never forget June of 1978. That's when the banking system began to offer money market accounts. Now, Americans didn't know what the money market was, but bankers and savings and loan people educated them and gave it legitimacy. So the banking community really started these things.

I remember in California they used to call them T-Bill accounts. People would go to their local savings and loans and plunk down their $10,000, and the S&L would say, "This is your T-Bill account." What the person actually got was a six-month CD tied to the T-Bill auction on Mondays. There wasn't actually any T-Bill industry that individuals had access to, but these accounts made people feel as though they held T-Bills.

So T-Bills got a great reputation, and the credibility of that rubbed off on the money market funds such as Capital Preservation Fund.

I should point out in all truth that the Reserve Fund was the first money market fund. Capital Preservation was second. So we should give Bruce Bent and Harry Brown their due rewards. During the first wave of growth they went to $500 million and we went to $50 million. But today we have $10 billion plus in assets, and they have something like $3 billion. They didn't diversify like we did.

Griffeth: That's right. You came out with other innovations: T-Note funds . . .

Benham: Yes, let's pause on T-Notes. We created the T-Note fund. It was not a fund that offered any bells or whistles. It just simply collected Treasury Note income, and distributed it to shareholders. But we had to fight a tax battle over it in California. It used to be that if you held a Treasury security yourself, the income you received wasn't taxed by the state. But if you held it through a fund, it was. The Franchise Tax Board used to argue and believe that with a Treasury mutual fund, whether it's a T-Bill or T-Note fund or whatever it was, the income in that portfolio changed its color as it came through to shareholders. Initially, it might have been Treasury income, but when those dividends popped out of the fund, they changed their color and therefore they were taxable.

So we waged a tax battle to convince California, and it took us six years and several hundred thousand dollars. But we prevailed in the California Supreme Court. And now, of course, T-Bill funds, Treasury Note funds, zero coupon funds, and long-term Treasury funds in California all enjoy the tax pass-through as if you held the vehicle directly. I'm glad we fought that battle.

Griffeth: What role should a fund such as Capital Preservation play in someone's mutual fund portfolio? Is it just a place to park your money when you want to go to "cash"?

Benham: It truly does play a role in people's portfolios. It gives them comfort. There are a lot of different personalities when it comes to investing. There's a variety of different types of personalities that don't like to assume risk. We're either given a disposition that can take risks or one that's very conservative. Some of that might be heredity, some of it is learned, as it was in my case. But we're all created somewhat differently, so I think T-Bill funds can play a variety of different roles depending on what you're trying to do.

In fact, one of the biggest mistakes people make, Bill, is that they don't distinguish between savings vehicles and investment vehicles. Savings vehicles include money market funds, T-Bills, CDs, savings accounts where you don't assume any risk of your principal. Last year [1993] and in 1992 a lot of people forgot about that, and they took their savings money and put it at risk in investment vehicles.

Griffeth: In order to achieve a higher yield.

Benham: Of course the big problem is if you don't make that distinction, just when you thought you didn't need your money, invariably you end up needing it when the markets are down, and you are left with a bad taste in your mouth about the markets.

Griffeth: So part of your business is not only to provide a service but to educate your shareholders at the same time.

Benham: It surely is. We do about 20 seminars a year for our shareholders around the country. We give them patience lessons, we give them diversification lessons, and of course we talk about the distinction between savings and investments. We teach them that the farther you go out on the yield curve the more your money moves wildly up and down. And that by being in the intermediate portion of the curve, you can reduce your risk and capture more income. Those are the sorts of things we try to do, and there's a hunger for that type of information, Bill. That's what makes CNBC so successful, and it's what makes your books successful. There's a hunger for straight ahead information that tells people how it is. They're tired of mumbo jumbo. They want it condensed down to regular English. People are pretty bright if you just talk to them.

Benham on Derivatives

Griffeth: Let's talk about derivatives. They've been blamed by Wall Street and Main Street for causing market volatility, especially in early 1994. You have, I know, gone out of your way to make sure your investors know that your money market funds don't use derivatives. Talk about that. Is there is a misunderstanding about what they are to begin with?

Benham: Yes. You know how we're not supposed to take drugs. All drugs are not created equal. Heroin is a drug. Aspirin is a drug. You wouldn't argue that an aspirin now and then was bad for anybody. Likewise, all derivatives are not bad. Some of them are like salt and pepper. They can actually enhance your stew.

——— ◆ ———
"All derivatives are not bad. Some of them are like salt and pepper. They can actually enhance your stew."
——— ◆ ———

The problem is that with some derivatives, you just don't know their true value. In fact, a lot of portfolios have been offered derivatives by sellers who don't know the instrument's real true value. Then it becomes a salesmanship game. A lot of lying goes on in the sales process about what the instrument is worth today and what it will be worth tomorrow if rates change.

Then the nasty problem is that the community that sold the derivatives to the portfolio managers is not now standing ready to buy them back and provide liquidity. They figure they made their money selling them. And if you were dumb enough to have bought them, now that you want to get out of them because you are having a run on your fund with people redeeming on you, hey, go find somebody else to buy them.

Griffeth: But what about the aspirin-type of derivatives? Do you have to avoid them too because the whole group has a bad reputation?

Benham: No. We have derivatives in some of our portfolios. In fact, in our stock funds we buy S&P [futures] contracts if we get money wired in late in the day. We want to stay fully invested in case the market moves. We'll put that new money to work in an S&P 500 Index position. Now that's a derivative, Bill. Would you call that irresponsible investing? Of course not. It's just an example of an aspirin-type use of a derivative.

Mutual Fund Boom

Griffeth: The mutual fund boom of the last few years certainly has been good for your business. You've grown tremendously adding new funds in the equity area where you didn't have them before. But you mentioned before about people getting out of CDs looking for areas where they could get a higher degree of income without thinking about the extra risk they were taking on.

Is the mutual fund boom a dangerously speculative one? Or how much of it is people investing for the long term, for retirement, or for their child's college education?

Benham: I vote the latter camp. I'm quite aware of the demographic changes that are in motion in our economy today with the aging of the baby boomers. And our industry is very much a growth industry as we accommodate these types of people. We have good demographics supporting our industry up through the turn of the century and beyond. Probably to the year 2010.

Meanwhile, our government's finances are in disarray. Many people question the reliability of Social Security when they turn 65. Frankly, I've already determined in my mind that

I'm not going to rely on it. I think it'll be taxed away by the time I retire, and that's only seven years from now. I'm scheduled to retire at age 65. This, of course, lights a fire under many people and causes them to try to find an alternative way to grow some wealth for retirement. And money markets, stocks, and bonds, and annuities, and all sorts of things are where they are looking.

The other phenomenon in motion is the international trend of investing. Americans are discovering that there is something beyond dollar-denominated investments. They are finding that not only does their wealth grow faster, it doesn't have the wild volatility year to year. It trims down your volatility year to year if you have, say, 20 percent invested in foreign securities.

I know there's anxiety about too many people who are in this area who don't know what they're doing. Frankly, I think there is some of that, but I think by far the majority of the people do, in fact, know what they are doing and they are very patient.

Griffeth: Do you foresee a time when we will finally get the one-stop financial services shops that were promised in the early 1980s, but never really materialized? I mean, will I ever be able to save and invest my money, borrow money, and pay my bills through the same financial services company?

Benham: It's becoming more and more like that. You know, Charles Schwab and Fidelity and Merrill Lynch are all very close to this thing you're talking about now. Schwab has a bank, as I understand. Merrill Lynch owns a bank. There are a lot of things that you talked about that are already here.

Griffeth: Last year [1993] at the Investment Company Institute Convention, Michael Porter, a Harvard professor, delivered a speech about the price competition in the mutual fund industry. He predicted that load funds would go by the wayside because companies would not be able to compete effectively if shareholders had to pay obvious fees either up front or as they exit funds. Do you foresee the day when we will have all no-load mutual funds?

Benham: No, I don't. I foresee the day where we will have more no-load funds than we have today, but I can still see the need and the justification for charging higher expenses. There are plenty of people in America involved in other areas of endeavor who are not enlightened about finances, and they need somebody to rely on. They may have piles of money, but they don't know what to do with it, and I think that's where salespeople come in. Salespeople who earn commission dollars and fees justify their work by taking Mr. Jones out of the dark ages and bringing him into modern times by having his money work for him in an appropriate way. He is much better off even though he's out a small commission.

WILLIAM M. B. BERGER

Birth Date: November 3, 1925

Education: Yale University, B.A. in English

Hobbies: Reading, trout fishing

Alternate Career: Architect

*T*here are actually two Bill Bergers.

One—descended from a Civil War hero—wears cowboy hats and leather jackets and spends time on his ranch in Colorado and at his family retreat in Maine.

The other—descended from a family of bankers—wears pinstripes, spends a couple of months each year in Manhattan schmoozing with the rest of the financial community, and runs a couple of the best known (and best performing) mutual funds in the country.

Or at least he used to run the funds. At the time we conducted the interview for this book, the second Bill Berger was in the process of easing himself out of the fund business so that he could spend more time being the first Bill Berger. In 1994, Berger announced he was selling his stake in Berger Associates to Kansas City Southern, the erstwhile railroad concern that had purchased Tom Bailey's Janus funds in the 1980s. Perhaps mindful of the hard times those funds experienced when Bailey stepped aside, Berger was quick to publicly calm his shareholders by pointing out his own money would remain invested in his funds.

Whether he is wearing leather or pinstripes, Bill Berger is a true pioneer. As you'll read, his family started the first bank in Denver in the 1860s. Almost a century later, in 1959, he started the state's first mutual fund, the Centennial Fund. Then in the 1960s, his Gryphon Fund was among the so-called "Go-Go funds" that sought higher than average growth by investing in smaller than average companies.

In the 1970s, Berger was asked to take over the management of a couple of troubled funds, the 100 and the 101. His 20-year record of managing them (they were, of course, later renamed the Berger 100 and Berger 101) has been distinguished. The Berger 100, for example,

41

outperformed the Standard & Poor's 500 Index 13 out of the 20 years, it was in the top 1 percent of all growth funds in 1989, and in the top 1 percent of all mutual funds in the country in 1991, according to Morningstar.

Berger does not suffer fools gladly. He has strong opinions on a number of issues, and he rarely—if ever—follows the conventional wisdom, especially when it comes to investing.

I called Berger in Maine, where—as is his custom—he was spending the summer. During our interview, he talked about investing in tennis balls and eggs, about why he is still very bullish on the stock market for the long term, about why he sold his company to Kansas City Southern, and about why he isn't so happy about where the whole mutual fund industry seems to be heading.

JULY 26, 1994

Banking and Mutual Fund Pioneers

Bill Griffeth: Money management is practically in your genes. Talk about your great grandfather and the Colorado bank he founded.

Bill Berger: Actually it was a great great grandfather, Christian Kountz. He came over in 1820 from Saxony as a young man of 26. He started out in Ohio and had nine children. They scattered around the country from Kountz County, Texas to New York City. They were the early treasurers of the Metropolitan Opera and members of the list of 320-some names that became famous as The Four-Hundred. They were very much involved with the social world at the end of the last century.

They had banks in different parts of the country. The First National Bank of Omaha, for example, was a Kountz bank. There was also a bank in Colorado Springs, and one in Cheyenne, Wyoming, I think. There were Kountz Brothers in New York, of course. All of them have changed their names.

My great grandfather, William Berger, married Margaret Kountz and he was involved in the bank in Denver. As was my grandfather and my father and myself.

Griffeth: You all worked for the same bank?

Berger: Yes.

Griffeth: Then you decided you didn't want to be a banker?

Berger: I was a banker for ten years, and I was brought up in it. It was in my system, as if I was attached to it by an umbilical cord. I loved what I was doing in the trust department.

Then in 1960, I invented a scheme where people could transfer assets through a newly formed mutual fund—that's for common stocks—and take back shares of the fund without incurring a capital gains tax. This fund, the Centennial Fund, was the first of what were later called exchange funds or swap funds. About a hundred million dollars was collected in 1960–1961 by this scheme of mine. And then all the big boys followed me very quickly into the game.

I got bored with that after doing two of those [funds], and so I started a "performance fund"—the Gryphon Fund—in 1962. It was one of the leaders of the pack in terms of performance. The only other one at the time that performed well was the Templeton Growth Fund of Canada.

Griffeth: What do you mean by performance fund?

Berger: Well, the detractors called them "Go-Go funds." It was the first time that people thought of performance as something that they wanted. Prior to that time, people bought mutual funds usually under front end loads. And then the salesman got half of the first year's payment as his commission—for getting people started.

They [the older, more traditional mutual funds] sold common stocks in those days—from American Telephone to U.S. Steel and Woolworth—from the familiarity of the names. FIF—now INVESCO—was built that way, and Hamilton—now Oppenheimer—was built that way. IDS was built that way. Rural people, the farmers—and some city people too, of course—bought those funds. They bought them because they recognized the names.

But common stocks were no darn good in the 1940s and 1950s. They were waiting for the postwar [World War II] depression, so people only owned about 20 percent of their financial assets in common stocks.

(Oddly enough, that's the reason for my bullishness today. The fact that after we got up to 36 percent or so [of financial assets in common stocks] in 1968, and then pulled back to a range of 18 percent or so in 1974, we only recently went above 20 percent again. So my theory is that they [investors] still fear common stocks. They don't yet own them. We still have a period of greed ahead of us. Right now we are still in the fear part of the cycle, and we have been for 20 years.)

So anyway, the detractors called our performance funds the "Go-Go funds." But the public liked performance. It was the first time people started being measured. We measured ourselves, I measured myself at the bank with the averages. It was unheard of that anyone ever measured themselves against the averages. They never thought you had to produce performance for the fee you charged.

I've always said let's charge a little higher fee and produce better performance. I didn't like hearing about the so-called clearing house fee schedule, where the banks met sort of secretly so as to avoid antitrust implications. They set their fee at one half of 1 percent for everybody, whether they did a good job or a bad job. I always thought that was stupid. The trust departments spent enough on investment people out of the fees they took for investment management. It is still a major bone of contention of mine. I believe that if people pay a fee for investment management, a healthy portion of that should go for the brains that provide the investment management.

◆

"I've always said let's charge a little higher fee and produce better performance."

◆

Griffeth: So what you essentially did, you put together what would now be called aggressive growth funds.

Berger: Yeah. Exactly. But I didn't think of it so much as being aggressive; I observed what was happening out there and I observed that the more profitable companies were the most prudent to own. Younger and newer companies were apt to be more profitable than the Erie Railroad.

Griffeth: Where did you find your shareholders at that time? Were you able to attract the farmers and others who were in the value funds to begin with?

Berger: It took a bit of doing. I learned the hard way.

At that point, I went over to Salt Lake City the day of President Kennedy's assassination to see if the Eckles Brothers would sell FIF. It turned out they would. So my group bought it.

[In 1966] I merged with Founders. So I had Gryphon Fund, which I started in 1962. It's now the Founders Growth Fund. The Meridian Fund, which was an income fund for doctors, is now Founders Income Fund. Founders Special is a little insurance fund I picked up while I was there. So I left FIF, now INVESCO, and went back on my own for a while.

Griffeth: What year was that?

Berger: 1966. I merged with Founders in 1966, then I left there in 1969.

Berger Associates

Griffeth: And where did you go from there?

Berger: Berger Associates. And then it became Fleming Berger Associates with a partnership of Fleming of London. Then the 100 Fund and the 101 Fund directors brought us those funds, and we started managing them September 30, 1974. They were started by a man named Bill Tempest who left FIF at the time I went there. Very nice guy.

Griffeth: And how is it the 100 and the 101 came to be the centerpiece of Berger Associates?

Berger: The previous management company became insolvent.

Griffeth: What was the problem? Was it the performance of the fund or just mismanagement, or what?

Berger: Oh, I'd rather not, it's one of those . . . they're all dead or dispersed now.

Griffeth: Well, did you have a project on your hands, managing these funds to begin with?

Berger: No, it was just the funds. When we started talking to them the funds were $60 million; by the time they were delivered they were $18 million.

Griffeth: What did you do with the funds to begin with?

Berger: Well, we managed them for 15 years, and they were still stuck at $18 million. That's when the fund directors said, "Look, you've increased each of the original shareholders' assets by six times but we still have the same amount of money in the funds. What's going on here?" We said, "Well, things don't sell themselves." So they said, "Do something about it." So we looked into it and decided that a 12(b)1 fee was the best way to do something about it. It paid for answering the phone, and it paid for the stuff that we sent out to prospective shareholders.

Griffeth: When did the funds start to take off?

Berger: As soon as we voted in the 12(b)1.

Griffeth: So, what you're saying is performance is not the only thing that will attract people. You have to get the word out there and do some marketing as well.

Berger: Exactly, if they don't know where to phone you, nothing happens. Lots of people have produced good performance just as I did for years, and they have not seen it rewarded.

Griffeth: Did the funds' prospectus fit your investment style?

Berger: They very much liked our investment style. That's why they came to us.

Griffeth: You didn't have to do a lot of changing then when you took the funds over.

Berger: No, because they had fairly standard investment clauses. The fund directors liked our concept of sticking with the most successful, profitable companies, which we still do. Which I did at the bank.

Berger's Investment Philosophy

Griffeth: Let's talk about that investment philosophy. Where did it come from? Is it something you learned from your father and grandfather, or is it something you designed yourself?

Berger: Well, when I was on the investment committee at the bank, I got to travel to investment conferences across the country, trust conferences. There would always be a collection of investment men and the question would invariably be asked of the investment panel, "Well, if new money came in today, how would you allocate it?" They would always say, sounding very wise, "Well, if new money came in today we would put 50 percent of it in bonds and 50 percent of it in stocks." This was always the case. And even our own investment group would sell off perfectly good stocks just to put the money into bonds.

I noticed that my uncle George's account, which was a custody account and not managed by the trust department, was 99 percent in common stocks and 1 percent in a few tax-free municipals. I noticed over the years that it had grown where the others hadn't. He invested in drug stocks in the early 1940s, for example, and that sort of thing. He was somewhat of an avant-garde investor. So it occurred to me that common stocks were the best place to be, and I always felt that if you were going to be in common stocks you ought to be in the most profitable ones you could find. Companies that could earn the most for their shareholders. In other words, all you own when you own a common stock—after you've bought it at probably several times book value—is that stream of earnings, what they can earn on this year's retained earnings that they don't pay out to you.

Bond rates were 2-1/2 percent at that time, so if the company could earn 12 percent, obviously you have a much better chance of having a successful trust account. I simply began to look for companies with a better rate of return, and these happened to be the newer companies. And it is still the case today. You've got to own the Wal-Marts of this world when they are bringing a good high rate of return and plowing it back into growth.

"You've got to own the Wal-Marts of this world when they are bringing a good high rate of return and plowing it back into growth."

When I was still at the bank, our clearing house trust department examiner worked with a Fitch stock guide. Fitch is long gone now, but as you know, it rated stocks A+, A, the same way as the others still do. Well, I had all sorts of [companies with a C ranking], and he felt some of these C's were terrible.

They included companies like AMP. I bought it at the bank at 2-5/8, and it's in the 1940s now. It turned out to be a very successful investment over the years. I had to buy it, because it paid a dividend. In those days you simply had to have a dividend. They didn't realize the dividends were taxed.

Trust accounting is still archaic. It penalizes the widow, and takes all the fees out of her income stream.

Griffeth: What made a company like AMP an A for you?

Berger: The fact that they could earn 15 percent retained earnings, or whatever it was.

Griffeth: Why wouldn't that be an A for Fitch?

Berger: Because it wasn't big enough, or it wasn't a familiar name, or whatever. I don't know how the hell they came up with their rankings.

Griffeth: [Laughing] Did you start your Go-Go fund, the Gryphon Fund, because you found a plethora of stocks that would fit that style of investing, or did you simply want to strike out on your own and give it a shot?

Berger: I forget what it said in the prospectus. I'm rather curious now to go back and see what on earth it was we said. Actually, we bought the same sort of things I bought at the bank. They performed well, and in 1964 it was the number four fund in the country. Templeton was number two.

Marketing vs. Performance

Griffeth: One of the other fund managers in this book told me he felt the boom in mutual funds the past few years was more symptomatic of the ability of brokers to sell the funds than it was the great performance of the funds. Do you agree?

Berger: Someone once told me, "We have all now educated the public on the desirability of funds, and now we'll be competing with each other." Which means the marketing people in each organization will always in a way be at odds. Well, not at odds exactly with the investment people, because they both need each other. Each one is always trying to claim the one is more important than the other. I've done both, and as an investment

guy I was insistent that the investment people were more important. As a marketing guy I would have to say investment guys
have nothing unless the marketing people do something about
it. So it's an interesting dichotomy.

But overseeing all of it are the bean counters. They are
always trying to hold back the creative people, both the
marketing and the investment people. Bean counters are
constantly trying to either figure out ways of holding them back
or figure out ways of exploiting them. Since they are not
creative, that's all they have the sense to do. Some of them can
be very clever at it. (Don't get me off on that subject.)

But I think before this whole thing is over, Bill, we are going
to see absolutely ridiculous things going on. I don't know what
form it will take, but there will be people willing to take uncon-
scionable chances with other people's money to try to win the
stock performing slot.

I remember in 1966 or 1968, I went down to the Contrary
Opinion Forum in Chester, Vermont. A group of us always met
first up in Montreal and had a little private meeting up there. Ed
Johnson, [Edward C. Johnson II, who founded Fidelity] was part
of the group. He said, "You know, I have more funds in the
incubator. I'm going to call them Salem, Essex, Magellan and
Contra" (that one after the contrary opinion forum that we were
heading down to). He said, "I don't know which one will work,
but one of them will work and then I'll trot it out and I'll have
a good record and I'll sell it [to the public]." Of course, Magellan
and Contra are two of their biggest funds today.

But anyway, you'll see more incubator funds, companies
starting a whole flock of funds just to have one they can trot out.
You will see portfolio managers lionized the way rock stars are
today. Even though I think the pendulum may swing away from
individual managers. I have long been a proponent of recogni-
tion of individual managers. And, of course, by the time we
finally seem to be able to accomplish that, we have reached a
point where no one can do it on his own anymore.

There are so many [job] opportunities out there today
compared to what there used to be. You have to have more
analysts, more staff, more people on the road, more people
going to seminars to keep track of all these new opportunities.

There are so many more industries and disciplines that you have to follow. No one can do it on his own anymore.

The fund manager can be the orchestra leader. As I always say, all of us who manage money are reading the same music, it's just that some of us conduct the orchestra differently. It's a very fine point that separates the good conductor from all those directors of high schools across the country who are just waving a baton. You have to hope that nobody ever discovers what the difference is, because the world would be a rather uninteresting place if the Japanese could write an instruction manual for orchestra conducting. The fact is we do all read the same music, each of us just interprets it differently.

> "... All of us who manage money are reading the same music, it's just that some of us conduct the orchestra differently."

Tennis Balls vs. Eggs

Griffeth: Are you saying that eventually you could see mutual funds becoming like tulips?

Berger: No, no, there's no way they can do that.

Griffeth: We had a fellow on our program one night who owns 44 different funds. I mean, there are plenty of people out there who buy and sell funds like they do stocks.

Berger: I don't think there are too many people who will do that, but enough of them will do it to keep the thing lively. The biggest problem will be that instead of competing with the public, which is what we did years ago, we will be competing amongst ourselves. The public owns $3.5 trillion in common stocks including $700 billion in equity mutual funds. I think that by the time this is over equity mutual funds will be over half of what people own and at that time people may own $6 trillion in common stocks.

So it's going to be a very big industry, and there is going to be a lot of talent, all trying to outsmart each other. There are some very, very smart minds at work. It's not going to be easy at all. There will be a lot more opportunities, but it has always been hard work. It's just harder work now with all the competition.

There's a problem of relative strength, you see. There are too many people climbing on the band wagon here at the end of the cycle. And how many of them know when to get out of the game in each down cycle in the market?

It's a matter of tennis balls and eggs. In 1962 it looked as if Putnam Growth and Fidelity Trend and Wellington Equity and other funds were much the same. But it turned out that some of them were tennis balls and some were eggs. Wellington Equity was an egg, for example. It never bounced. And look at some of the other prominent funds from that time. Ned Johnson [Edward C. Johnson III, the son of Fidelity's founder and current Fidelity chairman, who managed the Fidelity Trend fund in the 1960s] was a better manager, in my opinion, than Gerry Tsai ever was [Tsai managed the Fidelity Capital fund before moving on to the Manhattan Fund in 1966]. Johnson was a brilliant fund manager, and he proved that he was a tennis ball.

We were a tennis ball, fortunately. I've forgotten whether Putnam Growth was a tennis ball or an egg. But it is an important distinction to make: everybody goes up as much and everybody comes down as much. It's the bounce that then counts.

Griffeth: Because of the tremendous growth of the industry and the number of funds to choose from, how does an individual investor determine before she gets in whether she is investing in a tennis ball or an egg?

Berger: It is exceedingly difficult. It's very hard for me to determine what the funds might do even when I think I know. There are about 2,000 equity funds making up this $700 billion so the public has as difficult a problem figuring it out as we do figuring out which common stocks to buy. The best thing to do of course, is to get rid of the 90 percent that are mediocre. Rankings and ratings can help you do that. Chances of a fund with continuing good performance are better than finding the turnarounds that are out there. It's the same with common stocks. So if you narrow it down to the top 200 funds you still have your hands full, and then you really have to go to work.

I think you have to find that fund whose philosophy you can understand, because through understanding comes comfort, through comfort comes the courage to hang in there. The biggest problem in investing is control over one's own emotions, fear and greed. We have it, the man on the street has it. It's the need for courage and not letting the conventional wisdom talk you into doing something stupid.

So I would submit that you have to find a fund whose investment philosophy makes common sense to you, that you understand, and therefore feel comfortable with it. If you are trying to find earnings that will bail you out regardless of what the screwy market does, not just trading stock, then it's terribly important to make the distinction between people who are trying to run portfolios of investments as opposed to people trading stocks. Now, what I said a moment ago about common strength is a handicap here because you also have to have the ability to be able to sell something that's done exceedingly well for you, say goodbye to it. If it's coming under distribution, or it has gotten vastly overpriced, you simply have to have the skill to do it and that's where you rely on the fund manager.

But to swing back to how you pick the fund. Risk, Bill, is a misnomer in this business. What we are really talking about instead of risk is work, hard work. It is not hard work to buy a Treasury Bill. You get a return without any work involved. You know inflation and taxes eat that return to nothing. The next step up is the long bond. Well, the only thing you know is it will be paid off at maturity; meanwhile it is going to give you a substandard return that fluctuates as much as—or more recently—more than common stocks. That doesn't do you any good. You have to go into the common stocks themselves. What I tell people is I don't like to talk about individual common stocks, but I do like to encourage people to write for the annual reports of the top holdings of the fund that they are interested in, or of companies they own shares of. Write the companies. Unfortunately we just put so little money to work per shareholder we can't do it. If shareholders will write some of the companies we own and get their annual reports, they will learn more about investing and more about what we're trying to do than we can tell them in a thousand regulated words.

Reputation vs. Performance

Griffeth: As you pointed out, fund managers are now competing against each other, not just against the public. And they are trying to increase their returns and outperform their fellow fund managers with derivatives, among other things.

Berger: Reaching for yield is a disaster. And to reach in the name of extra performance is just disgraceful.

Griffeth: But I guess it is a natural progression of the competition factor, isn't it?

Berger: I think anything that grows as fast as this business has will attract its share of charlatans. But let's face it. The remedy that's been used, which is dipping into massive sums of capital to make up for losses, is a precedent that will stop much of this nonsense from going much further. No good board of directors is going to run the risk of a management company having to step in with a couple hundred million dollars to bail out a fund. So this will be self correcting very quickly, I think.

It's like the old days of the banking business when—I think it was in the panic of 1893—our bank loaded up a wagon with gold and took it up to the First National Bank. They [the depositors] wanted to take deposits out of the First National, so we loaned them a wagon load of gold to put in the lobby so that people could see it and stop the run on the bank. In those days your reputation stood for something, because you didn't have the FDIC, and therefore every bank was on its own and free to do any damn thing it wanted to.

This [the mutual fund business] is still dependent upon reputation. I'm not so sure but in the long run that is a better regulatory mechanism than trying to have regulators that can invent ahead of time something to prevent all the chicanery that people can come up with.

The forefathers of this business, Fleming on down to the guys that started Massachusetts Investors Trust and State Street, they created a wonderful image, a wonderful reputation for prudence. And I'm not knocking those guys for the fact that they sold funds that made up the Dow Jones average in those days because of the familiar names. It did help people save money. In the last analysis that's our job: to help the American public save money on the one hand and allocate it in the best places for the country's good as we receive it. That's our role.

In any regulated business, like banking and savings and loans and insurance, there will always be problems, because the regulators cannot keep up with human ingenuity. Perhaps it's better to depend upon building a name that means something.

Griffeth: Let me play devil's advocate on this derivatives thing. In the early 1960s, as you pointed out, the prevailing wisdom was to go with brand name common stocks. And then a few young turks like Bill Berger came along and changed that concept and emphasized performance with aggressive growth funds.

I can understand how some of the veteran money managers at that time might have looked askance at that and wondered what these young fellows were doing and where it might lead. And I wonder now if, because of this competition factor, we aren't just witnessing the next level of competition among funds by the use of derivatives.

Berger: Well, I did use puts very successfully in 1987. Before Black Monday we bought puts at 5/8 that we then sold at $85. It was a hell of a good hedge. Some we sold at $50. What's that, about a hundred times our money? But somebody had to put up the money to pay for that.

Common stocks have their swings in price earnings ratios, but essentially common stocks in general have to track earnings. At some point they go from 15 times earnings back to 15 times earnings, up or down to get there. So we're all only as good as the economies we're investing in.

The rest of these—commodities for example—have a useful purpose in that they help farmers and metal extractors and others beat some of the strains of cyclicality. But derivatives are merely robbing from one person to pay to another. Hell, the Hillary Clinton thing [in which the First Lady apparently achieved a $100,000 profit trading cattle futures in 1978] meant somebody had to lose the money that she gained. It is a zero-sum game, whereas ours essentially grows because the economy grows faster than others.

An early investor in a growing company is productive in that he takes out the venture capitalist and holds the stock for a while until he sells it to the banks who like it after it has matured. But there's a purpose in it.

I can see hedging if you are hedging against an existing portfolio, but not when you're buying these things to try to make money. And there's the distinction, Bill. If these things are being used to hedge in a proper fashion, or to make it possible to do something that is useful and productive and protective, that's one thing. But to buy these things simply to try to outsmart the other guy, that's where you get in trouble, and that's where the misuse has come. People have tried to use them for the wrong purposes, to make money in them.

We buy puts for cheap insurance. We would never consider buying one with the idea of making money on it. We buy them like an insurance policy hoping we'll lose money on them. We don't need them, but we have them in case we do.

Mutual Fund Manager as Superstar

Griffeth: You are in the process of selling your share of Berger Associates to Kansas City Southern.

Berger: As you know in our industry it's not like owning a department store or a hardware store or something. You can't just leave it to your kids. It requires the business of people and you have to get a lot of people at the right time feeling that the best thing to do is to switch things around. They will benefit. I prefer to do it now while I can still oversee it, looking over it, instead of waiting until I'm completely senile!

Griffeth: [Laughing] We're in this period where mutual fund managers have become the stars of the show. I mean, that's essentially the premise of this book. In your view, should an individual invest in the manager or the fund?

Berger: You should invest in the philosophy. The managers are human. The managers need backup these days. The age of the boutique is over and Steinhart and Soros need a lot of help to do what they do. It's changed. You're writing a book just at the apex of this. This, I predict, will be the last book of its kind.

The trick is to find the managers who have been through more than one cycle. I've known an awful lot of good managers, but they lasted one full cycle, and then where did they go?

You've got to find the John Neffs. In terms of long-term records, he and I are about 100 basis points apart, and we do things quite differently. He's a master, he's an unusual person. I don't have to tell you that there are not that many John Neffs.

Make Way for the Next John Neffs

Griffeth: It brings me to my final question. With the consolidation, the conglomeration, the growth of the industry, what kind of relationship do you think mutual fund investors will have with their fund managers? Today, theoretically, we are still at the point where a fund shareholder can pick up the phone and maybe talk to a Bill Berger or whoever their fund manager is. Maybe we are getting a little too big for that, but what about the days when it will become truly an institutionalized industry?

Berger: It will make me throw up. It sounds awful. I hate to think of it going that way.

Griffeth: Is that where we're going, though?

Berger: I've always believed that my snapping at the heels of the Vanguards and the Fidelitys of this world has helped. Well, I shouldn't say Fidelity/Vanguard because they have always been right there snapping alongside me. But I think we've been a good influence on the industry in delivering a better product, and I think it should always be kept open for new guys to come along.

It shouldn't go the way of the big three automakers. Regulators would love to have only three fund companies to regulate. But look where that brought automobiles worldwide.

No, somehow we've got to keep the industry open to all people. It shouldn't cost people a lot of money, the product has to be able to weather good and bad times, and standards of management have to be kept high.

I guess that's the key to it, Bill. We've got to make it possible for the next generation's John Neffs to make it. Whatever it takes to do that.

PHILIP L. CARRET

Birth Date: November 29, 1896
Education: Harvard, 1917
Hobbies: Travel
Alternate Career: Journalist

*P*hilip Carret is like a walking piece of mutual fund history. He was there when the first American mutual fund was born. In 1924, he was working as a feature writer for Clarence Barron, who went on to buy Dow Jones & Company (the publishers of The Wall Street Journal) and for whom the weekly financial publication Barron's is named. And, as Carret related in the conversation you're about to read, a group of entrepreneurs frequently visited one of Carret's editors, Herb Cole, seeking his advice on how to start a fund that would pool together money from a number of shareholders and invest it on their behalf. The fund they were discussing became the Massachusetts Investors Trust, the first open end mutual fund started in the United States. (MIT, as it was known in the fund industry, is profiled on page 11.)

Carret paid close attention to the discussions he overheard in the newsroom, and he carefully tracked the progress of the new fund. Then in 1926 he started his own fund with $25,000 he collected from family and friends. It enjoyed a modest amount of success, and Carret managed it for 25 years until he sold it to an investment company in 1951. Today the Pioneer Fund has more than $2 billion in assets, Carret is its chairman emeritus, and he still sits on the board of directors of the Pioneer family of funds.

During Carret's long career, he was a bond salesman, a financial journalist (a series of articles he wrote for Barron's in the mid-1920s became the classic text The Art of Speculation), the president of a major publishing company (the American Book Company), and of course, a mutual fund manager.

I interviewed Phil Carret for this book in the mid-town Manhattan offices of Carret & Company, the money management firm he founded in 1963. We sat in the company's boardroom at the long

57

directors' table. At one end was hung a large framed color photo-graph of a younger Philip L. Carret. His assistant served us coffee in bone china cups on a silver platter.

At the time of our interview, he was a spry 97-year-old preparing for his annual month-long sojourn to Europe. It was a trip he used to take with his wife, Betty, until she passed away in 1985 after 63 years of marriage.

Phil Carret is not the most successful mutual fund manager who ever lived. But the simple wisdom he espouses here is a valuable addition to this book. It speaks to a time when there were no computers on Wall Street, when greed may indeed have been good, and when young men (and perhaps a few young women) in the business still used words like "prudence" and "value."

June 7, 1994

The Money Mind and Greed

Bill Griffeth: You titled your autobiography *A Money Mind at 90*. What is your definition of a money mind?

Phil Carret: Well, the money mind belongs to someone who thinks in terms of what something will do to the stock market. For instance, I remember a few years ago I was driving down the road and saw for the first time a North American Van Lines van moving furniture and realizing that I had seen increasing numbers of them on the road. So I took a look at North American Van Lines, whose stock was then available. (It was later bought by Pepsico.) I don't remember whether I made much of a profit on it or not, but I bought it because I had seen it and realized it was in a growing business.

Griffeth: Norman Vincent Peale wrote in the foreword of your book that the money mind concept should not be interpreted as an example of greed. But if you're continually looking for ways to profit, isn't that a form of greed?

Carret: Well, it depends on your definition of greed. The Greeks had a moral quest: "Moderation in all things." And I think a certain degree of greed is a constructive phenomenon. Carried to excess, it's a vice. For example, I think one drink before dinner maybe four or five times a week is probably good for people, certainly those past the age of forty. But excessive use of alcohol is a disaster for society and the individual.

Griffeth: There is a famous line from the motion picture *Wall Street* that "greed is good." That got the movie makers in trouble at that time. Are you saying a certain amount of greed *is* good?

Carret: Yes. If you didn't have a motivation for being in the stock market, then investing money would be a very dull operation.

Wall Street in the 1920s

Griffeth: You were a financial journalist in the 1920s. That was a pretty heady time for Wall Street, wasn't it?

Carret: Yes. I worked for a little daily paper called *The Boston News Bureau*, which started originally as just that: a news bureau which collected financial news in Boston. It was a very constricted financial district which covered just a few blocks. The news was put on bulletins about, oh, maybe three by five, and they were clipped to clip boards. And Clarence Barron, who started it, had a fleet of boys who ran around every fifteen or twenty minutes during the day to paste these things up on the clip boards. And then people started asking for a record of it, so he started publishing a newspaper called *The Boston News Bureau* which was known in my day as *The Summary*. In other words, it was the summary of all these bulletins. And then his son-in-law, to whom I was quite devoted—Hugh Bancroft—got the idea of taking the same material and putting it into a weekly paper which became *Barron's*. He named it for his father-in-law, but old man Barron was not particularly interested in it. He occasionally wrote an article for it.

Griffeth: Did he name it *Barron's* to convince his father-in-law to go with the project?

Carret: I don't think so. But I'll never forget how the old boy once wrote an article about railroads. And he made the statement that there were more railroads entering the city of New Orleans than Chicago. Of course, I saw the galley proofs before it was published, and it didn't sound right to me, so I got out Mr.

Moody's Railroad Manual and I counted and there were twice as many railroads entering Chicago as New Orleans. So I went to Mr. Bancroft just before the thing ran, and I said, "The old boy made a mistake."

"Well," he said, " I think we'd better let it stand." So that's the way it was published.

Griffeth: There's something to be said for being the boss.

Carret: Yes! And to my great surprise we didn't get a single letter pointing out the error. [laughing] That's very funny!

Griffeth: [also laughing] Yes.

Carret: Of course, things have changed dramatically over the past 60 or 70 years. In the old days news was hard to get. I mean companies were not too enthusiastic about baring their souls to some reporter and having what they said published on a page of a newspaper. That has all changed, of course, and now they are very anxious to get any publicity, whether it is favorable or unfavorable.

There is the famous case of McKesson & Robbins which had a disaster on its hands when it was discovered that the CEO was a famous crook who had changed his name. He hadn't lost his old habits, however, and he had cooked the books quite a bit. When that was discovered, Sidney Weinberg of Goldman Sachs, who was on the board, insisted on having a special meeting of the board at which Mr. Coster did not appear. And Sidney Weinberg, so the story goes, had just moved that they fire him, when the phone rang and word came that Mr. Coster had shot and killed himself. Weinberg is supposed to have said, "Well, I still move that we fire the S.O.B.!" [laughing]

But the company suffered not at all. It was just publicity of a sort. People didn't remember what they'd read about McKesson & Robbins, they just remembered the name. They read the name and therefore that was favorable.

Griffeth: And now with television and computers, financial news is reported instantly. Does that speed up the cycles in the stock market? Does it compress the activity?

Carret: I suppose.

Griffeth: Is that good or bad?

Carret: I've always thought that we'd be better off if we had more frequent and smaller recessions because a long recession, of course, is devastating to the economy and many investors. It causes a lot of people great damage financially and mentally. If you had a reasonably frequent recession why, you'd get out of that. On the other hand, of course, the politicians do everything they can to prolong a period of prosperity and to hell with the aftermath. That can be left for the next administration.

Investing $100,000 for Widows

Griffeth: You had a contest at *Barron's* called "Investing $100,000 for Widows."

Carret: It was a very interesting contest. We had three members of the staff, including myself, who went through the entries. As I remember there were about a thousand, and we picked out what we thought were the best eight to ten. And then we had three prominent commercial bank presidents from the leading banks in Boston act as the final judges.

Griffeth: Do you remember which portfolio won the contest?

Carret: No, not particularly.

Griffeth: Well, let me ask you this: You conducted this contest back in 1926. How would a widow's $100,000 portfolio in 1926 differ from a widow's $100,000 portfolio today?

Carret: I think it would have more emphasis on bonds, somewhat less on stocks.

Griffeth: When?

Carret: In the earlier period.

Griffeth: Why?

Carret: Well, that was the conventional wisdom in those days. In 1920, say, when I was just getting started the general theory in New England was that if you had $100,000 you could invest it at 6 percent, receive an annual income of $6,000, and live quite comfortably. Now remember this was a period when the income tax was just beginning, and before inflation really took hold.

Griffeth: In other words, your money has to work harder today than it did seventy years ago. So today the emphasis has to be on equities. Is that why we are seeing this boom in mutual funds?

Carret: I think the boom in mutual funds has a lot to do with good salesmanship. They're a profitable item for the retail brokers.

Griffeth: So part of the boom is the result of Wall Street convincing Main Street that it needs mutual funds.

Carret: Yes. And I'm a great believer in mutual funds. I think they are a very sound form of investment for the average individual who doesn't have the time, or the expertise, or the particular emotional interest in investing.

◆

> "*I'm a great believer in mutual funds . . . they are a very sound form of investment for the average individual who doesn't have the time, or the expertise, or the particular emotional interest in investing.*"

◆

First American Mutual Fund

Griffeth: You were working at *Barron's* when the first American open end mutual fund was invented, and in fact, you knew the people who started it. Tell that story.

Carret: Well, my desk was right under Herbert Cole's, the editor of *The Boston News Bureau*. He sat on a little platform like a teacher in a schoolroom. And he frequently used to receive calls from one Sherman Adams, not the one who became prominent during the Eisenhower administration. This Mr. Adams and some of his business associates used Mr. Cole as a sounding board for an idea they had to form an investment company. It eventually evolved into the Massachusetts Investors Trust [the first American mutual fund].

I used to listen to their discussions, and it sounded very interesting to me. So I got a little family money together [$25,000] and started a very small investment trust with the rather ambitious title of Fidelity Investment Trust. It later became the Pioneer Fund.

Griffeth: You didn't call it the Pioneer Fund to begin with?

Carret: No.

Griffeth: Where did the Fidelity name come from?

Carret: I dreamed it up. Bad name.

Griffeth: It was in 1951, then, that you renamed it the Pioneer Fund. Where did that name come from?

Carret: I suppose I dreamed it up, too.

Griffeth: Because you were a pioneer.

Carret: Yes.

Griffeth: I have here a copy of the first portfolio from 1928 of the original Fidelity Investment Trust. [*I hand him a copy of the original portfolio, shown on pp. 64–65*] Are you the kind of money manager who remembers every stock and bond you ever bought?

Carret: No. [*He carefully studies the list of stocks and bonds in the portfolio.*]

Griffeth: What was the theory or the investment philosophy behind that original portfolio? Did you have one?

Carret: I don't suppose so. I just wanted to find things that made sense and gave a reasonable return.

Griffeth: I also have a copy of the first letter you wrote to your shareholders. It referred to your first ten months of operation from March until December 31 of 1928. It shows a portfolio worth between $54,000 and $60,000. I notice it was populated with a lot of convertibles and bonds. You recognize the names?

Carret: Oh, a few, yes. Boy, I didn't remember that the Hood Rubber Company had any convertible bonds. Some of these things I don't remember at all.

Griffeth: Did you choose the original portfolio, or did you have a staff with you?

Carret: I was it.

FIDELITY INVESTMENT ASSOCIATES, INC.
PORTFOLIO
December 31, 1928

Shares	Security	Cost	Market
25 shs.	Alabama, Tennessee & Northern R.R. pfd.	512.50	500.00
10 units	American & Foreign Power 2nd pfd. & warrants, 50% paid	665.00	2,867.50
25 shs.	Auto Sales, pfd.	828.75	962.50
$1,000	Bates Valve Bag deb. 6s, 1942	2,071.50	2,150.00
15 shs.	Bates Valve Bag	900.00	900.00
5 shs.	Booth Mills	615.00	650.00
5 shs.	Boston & Maine pfd. "C"	456.00	600.00
$1,000	Budapest 6s, 1962	879.50	921.15
20 shs.	Canada Dry Ginger Ale	1,908.13	1,980.50
50 shs.	Consumers Co. cv.	560.59	490.00
10 shs.	Crowell Pub.	1,047.50	2,000.00
50 shs.	Debenhams Secs.	2,113.75	1,912.50
2 shs.	Denver & Salt Lake Ry	69.32	250.00
20 shs.	Eastern Mass. St. Ry pfd. "B"	1,312.25	1,360.00
20 shs.	Electric Bond & Shares Secs.	1,620.25	3,590.50
$2,000	Federal Water Service 5-1/2s 1957	2,074.00	2,100.00
10 shs.	Firestone Tire & Rubber	1,720.00	2,422.50
10 shs.	First National Plc. pfd.	1,048.75	1,040.00
15 shs.	Fleischmann Co.	878.25	1,346.86
5 shs.	Folmer Graflex Corp.	00.00	1.00
$1,000	Great Cons. Elec. Power 6-1/2s 1950	957.00	940.00
$1,000	Hood Rubber cv. 5-1/2s 1936	957.00	940.00
$2,000	Iowa Central 1st. 5s 1938	944.00	800.00
50 shs.	Iron Fireman Mfg. Co.	1,050.00	1,225.00
5 wts.	Karstadt (Rudolph)	720.00	825.00
20 shs.	Loew's Inc.	962.25	1,270.00
10 shs.	Ludlow Mfg. Assoc.	1,803.79	1,850.00
25 shs.	Maytag $3 pfd.	1,225.00	1,121.85
15 shs.	Minneapolis Honeywell Reg. pfd.	1,640.75	2,250.00
10 shs.	Missouri Pacific R.R. pfd.	1,091.25	1,197.50

FIDELITY INVESTMENT ASSOCIATES, INC.
PORTFOLIO
December 31, 1928

Shares	Security	Cost	Market
150 wts.	Monteontini	00.00	1.00
50 shs.	National Shirt Shops	1,200.00	850.00
15 shs.	New York, Chicago, & St. Louis	1,404.61	1,250.00
10 shs.	North Carolina Jt. Stk. Land Bank	1,400.00	1,230.00
15 shs.	Northern Pacific Ry ctf. dep.	1,383.00	1,580.62
$500	Oklahoma Natural Gas 1st. 6s 1946	503.41	480.00
$2,000	Pan American Pet. & Tr. cv. 6s 1934	2,069.00	2,120.00
20 shs.	Penn. Ohio Edison warrants	88.60	680.00
$1,000	Pirelli Co. cv. 7s 1952	1,062.00	1,180.00
10 shs.	Public Service No. Ill.	1,850.00	2,050.00
$1,000	Public Utilities Co. Evansville 6s 1929	1,005.00	1,000.00
$1,000	Snider Packing cv. 6s 1932	1,070.00	945.00
50 shs.	Standard Oil N.J.	2,351.25	2,750.00
10 shs.	United Sts. Improvement	1,135.00	1,681.25
$1,000	United Steel Works 6-1/2s 1947	972.50	880.00
$1,000	Upper Austria cv. 6s 1930	965.00	960.00
10 shs.	Washington Ry. & Elec.	1,172.63	5,000.00
10 shs.	Wilson & Co. "A"	304.00	250.00
		$54,343.99	$67,527.32

Griffeth: What was the allure of convertibles?

Carret: Well, a convertible is a somewhat more prudent way of buying common stock, depending on the premium you have to pay. And very frequently a convertible bond or convertible preferred will give a higher yield than the underlying common and if it sells, say, at a 15 percent premium well, that's worth paying. If it's selling at a 50 percent premium the conversion isn't worth very much. But I still consider convertibles a very good way to buy common stocks when the figures are right.

Griffeth: Also a conservative way to get good income within a portfolio.

Carret: Yes.

Griffeth: In your letter to your shareholders you wrote, "The first ten months of operation provided a prosperous period for Fidelity Investment Associates Inc. Profits would have been larger if a less conservative policy had been followed by the board, but the management deemed it sound policy not to resort to bank borrowings and to maintain a substantial investment in bonds and preferred stocks under the conditions which existed." Why the emphasis at that time on bonds and convertibles?

Carret: I thought the market was rather high.

Griffeth: This was in 1928, so it probably was.

Carret: Yes.

The Crash of 1929

Griffeth: How did you weather the crash of 1929 with the fund? Did you take a big hit?

Carret: Oh, sure. Our portfolio went down just like everyone else's. I had done a little bit of hedging. Somewhere along the line, for example, I remember buying Homestake Mining, and I think I went short some other mining stock that I felt was too high. And that worked out pretty well. Gold, of course, was very popular and in great demand. It always is when everything goes to hell. There was a time, of course, when gold had a fixed price, but Mr. Roosevelt ended that.

Griffeth: Was that a good idea?

Carret: I think it was a very bad idea. I think we'd be much better off if we had a currency that was based on gold as we did for decades.

Griffeth: Why?

Carret: Because you don't have inflation under those conditions. Inflation is very bad. It pushes up the cost of living. They used to talk about the high cost of living back when things only cost about a tenth of what they do now. And that's what the public sees as the high cost of living. Their incomes stay more or less fixed and the cost of what they have to buy tends to go up and it makes people unhappy and usually results in a change of the administration in Washington.

Griffeth: That's not always bad.

Carret: [laughing] Sometimes it's good!

Griffeth: Are we at the point of no return to go back to the gold standard?

Carret: I don't know when we'll get back to it, but I think we will.

Marketing a Mutual Fund

Griffeth: How did you find new shareholders in the early days? Did you market the fund?

Carret: No, I didn't market it. One of my weaknesses of character, if you will, is I'm not very good at that. So the way it worked was a friend who owned some shares would mention it to somebody else and they would come to me and say, "I understand you have a pretty good fund. Can I buy some shares?" And I would say, "Sure." The fund had no loads. No one profited from the transactions of buying and selling shares.

Then when the fund got up to a few hundred thousand dollars, a screwball—I thought he was a screwball—came to me and said, "You have a fund with a remarkable record. Why don't you do something about it?"

I said I was too stupid, or too lazy, or too something.

He said, "Well, let me do it."

Being a conservative and cautious Yankee, I said, "How much will it cost me?"

Well, he must have been in terrible shape financially, because he was willing to do it for a very nominal amount on a drawing account basis. So I said, "Go ahead."

Eventually, he got the fund up to maybe $800,000, and gradually I got involved in finding more people to sell it. And I was going out and doing a certain amount of selling myself, usually not with any great degree of success, but I made some good friends in the retail business.

Usually these sales meetings annoyed the hell out of me because each brokerage house would give me ten minutes in the morning to talk to a bunch of registered reps who had gone through my portfolio the night before. And they always found one stock that was a lemon. You know, there are always some lemons. Nobody could have a hundred securities in a portfolio and not have a lemon.

Well, in those days the usual culprit was First Consolidated Publications Preferred. This was a newspaper chain that had 14 papers at that time. I went to see the company's treasurer one time after they had just sold one paper for many millions of dollars, even though it was losing money. (A newspaper is a strange animal because if there are two newspapers in a town, why, one of them will pay a lot of money to buy the other and kill it.) So after the sale of this particular newspaper, I said to the treasurer, "I think the shareholders would be very happy if you did a deal like this every year."

"Well," he said, "we would only last 14 years at that rate."

I said, "Who cares, as long as the stock brokers make some money out of it!"

So I went in one time to see this brokerage firm out in Los Angeles. And sure enough, one of the brokers said with a kind of a malicious grin, "How are you doing with First Consolidated Preferred?"

And I said, "Oh, we just sold it at a handsome profit." I had gotten so tired of being needled about it that when it got to 25 and they called, like an idiot I let them have it. We made a fair profit on it, but a year later they called the whole bundle of it at 50. So I should have kept it, obviously.

Investing with Computers

Griffeth: We had a mutual fund manager on our TV program who said investors should set a price target for a company they invest in and when it hits the target no matter what the momentum is, no matter what the earnings are, they should get out.

Carret: Great mistake. You have to keep revising your ideas as you go along. Is the rise in the stock justified or not? If it is, why, how far is it going, you don't know. How far is the company going, don't know that.

Griffeth: His philosophy was based on a computer model that considers a number of different criteria. He then sets a price target for the stock, and when it is achieved, he gets out. What do you think of the computer-based money managers these days?

Carret: Nonsense. I am a member of the New York Society of Security Analysts. In fact, I'm one of the founders. And they publish what they call *The Analysts' Journal.* Have you seen it?

Griffeth: No, I haven't.

Carret: Well, it is full of articles written by analysts, I think, for their own amusement or to impress others in the field. They have no practical value at all. They have these long mathematical formulas. Now maybe some pension fund or something like the Rockefeller Foundation with billions of dollars, might get some use from a mathematical formula, but I doubt it. And for the

◆

"You don't analyze a stock by writing out equations of A and B and Q and P and putting them all together. It's nonsense."

◆

average individual, it's utter nonsense. You don't analyze a stock by writing out equations of A and B and Q and P and putting them all together. It's nonsense.

Griffeth: But you know that many successful investors say that you must take the emotion out of investing.

Carret: Oh, yes.

Griffeth: Don't mathematical models remove human emotion from the investment process?

Carret: Yes, they take the emotion out. And they take all the common sense out, too. It's very good to take the emotion out, but not the common sense.

Mutual Funds and the Individual Investor

Griffeth: People today, we find, are starting to buy and sell mutual funds the way they used to buy and sell stocks. We had a gentleman on our TV program one evening who owns 44 different mutual funds. What role should a mutual fund play in an investor's life?

Carret: It depends on whether the investor is sophisticated and has some degree of financial expertise or not. If he has none, why, mutual funds are ideal for him. If he has some, why, a mutual fund can certainly play a role in his affairs, but I look at a mutual fund as being ideal for the average investor. If he wants to take the time and has the interest and will do some studying of finance by buying a few books and reading them and trying to make some sense out of them, he can do better with individual securities than the average mutual fund is likely to do for him. A mutual fund takes the role a savings bank used to play when you got 6 percent on your savings account and we didn't have any inflation.

Griffeth: How do you choose a mutual fund to meet your needs?

Carret: You look over the track record.

Griffeth: Right now there are a number of services that rate mutual funds based on various criteria such as portfolio turnover and the amount of risk that a fund assumes.

Carret: How do they measure that?

Griffeth: Well, they adjust the portfolio's performance for risk. The volatility.

Carret: The beta.

Griffeth: The beta. Exactly. I mean, there are an awful lot of sophisticated criteria used to rate mutual funds.

Carret: Yes. Well, it's like the old story of the preacher who kept the handwritten sign in his pulpit that read KISS. One of the parishioners saw it and asked the preacher where he got it. The preacher said, "My wife gave it to me."

"Oh, isn't that nice, very sentimental."

"No," the preacher said. "It's not sentimental at all. It means, 'Keep it simple, stupid!'"

Griffeth: All the sophistication, all of the computer models, the mathematical models, the various investment systems, aren't necessary?

Carret: They don't do me any good. I don't understand them, so to me they're no good.

The 1920s vs. the 1980s

Griffeth: You experienced the stock market crashes of the 1920s and the 1980s. How were those periods different?

Carret: The 1920s were much more speculative, because the market was affected to a great degree by pools. In those days, wealthy entrepreneurs would get together and pool their money and they would "paint the tape." For example, they would start buying Radio Corporation of America, which was one of the great speculative favorites of the 1920s. (And remember, a member of the stock exchange could do this very cheaply.) So they would buy and sell large amounts of a stock, and people would see the trades on the [ticker] tape and they would say, "Oh, geez, there must be something going on."

So then they would start to buy it and eventually if the stock went up enough, why, the insiders would unload and the pool would make a handsome profit. The SEC has pretty much put a stop to that sort of thing; I don't think it goes on at all as far as I know.

And now we have a tremendously broader market. I don't know how many stocks were listed on the New York Stock Exchange in 1929, but it was probably a few hundred at the most. And now you have thousands on the stock exchange. Plus you have an over the counter market [now called NASDAQ] that is tremendous. And you have what used to be called The Curb [now the American Stock Exchange], which is a fair size market, to say nothing of the Midwest Stock Exchange, the Pacific Coast Stock Exchange, and so on. So you have an enormous market.

Griffeth: Not to mention the London Stock Exchange, for example, where U.S. stocks also trade.

Carret: Yes.

Griffeth: An awful lot of people today who are retired remember the Depression and the crash. And we are told statistically that people generally are too conservative with their investments for retirement. They don't take enough risks to keep up with the rate of inflation. Are they needlessly doing that because they fear we could have another 1929?

Carret: I suppose, yes. I don't know how you'd reassure them. Although, it will be very bad when they lose their caution.

Griffeth: Are people too cautious with their investments?

Carret: Usually, yes. You can't make money without taking some risks, you just have to be sure that it's an intelligent risk.

Young Mutual Fund Managers

Griffeth: Last question. When you were on my television show recently, you said you wouldn't invest in a fund that was run by a 28-year-old.

Carret: Obviously, it's an advantage to have had experience. It may slow you down, but that's not always bad. But to have had no experience and to know nothing about depressions, panics, major spills in the market, except what you read in some book, is something of a disadvantage.

Now, not everybody has to have experience to gain wisdom or some degree of it. Some people are born with "an old head on young shoulders," or something like that. But in general, I myself would feel some hesitancy about entrusting money to a 28-year-old.

NOTE: In his book The Art of Speculation, *first published in 1930, Carret summarized his views on how to be a successful investor with "Twelve Commandments for Speculators." I think they provide a fitting end to this chapter.*

Twelve Commandments for Speculators

1) Never hold fewer than ten different securities covering five different fields of business.

2) At least once in six months reappraise every security held.

3) Keep at least half the total fund in income-producing securities.

4) Consider yield the least important factor in analyzing any stock.

5) Be quick to take losses, reluctant to take profits.

6) Never put more than 25% of a given fund into securities about which detailed information is not readily and regularly available.

7) Avoid "inside information" as you would the plague.

8) Seek facts diligently, advice never.

9) Ignore mechanical formulas for valuing securities.

10) When stocks are high, money rates rising, business prosperous, at least half a given fund should be placed in short-term bonds.

11) Borrow money sparingly and only when stocks are low, money rates low or falling, and business depressed.

12) Set aside a moderate proportion of available funds for purchase of long-term options on stocks of promising companies whenever available.

Source: The Art of Speculation, *by Philip L. Carret. Used by permission of Fraser Publishing Co., Burlington, VT.*

MARIO J. GABELLI

Birth Date: June 19, 1942

Education: Fordham University, B.S. in Accounting (Summa Cum Laude) Columbia University, M.B.A. in Finance and International Banking

Hobbies: Golf, trap & skeet shooting, opera

Alternate Career: "Movie Making"

O *ne evening when Mario Gabelli was my guest on CNBC, I mentioned to him how much I thought he looked like David Letterman.*

"I don't know about that," Gabelli, always the businessman, said, "but we would welcome his account."

Gabelli was born to run a money management company. He is a shrewd businessman with one of the quickest investment minds on Wall Street, a master marketer, and—as you'll see from our interview— he is prone to making bold, sometimes outrageous statements. He also has a rather irreverent sense of humor. The last sentence of his official biography reads, "He does not read novels, preferring 'the fiction found in most annual reports.'" Needless to say, his annual contribution to the Barron's Roundtable is always informative and entertaining.

He is the founder, chairman, and chief executive of Gabelli Funds, Inc., which is based in Rye, New York. G.F. includes money management services through GAMCO Investors, mutual funds through Gabelli Funds, and broker/dealer services through Gabelli & Company.

Gabelli is a fundamentally oriented stock picker from the Graham & Dodd school. In fact, he prides himself on having developed a Graham & Dodd-like method of determining the value of a publicly traded company before it is taken private in a leveraged buyout. You will read about his Private Market Value method during our interview.

But Gabelli is probably best known to the public as a prodigious investor in—and owner of—media and telecommunications companies. He was an early champion of companies involved in cable

TV and cellular telephone. And his mutual funds and separately managed accounts combined were the largest individual shareholder in Paramount Communications during the protracted 1993 takeover battle for the company between Sumner Redstone's Viacom the—eventual winner, of course—and Barry Diller's QVC Network.

In early 1994, Gabelli lost his star fund manager when Elizabeth Bramwell left to start her own money management company. Even though neither Gabelli nor Bramwell ever commented publicly on the reasons for her departure. And when I interviewed Gabelli for this book in the summer of 1994, he still had not found a new manager for his growth fund.

During our interview, Gabelli talked about how and when he first became interested in media companies, about his version of the Information Superhighway of the future, and about turning mutual fund managers into stars.

AUGUST 16, 1994

Graham & Dodd & Gabelli

Bill Griffeth: How did you decide to come to Wall Street?

Mario Gabelli: I was already buying stocks when I was 15 years old and maybe even younger than that. I started off by buying Hunter Mountain Ski Resort in the early 1950s. I kind of enjoyed the market, I enjoyed the intensity. I would read the Wall Street Journal in high school. So Wall Street to me was just kind of an extension of what I had already been doing. It was kind of a passion.

I went to Columbia to get the credentials to get on the dance floor on Wall Street. Roger Murray got me interested and hooked me into security analysis. I always knew I liked Wall Street. I didn't know what facet, though, until I took a security analysis course and, bang, I loved it.

Griffeth: He was your professor at Columbia?

Gabelli: Yes, he was the Graham & Dodd security analysis professor. He edited one of the editions of Graham & Dodd's *Security Analysis.*

Griffeth: So that's where you were bitten by Graham & Dodd.

Gabelli: Yes. That's it.

As an aside, Bill, I have four videotapes of Roger at the age of 86 lecturing for one hour and 20 minutes at the Broadcasting Museum. And I offer these lectures to anyone interested in them for free, particularly universities.

At Columbia we awakened a fundamental security analysis course now taught by Greenwald, and of which I am a guest lecturer.

Griffeth: What was it about that system of investment analysis that attracted you?

Gabelli: Well, I had a great marketing flare for some of the businesses I was running while I was in school. Plus, I had an accounting background. So it all came together in terms of the dynamics of the business. It lent itself to my very strong accounting and finance background of running numbers, looking at spread sheets, reading annual reports, tearing them apart. It was just exactly what I was looking for.

Griffeth: Did you use it when you were working for Loeb, Rhoades and William D. Witter?

Gabelli: Well, no. At Loeb, Rhoades I really was not on the academic side of the world. When I joined Loeb, Rhoades in June 1967 Michael Steinhardt had just resigned on a Friday and I walked in on a Monday morning. I was originally going to work in a different area, but they turned to me and said, "Michael just quit on Friday, so you are now the automobile analyst and the conglomerates analyst because Michael covered it."

So what I did basically was market-oriented research as opposed to fundamental security analysis. That means you try to find undervalued companies, but you are also responsible for following a traditional niche at a sell side brokerage firm. So I was the automobile and farm equipment and industrial products analyst in 1967 and 1968.

In 1969 another analyst left and I became the broadcast analyst, which meant that I followed all the movies and entertainment stocks as well as business service companies. And that's how I got into cable and broadcasting and media.

Private Market Value

Griffeth: You certainly developed a wide area of expertise.

Gabelli: During that time, Bill, I was responsible for consumer cyclicals, like the autos, for example; producer durables like farm equipment; and growth companies in business service and media and entertainment. So I had an array of companies that were non-tech, non-drug, and non-bio. (And by the way, there was no word "bio" being used at that time.) At Loeb, Rhoades the emphasis was much more cyclically oriented from a top down point of view.

Then I left Loeb and went to William D. Witter where I was a sell side analyst, and I headed up a team of which Elizabeth Bramwell was a member and of which Sue Byrne was a member. We did research on small cap companies.

It was because of what happened in the stock market of 1973 and 1974—that real debacle—that people were wondering, "Why do I want to own stocks?" So during this time I developed a concept based on the premise that there are wealthy families out there that want to buy businesses and there are wealthy groups of individuals and corporations that want to buy businesses. What do they look at? They look at the intrinsic value of a company. And when they took a public company private they would do what I would call a "private market value" transaction. I coined that phrase very early in the process, and I promulgated it among the professionals in the investment business.

So what I have added to the Graham & Dodd school is what they called intrinsic value. I called it private market value, or the value of a public business being taken private. And I wrote up research reports during that period of time, and that's kind of where I became well known back in the late 1970s. I caught the LBO [leveraged buyout, where public companies are taken private] mania very early in the process.

Griffeth: Can you give me, in English, what the private market value method is?

Gabelli: Well, what you try to do is a financial analysis of a company. You start off with the industry it is in. Let's say it's broadcasting. You ask yourself, "What's broadcasting going to do for the next eight to ten years? What's it likely to do in the context of an inflationary environment? If inflation is 5 [percent] what will happen to revenues? What happens if the dollar goes up or down? What does the company earn at the TV station level? Why would someone want to buy it? What are the constraints on that purchase? What is the value of that cash flow? What happens to that cash flow eight years out? What would people pay eight years out?

And after you answered those questions, you said, "Okay, if I've got Taft broadcasting, or Lin Broadcasting, or Chris Craft selling in the public market at $10, what would be the value of the pieces affected by taxes, what would someone pay today and what would they pay five years from now? Whether an industrialist is buying it, or an LBO group, a financial buyer, or a strategic buyer or synergistic buyer, what would they pay?" And that's what I call the private market value.

◆

"What makes a great diamond is cut, color, carets, and clarity . . . all four of them together make a perfect stone. So, too, a great stock."

◆

Griffeth: And you use this method of valuation on the companies you put in your funds today?

Gabelli: Yes. Plus we add one other element to the methodology, which is earnings per share. So we look at the earnings per share, we look at cash flow, we look at private market value and we look at management and blend them together like a diamond.

What makes a great diamond is cut, color, carets, and clarity. You know all four of them together make a perfect stone. So, too, a great stock. When you have all of these elements of the valuation process, plus good management, then we take a look at that company.

Gabelli & Company

Griffeth: Tell me about the founding of Gabelli & Company.

Gabelli: While I was at William D. Witter we were taken over by Drexel on August 29, 1976. And believe it or not, Bill, that day was going to be the first I ever took time off to play golf. I got a call at home from my research director. He says, "Mario, you've got to come in this morning." I said, "Come on, I'm going to play golf!" He says, "You'd better come in. We just sold ourselves out."

Griffeth: [Laughing] That's enough to affect your golf game forever!

Gabelli: [Also laughing] Well, you certainly keep your head down!

So what happened is, within 30 days Drexel took us over. Tubby Burnham was the patriarch at Drexel at the time. He's a nice guy and a good investor (Mr. Loeb was the same way), but I didn't want to work for a big firm.

So I had breakfast with a guy from Denver, a guy by the name of Dick Goldstein. He said, "So Mario, what are you going to do?" I said, "Well, I'm interviewing with this firm and that firm." He said, "What, are you crazy? Why don't you start your own firm?" At that point, I had not really focused on it. But bang! Within 90 days I was in business.

I made a mistake, though. The basic fundamental business I started was a sell-side brokerage firm. I knew I could make money for the customer, but I wasn't sure how they would pay me.

I tried to raise a million dollars in capital and wound up raising $75,000. Some of my neighbors would knock on my door and say, "Mario, I'll give you $50,000." Then the next morning they would knock on my door and say, "I want it back!" [Laughing] That happened two or three times.

So I raised $75,000, plus I put in some Lin Broadcasting stock that I had bought, which had done quite well. And that's how the firm got started as a sell side firm as opposed to a money management firm.

I backed into money management when Honeywell in 1980 or 1981 knocked on my door and gave me $10 million and everything took off. Because internally it said to us, "Hey, if Honeywell is willing to give us the 10 million bucks we must have something the rest of the world doesn't." And so we grew from there.

"Packaged Products"

Griffeth: When did you start your mutual funds?

Gabelli: We found we couldn't handle small accounts for lots of friends, so I started the Gabelli Asset Fund. It was a way for individuals to buy into our style. You know, a guy calls up and says, "Look, I want you to handle this $25,000 account for me." But we had no place to put it. So we put it into what is called the Gabelli Asset Fund, a no-load, open-end fund, and that's how it got launched. And then we launched the closed-end fund, which was the Gabelli Equity Trust.

And then I convinced Elizabeth [Bramwell] that growth stocks were In. But nobody would believe me that growth was going to be fashionable again. I said to Elizabeth, "You've got to run my growth fund for me." She was my research director at the time, and I told her, "If you are going to do it, Elizabeth, you've got to let me make you a star."

Griffeth: You wanted to cultivate her as a personality in the public eye?

Gabelli: Yes, the same way we are doing it now with Caesar Bryan and some of my other money managers. We had to do that because it was the only way to compete against Dreyfus and Fidelity and Vanguard at the time. It's a way to get shelf space.

Griffeth: You can't do it just with a decent track record?

Gabelli: No. You've got people with no record who have shelf space. The shelf space I'm talking about for no-load funds is, for example, the inside cover of the *Wall Street Journal*. That's where they advertise. They don't sell performance, Bill, they sell shelf space.

Griffeth: But performance can become the marketing tool of a fund. It has to have marquee stocks in the portfolio to attract people as much as anything, doesn't it?

Gabelli: I would say the following: If you gave me an average performing fund, labeled it a growth fund at a time when growth is in vogue, gave me the inside cover of the *Wall Street Journal* as an ad space, I would grow that fund phenomenally.

> "... I could pick a fund with nobody's name on it, create a personality for that individual—even if he's got average performance—and create a very attractive business."

I hope I don't offend anybody, but let's take Lou Rukeyser. Lou has learned how to market, and he's got some guy working for him who knows mail order marketing techniques. If I got that guy to be my partner, I could pick a fund with nobody's name on it, create a personality for that individual—even if he's got average performance—and create a very attractive business.

I think you could create a great business if you got lucky and found another Peter Lynch. I found Sue Byrne, and she's going to do a great job for me. I found Elizabeth. I mean, I created Elizabeth. I think Caesar [Bryan] is going to do a great job, but his niche is much more volatile. I mean, gold stocks are terrible. If I had a guy like Mark Mobius, he'd be terrific. And I'll find him. [*NOTE: Turn to page 149 for more on Mark Mobius.*]

Griffeth: You know, there are people who feel that marketing funds the way you are talking about draws in a number of investors for the wrong reasons.

Gabelli: Well, that's a different issue. The flow of funds into equities at the wrong time of the cycle is part of what Charles Mackay wrote about in his book, *Extraordinary Popular Delusions and the Madness of Crowds* back in the 1850s. The problem today is valuations have gotten ahead of themselves because of the flow of funds, but I think the fundamentals could catch up.

For example, 1991 was a disaster for those who bought health care stocks. But if you had bought a value fund in 1991, you would have made a lot of money. So I'm not sure that I would share with you a broad-brush comment that there is a mania that could result in everybody losing money.

Griffeth: Here is what I'm saying: Individuals should be investing in mutual funds for retirement or for a child's college education or whatever. And yet, some of them find themselves buying 20, 30, even 40 mutual funds sometimes simply because they have seen the fund manager's picture in the newspaper or they have seen that fund manager on television. In other words, they are buying the fund manager, they are not buying the fund's concept and matching it to their needs.

Gabelli: Yes, okay, then what you have is people buying toothpaste.

Griffeth: Which is what mutual funds are becoming, don't you think?

Gabelli: They are what I call "packaged products." I use that word precisely for that concept, namely that the consumer is very comfortable buying toothpaste as opposed to simply putting baking soda on his toothbrush.

There is no question that John Neff's Vanguard/Windsor or Peter Lynch and Fidelity Magellan were packaged products. You know, those guys have staying power.

Savings Vehicle or Fad?

Griffeth: But how long can this marketing and packaging go on before the mutual fund industry goes beyond its purpose of providing a savings vehicle for the masses, and instead becomes a fad? Where do we go from here?

Gabelli: The way I look at it is very simple. The United States, Germany, Japan, and England have aging populations. In the United States, we have augmented a government mandated retirement system, Social Security, with a private system. We know it as either corporate pensions or 401(k) plans. I think you are going to start seeing a lot of that in Japan, Germany, and England. You are going to start seeing mutual funds in these countries sprout.

So, yes, you've got this growth in the United States, but I think you are going to see an enormous amount of private savings in these other countries. You are seeing an aging of the population in these four countries, and you are going to start seeing mutual funds accelerate, not from the point of view of investing in these countries but from the point of view from the excess assets that are going to be accumulated looking for returns.

◆

"I think the system will do fine, the [mutual] funds fill a need for people, as they are getting older, to have savings."

◆

So the real question is, over the next 20 years, as these four countries continue to generate excess capital and this capital migrates toward private investments, how does an investor earn a double digit return in a single digit environment? I still believe that, just as good managements at General Electric and Cap/Cities and Honeywell and Ralston Purina can attract my attention as a fund manager, I think well-run, well-conceived financial approaches trying to achieve—on a risk-adjusted basis—these double digit returns can do well.

On the other side of the coin, there are guys who are going out and putting together packaged products with big fat fees and, in some cases, with more risk than is necessary. Certainly, the foggiest out there need to be examined.

Griffeth: If investors get into certain funds because the risk was misrepresented, aren't they the ones who will head for the exits in a hurry at the first sign of a market correction, leading potentially to something worse?

Gabelli: My own sense of it is that there will be, at the margin, a flow of funds away from mutual funds due to a market correction. You will have a major concern at some point in time with some mutual funds. I can't tell you when, I don't know which fund, and I don't know which area. I would be more wrong if I were to say that it will never happen.

There is no question that some of the banks and some of the other intermediaries selling mutual funds are hiring salesmen who could have been selling shoes the week before. That always lends itself to abuse, because when some guy walks in they are going to say, "Come on in. I've got to make my quota today. What do I care about your problems five years from now?" That is a problem.

But on balance I think the system will do fine, because the funds fill a need for people, as they are getting older, to have savings. It's a very convenient way to have savings.

The Gabelli Funds

Griffeth: Let's move on. In your family of funds, some are load funds, some are no-load. Why?

Gabelli: We are not as good at managing a business as we are at picking stocks. When I started the asset fund and the growth fund I said I wanted them to be no-load. Then what happened was Shearson came along and said, "Mario, we want to do a road show and we want to raise a fund for you in the value category, and we will place $1.1 billion." It was one of the largest initial underwritings that any fund manager on Wall Street has had with one underwriter. Shearson did not syndicate it. So that's how I got into the load business, because Shearson came to me and said, "We want to do load funds." So the value fund is a load fund because it was born that way through Shearson.

Some of my other funds are designed to become load funds after they have been in business for a couple of years, in part, to slow down the money coming in. My small cap growth fund, for example, has had a phenomenal record, and I converted it to a load fund and absolutely no money has come in since then. At $200 million, it's the right size, it's now fully invested and I may shift it back to a no-load product.

Griffeth: Your convertible securities fund is closed to new investors, but it only has about $120 million in it.

Gabelli: What happened there, Bill, is very simple. In December [of 1993] or January [of 1994], I said to myself 1994 is going to be a tough year. I think interest rates are going to go up, which is going to hurt the bond feature of the converts [convertible securities] and therefore stock prices are going to be lackluster, and that will hurt the premiums. I didn't want to take any more money in so I shut it down, even though it only has $120 million. Another thing that caused me to close the fund was some of the converts that I bought cheap were being called because companies like Bershire Hathaway and IBM called in their converts as bonds rose or the stocks rose. So I was losing merchandise as fast I could find new ideas.

But recently the reverse has happened. The stock market has come down, interest rates have gone up, and so all of a sudden I'm starting to find converts that have a better risk reward, better yields, and conversion premiums have dried up. So maybe I made a mistake. Maybe I should have left it open. I'm not going to reopen it, though.

Griffeth: Ever?

Gabelli: I don't think so. I think this convertible fund is closed forever, and I'll tell you why. I'm thinking of asking the shareholders to make it a closed-end fund. I haven't decided yet.

Griffeth: Give me a sense of your company's investment decision making process. Do you have a morning meeting where you go over buy and sell candidates, for example?

Gabelli: Here's how we do it. We run $8.5 billion, all in equities. About half of that is in the mutual funds, the other half is in 850 separately managed accounts. And as a group, we all work off a centralized research list of companies. And we are constantly looking for change within the context of our companies, knowing full well the changes in value are very slow in coming. We are constantly having our scouts go out and report back. Our scouts are analysts who tell us what they found after going out and seeing the companies or seeing their competition.

Then, there is also an exchange of ideas within the office. Today, for example, I tried some of Church & Dwight's new toothpaste, and I may even report on that tomorrow. Somebody else may come in and say, "Hey, I just saw *Forrest Gump*" and we'll discuss what it may do for the production company that made it. So we have an interplay of dynamics. Someone else will come back and say, "Hey, at Gencorp, Aerojet General is being discussed as a possible spinoff." That's a catalyst. That's what we like. Our methodology is then to run spread sheets on the company so we will know what Gencorp is suppose to do for the next five to seven years. And then when a catalyst develops that we kind of are intrigued about, the analyst following Gencorp will comment on that, and we may then sit down and say, "Should we buy more Gencorp, or should we sell Gencorp?"

Griffeth: So you seem to be saying that your investment ideas come from your own experiences.

Gabelli: Yes, we are basically very narrow analysts. We define certain areas of competence. For example, media and entertainment are obviously two of our strong suits. But then, as another example, when I go to the airport and I start seeing people queue up for coffee at $2.50 at Starbucks I start looking for things like changes in consumer habits and consumer tastes. So sometimes a lot of the things we do are right in front of us.

We are fairly comfortable on cyclical things like outboard engines, given my background we think we know how to understand and value and we also understand the replacement part of cycles for refrigerators. What is very hard for us as analysts—and therefore we tend not to invest in them—are products that create new markets, like drugs. We were very, very good in cellular, but that was an outgrowth of what we knew in telecommunications. We felt that people who use the telephone a lot would make the seamless transition to becoming heavy users of cellular if the quality was there.

The ideal candidates for us are franchises where there is pricing power. We think the *Wall Street Journal* is an example of pricing power in a franchise. We think the *New York Times* is. We think that occasionally companies like Marlboro and Coca Cola become question marks because you are always worried about the old classic. And by the same token you wonder whether or not a single product company like a Snapple Beverage is a fad within a secular trend toward people disposing of a portion of their disposable income.

Another good example of a fad is we don't tend to buy the fifth river boat company in Natchez. Some of my friends are from Natchez, so I'm not knocking Natchez. I'm just saying that we would buy a company if a guy had a singular gaming franchise in New York City. So we do try to make distinctions.

Also, the companies we go after have historically been in the United States and it's only within the last five years that we're reaching offshore to find businesses. We kind of believe the Vancouver Telephone Company, for example, is pretty decent now that new management is in place and we can buy it at 3 times cash flow.

The ideas are clustered in industries where there are strong buyers, and we try to find companies that have strong brand and franchise names.

The Media Bug Bites

Griffeth: The theme, or industry, with which you have been most closely identified over the years is, of course, the media. Do you remember when that bug bit you?

Gabelli: I was basically assigned the task of following the media industry in 1969 . . .

Griffeth: Yes, but you also followed autos and other areas as well. Why did this one stick?

Gabelli: What stuck to me was when I went to Japan to calculate the ability of the American industry to compete against the Japanese in 1979–1980, it was apparent to me that we were not going to win. We had to redo the whole industrial fabric of America.

And then when I looked at our broadcasters and how, among other things, they could grow cash flows at an exhilarating rate—plus the fact that they were tied to the consumer sector of the U.S. economy—it was apparent that it was automobiles no, broadcasting yes. So that's what really drove home the notion of being in broadcasting. And that drove me to cable. Cable really became a great idea when the satellite was able to deliver HBO. I jumped all over the cable stocks in 1977 and 1978. I was one of the first to analyze the value of an unbilled franchise and that's how I acquired an understanding of the value of cellular because I was one of the first to do unbilleds. That's why I knew the value of a cellular franchise then, and it's why I know the value of an SMR franchise now.

The concept of global telecommunications, global media, global entertainment just makes a lot of sense to me. I think MTV is a classic example. In the United States, there are 60 million homes that have it. There are 60 million in Europe, 70 million in Latin America, and another 60 million in Asia that will have it within two or three years. I mean it's just terrific for eyeballs, and it travels well. ESPN sports travels well, also. And it's my job to figure this out.

Griffeth: The telecommunications concept runs through all of your funds. I mean you really, in some cases, have a group of de facto media funds.

Gabelli: If one was very analytical, 10 percent of the stock markets around the world are telephones. If you take Japan, 16 percent is telephone. If you take Peru, 50 percent is telephone. Mexico has 34 percent. So if you look at the world markets, they are 25 percent telephone, cable, broadcasting, entertainment, and media.

In the United States, telecommunication is only about 8 or 9 percent of the market, and I may be 20 or 25 percent. So that's why my funds may look like they are overweighted in that sector.

Mr. Gabelli's Information Superhighway

Griffeth: So what is your version of what the infamous Information Superhighway will look like when it is eventually completed?

Gabelli: It is very simple. An individual who is 13 years old sitting at home will order up on his interactive TV a way to play the Sega Channel. Or he will get Wrestlemania on Pay-for-View. Somebody else in the house will be able to shop. Somebody else will be able to "go" to Hong Kong and order up a menu of travel services, see where the Mandarin Hotel is, figure out which side of the island it is on, get a picture of the Mandarin, figure out which room he wants, what kind of view he wants, what price to pay.

"So what I see is Sears & Roebuck of 100 years ago, and I see the youth of the future being trained on interactivity."

So what I see is Sears & Roebuck of 100 years ago, and I see the youth of the future being trained on interactivity. What I'm not clear on is the delivery system, whether it's over the air, whether it's cable, or something else. But it's going to happen. Consumers don't care who delivers it. They just want a high-quality service at a cheap price, and it's going to happen.

And the Microsofts of the world are going to be competing against the Paramounts for a share of revenue dollars from the consumer against guys like JC Penney and American Express. By the way, American Express could be in real trouble here because, in theory, the guy that has access to the superhighway will try to figure out a way to have his own credit card. But then again, American Express is smart enough to figure all of this out.

Interactivity is basically the same as when I was growing up in 1945. I used to go home and watch Flash Gordon, and Ming [the Merciless] would get up on that screen and they would talk to each other just like Dick Tracy. [Laughing] The future is the past.

Griffeth: But how long before all of this actually happens? For example, we were told long ago that we would have these individual computers in our homes, and it took a lot longer than expected for that reality to happen.

Gabelli: What's the difference if it's five or ten years or so?

Griffeth: Well, the difference is that the companies you are investing in have to realize those valuations and provide returns to your shareholders.

Gabelli: When you find companies like John Malone's Telecommunications Inc., when you find Time Warner, when you find Comcast, when you find solid managements with great cash flow franchises that are doing well, they are still going to bob and weave, but they will do well. That's the way you've got to look at portfolios. I'm not worried about two years.

The thing that distinguishes the Warren Buffets, the Graham & Dodds, the Mario Gabellis, is not a time frame like one month, three months, or six months. Instead, it is really about accumulating capital.

The other thing is—because we find so few quality companies that fit our image—we've become like postage stamp collectors. So Mario Gabelli's style has been akin to a postage stamp collector, which has a big virtue in that it allows profits that compound tax deferred. And in an environment, Bill, when you've got a 40 percent tax on dividends and a 28 percent tax on long-term capital gains a buy and hold strategy really compounds the benefit to the shareholder.

Paying Shareholders Back

Griffeth: Shareholders in your closed-end trust receive a very generous 10 percent pay out each year. Is that a marketing gimmick?

Gabelli: It was really not a marketing idea, but it was a desire to give the current generation of shareholders ballast with regards to the net asset value so that the public value [of the fund] would track the underlying private value. [*NOTE: In other words, he doesn't want the price of the fund to trade at too high a premium or too steep a discount relative to the fund's net asset value.*]

And you must understand one more element. Every regulated investment company, in order to maintain its tax conduit status, has to payout 90 percent of its dividends, interest, and realized capital gains. Our goal, as money managers, is to beat inflation plus 10 percent, to add 10 percent to the value of a client's portfolio so that if inflation is 4 percent we should be able to do 14 percent.

Griffeth: But if the fund doesn't make the 10 percent, in order to meet your payout obligation you end up kicking some principal back to the shareholder.

Gabelli: Well, think of it another way. If we don't make 10 percent, what the manager is saying—rightly or wrongly or intellectually or arrogantly—is that if he doesn't earn the 14 percent he thinks he can earn on a long-term basis in markets that are going to gross 7, 8, or 9 [percent], he is then willing to give back some of the money the shareholders have entrusted to him.

You've got to understand one other thing. In a closed-end fund I don't get any benefit from paying out 10 percent. I'm not marketing the fund because I don't get any new money in. Unlike an open-end fund where money comes in, I can tell a guy I'm going to give him 10 percent but I don't get any money out of it. The fund's shares are bought and sold like any common stock, but the manager doesn't get any benefit out of it, Bill.

And there's something else I've done that we should talk about. I don't think there is one other equity product in the country that has guaranteed customers 6 percent [which Gabelli does with his ABC Fund]. I'm the first manager that's done that. That's not good business sense.

Griffeth: And you are willing to admit to it?

Gabelli: Yes, I have no problem with that. I'm not the best businessman in the world. I'm a pretty good investor. I would say I'm in the top 10 percent of investors in the world in the last 20 years in terms of returns. I'll compare our returns for 20 years with anybody. With an average annual 21 percent return compounded—including one down year in 1990—Gamco has got to have one of the best records during that time period of any registered investment advisor. I'm only talking unleveraged investments now.

One More Question

Griffeth: You are obviously highly intelligent and highly energetic with a lot of diversified interests. Is this company going to hold your interest until you decide to hang it up, or do you see yourself doing something else someday?

Gabelli: That's a very good question. You know, Mr. Loeb is about 93 years old. He still goes to the office every day, and he enjoys picking stocks. Mr. Gabelli has 41 more years to go to get to that age. And as long as I can buy and sell stocks, I'm going to do it. I think it's a great business. I enjoy it, I think it's fun, I think it's challenging, and I think I can deliver a return for the investor above the average that he can't do with an index fund.

WILLIAM H. GROSS

Birth Date: April 13, 1944

Education: Duke University, B.A.; M.B.A. from UCLA Graduate School of Business

Hobbies: Stamp collecting, running

Alternate Career: Accountant

*B*ill Gross has been called the best-known fixed income manager in the United States. He has also been called the Peter Lynch of the fixed income market. The fact is, Gross probably oversees the management of more fixed income investments than any single manager in the country. His Pacific Investment Management Company (or PIMCO) manages over $55 billion in fixed income securities. Of that amount, $46 billion is devoted to over 200 separate accounts managed for large corporations, states, cities, and several foreign countries. The other $9 billion is in eight separate mutual funds, including the Harbor Bond Fund, the PIMCO Low Duration and Low Duration II funds, the PIMCO Total Return and Total Return III funds, and PFAMCO (or Pacific Financial Asset Management) Balanced and Managed Bond funds.*

In 1994, when the Paine Webber U.S. Government Securities Fund ran into trouble because of excessive use of derivatives in order to achieve a more competitive yield, Paine Webber hired Bill Gross and PIMCO to take over management of the fund and restore the confidence of its shareholders.

For someone with the high-pressure job of managing so much money for so many important institutional clients, Gross is a surprisingly calm, soft-spoken, and accessible person. He is a frequent guest on CNBC, commenting on Federal Reserve policy and the direction of interest rates.

I called Gross at his offices in Newport Beach, California, one afternoon after the markets had closed. We talked about his rise from coupon clipper (literally) to fixed income powerhouse, about the four things he looks for when he invests in a bond, and about the proper use of derivatives in a portfolio. I also asked him whether the enormity of managing $55 billion ever gets to him. His answer might surprise you.

AUGUST 23, 1994

Coupon Clipper

Bill Griffeth: Let's start with your early career. You started with PIMCO right out of college, didn't you?

Bill Gross: Right out of UCLA Graduate School in 1971. I was looking for basically any job and a job specifically in the stock market. But I found one at Pacific Mutual Life Insurance in Los Angeles that offered responsibilities for private placement in bonds and such esoteric things as clipping coupons. In the old days we actually stored bonds in our vault down in the basement at our offices on Sixth Street in Los Angeles. And that was part of my assignment.

Griffeth: As the new kid you actually got to clip the coupons, huh?

Gross: Yes, it wasn't just an idle phrase. It was a reality I guess back then.

Griffeth: Most people that I know in fixed income didn't start out wanting to be there. They wanted to be in equities.

Gross: That's correct.

Griffeth: What is the thing about fixed income that most people don't aspire to?

Gross: Well, you know, I think as a young person you are more risk oriented. And back in the early 1970s and even today, the equity side is certainly more glamorous than the fixed income side. There's more action, so to speak, in terms of at least perceived movement in the marketplace. And it's a much more visible area. You can pick up the *Wall Street Journal* and get quotations on thousands of stocks, but the bond column and the bond quotes are sort of buried in the back.

And it's the same thing with quote machines in brokers' offices. Stock prices and stock information are readily available, but bonds are basically a pick-up-a-phone type of an event in an over-the-counter type of market.

So I think all of those things combined—the risk orientation, the visibility, and the information flow—lead young people into the equity arena first.

Griffeth: So when did it become clear to you that you would remain in the fixed income market?

Gross: Probably after about a year and a half. I was beginning to figure out that there was this huge hole, as in a line in football. There was a huge hole in the line on the fixed income side because most people shunned it. Most of the smart people were over on the equity side. And it seemed to me that, as active management was developing in bonds in the early 1970s, there was just a super opportunity to manage something that no one really wanted to do. In other words, there was very little competition and quite a lot of opportunity.

And so after about a year and a half I started managing some bonds for the Pacific Mutual Portfolio on an active basis in order to establish a track record. And, gosh, it wasn't another year and a half or two years until we got our first PIMCO client in Southern California Edison.

Griffeth: How much money did they bring in?

Gross: $50 million. But our real big break was about a year after that when AT&T selected us. I say "us," but there was only me as portfolio manager and we had a marketing person and a business person and sort of a staff of five or six. And we were encased within the much larger organization of Pacific Mutual Life. PIMCO was a subsidiary, and so it gave us some type of respectability.

But anyway, AT&T picked us as their first investment counselor on the bond side as well as their first investment manager west of the Mississippi. And once we had been picked by AT&T, it sort of opened up all doors I guess, and led to many more accounts over the years.

Griffeth: What kinds of fixed income instruments did you have to work with back then?

Gross: It was sort of a selected mix of private placements which, as you know, are sort of direct arrangements with the company issuing them, plus other corporate bonds, and of course government bonds.

And believe it or not, there weren't any mortgage passthroughs at that time. You know, the first Ginnie Mae passthroughs first came out, I think, around 1974 or 1975. So we didn't have the mortgage market to participate in. It was basically corporates and governments.

Pimco's First $50 Million

Griffeth: What year did you start managing these corporate accounts?

Gross: Southern California Edison was 1973 and then AT&T came in 1975.

Griffeth: So you started PIMCO right at the bottom of the stock market.

Gross: Yes, 1974 was a bottom and 1970 was a bottom just as I was getting out of school. In fact, bonds suffered throughout the entire 1970s in terms of a bear market. It turned out to be a pretty good training ground for learning how to suffer silently.

Griffeth: Did you make a conscious decision to focus most of your business on institutional clients, or did you simply take the money wherever it came from?

Gross: No, we made that specific decision. We were fortunate to have a business person—Bill Podlich, who is a partner right now—who was able to perceive in the early 1970s that our best niche, from a business and marketing standpoint, would be on the institutional side. It had numerous benefits for a fledgling firm. I mean, clients like AT&T and American Express and Philip Morris and RJR and so on, were basically aggregators of funds through their own corporate pension plans. In today's market, by contrast, if you are starting mutual funds and you have to advertise for new business, you know, that's an aggregation type of expense. But in the 1970s and the early 1980s basically our institutional clients themselves were aggregating for us at no expense to Pacific Investment Management Company.

In addition, there were a lot of consultants who were doing the same thing. In other words, all we had to do was make one or two visits to these major aggregators as opposed to advertising to the tune of hundreds of thousands of dollars. We basically had the aggregators working for us for free, and that was really the plan all the way—to utilize this aggregation element to efficiently pick up the large institutional business.

Griffeth: I'm curious. What did your fledgling company, as you called it, have to offer to the large companies like AT&T? Couldn't they very easily just go to a large Wall Street firm?

Gross: Yes, they could have. But, you know, the bond market was changing in the early to mid-1970s. Prior to that time, most pension money—certainly in the 1950s and 1960s—was managed by New York and Detroit banks. And there was a perception in the mid-1970s that that money had fallen asleep, so to speak. The feeling was that those companies were merely clipping coupons and not actively managing the bonds that were in the pension funds.

What we had to offer was a new form of management in which bonds were bought and sold. Now that doesn't necessarily mean we bought and sold at a rapid rate; you know, on a day-to-day or week-to-week basis, but certainly there would be some turnover during the year. It was a philosophy that was basically absent in most major institutions in the 1960s and 1970s. Bonds were simply bought and held. They weren't traded or turned over because they were considered to be income vehicles. For some reason, people didn't think about their potential to go up and down in price.

Now, the early 1970s and all the way up to 1981 sort of belied that entire theory, because these institutions saw the value of their bond portfolios collapsing. So it was this element, I guess, combined with the assumption that the trust banks had sort of fallen asleep, that led these major institutions to look in another direction. We had a very good record for our first few years. We weren't sage old veterans, but maybe it was that combination of youth and a good record and aggressiveness

"Bonds . . . weren't traded or turned over because they were considered to be income vehicles. For some reason, people didn't think about their potential to go up and down in price."

and enthusiasm and a changing era in terms of bond management that led to the rapid growth of PIMCO.

Griffeth: But are you putting all this pension money at more risk
by more actively trading it?

Gross: I don't think so. You know, I think what the market
proved in the 1970s was that there was certainly more than
enough risk just holding a portfolio of bonds in a substantial
bear market, and that managers who chose to run for cover in
such an environment might actually reduce risk and reduce
volatility.

The bond market, back in the 1970s, was still developing in
terms of its know-how and understanding. I mean, we didn't
have terms like "duration" and "convexity" and all of the technical terms that people use now. It sounds sort of infantile now
to even suggest it, but there was this perception beginning to
develop that if you held a portfolio of long maturity bonds
during a bear market—when prices went down—the value of
that portfolio might be, in some cases, cut in half, which turned
out to be the case. I mean, portfolios went from a hundred cents
on the dollar to fifty cents, not because of credit quality or
anything like that. It was simply because interest rates went up.

So that is why actively managing a bond portfolio began to
make sense, because it actually reduced the portfolio's risk as
opposed to increasing it.

"Master of the Universe?"

Griffeth: Let's talk about how you actively manage these
accounts. I know that you spend a lot of time in the trading
room, but you don't seem to be the prototypical "Master of the
Universe" that Tom Wolfe wrote about in *Bonfire of the Vanities*.
Tell me about your day.

Gross: Okay. Usually it starts around 5:30 A.M. at my home. I've
got a few quote machines like a Telerate and a Bloomberg
getting me up to speed first thing. Then I turn on your program
[CNBC] at about the same time I'm getting dressed and show-
ering. That gets me pretty well acquainted with what's going on.
Then it's a five-minute hop to the office here, so by about 6:30
or so I'm ready to roll, and we're trading.

Now we aren't necessarily trading a lot, but because of the huge cash flow that $55 billion generates at just 6 or 7 percent interest, you can figure out that that's another $3 billion a year just to reinvest. So there is a lot of money every day to put back to work, and we do that in every area of the marketplace, in governments, and corporates, and mortgages, and now international bonds and the like.

Griffeth: Do you hold a morning meeting? Do you have a group of traders sitting at their desks that you supervise? How does it work?

Gross: It's all done in this one very small trading room. I'd say it's no bigger than two large offices in midtown Manhattan. And all of us are in there together, about 14 individuals. Some specialize in certain areas of the market and some are basically generalists or portfolio managers, like myself, who put the pieces together.

What happens is the whole team is constantly on the phone with 20, 30, 40 brokers, and we are not shouting back and forth, but we are communicating with each other as to what we see, and what we like and don't like. It's not a question of having a lot of meetings, but there's this flow back and forth almost constantly that allows us to buy and to sell the particular pieces that we like the most.

Griffeth: We have already established that you manage a number of institutional accounts and some mutual funds. How do you decide what you are buying and selling for which account?

Gross: Well, we have extensive technology here that allows us to balance, or even out, each of our accounts according to the guidelines that we want to follow. For instance, if we wanted a portfolio with an average maturity of six years, we've got computers here that can tell us in about two seconds which accounts have higher than average maturities and which accounts have lower. That, in turn, tells us which accounts might need to buy some bonds and which accounts might need to sell some.

So we are greatly assisted by technology when it comes to managing these 200 accounts. We can get answers in seconds about where these bonds should go. And, as a matter of fact, if we wanted to we could simply let the computer allocate the bonds to the right places. The technology has come that far. But I sort of like to personally keep tabs on the accounts. I am 50 years old now, and I guess I'm the last to be fully assimilated into the computer age. So I do most of mine by hand, but there are a few people here who can just press a button, and the computer slots the bonds in the right places.

Griffeth: So you are not ready to cede control of your accounts to Hal the computer, huh? [laughing]

Gross: [Also laughing] No, I don't want to do that. Even if I wanted to, the brain cells are diminishing rapidly, and I'm not sure I could keep up with some of these young jockeys. But it works out pretty well.

I might mention that the reason I think we've been so successful here is that we take a longer term approach to the marketplace. When we first started PIMCO, I thought that since we're so young and so unknown we needed something different to attack not only the marketplace but the market itself in terms of adding performance. And what I felt was best was simply applying a little common sense.

I viewed Wall Street as very short term oriented, looking at two to three months' numbers, you know, fixating on one day's industrial production number or a housing starts number and those types of things. I thought that that was too short term oriented, because it tended to promote a herd type of mentality. It tended to allow for psychological whipsaws as some of the numbers came in good and then the next day came in bad.

What I thought would be better would be to take a longer term view, a two- to three-year view of the marketplace. We try to position ourselves—to be simplistic—in terms of a bull market, a bear market, or a neutral environment for the next several years as opposed to the next several months.

We have a one-week meeting every year where we just get away from the company, and we invite various astute economists and academicians to come give us their view of the world. Like, two or three years ago we had [Bill Clinton's Labor Secretary] Robert Reich and some others come speak to us.

We've had the Friedmans, Benjamin and Milton, and on and on and on.

So we tend to look at longer term factors to try and see where economies and financial markets are headed over the long term, and I think that's really kept us out of harm's way in terms of being whipsawed psychologically back and forth on a day-to-day basis.

Griffeth: Do you have that luxury because you mostly manage institutional money, which tends to take a long-term view?

Gross: Yes, that's a good point. It helps very much, because institutions tend to give you at least a three-year window in which to screw up, to put it bluntly. But an individual might look at a three-month or a six-month horizon and quickly bail out of a fund if he doesn't like it.

An institution will give you at least three years and I think that now, even with PIMCO having had such an excellent record for so many years, our window might even be stretched out to something like four years. So it gives us that luxury, as you say, of making a mistake for six months or 12 months and holding firm to a fairly long-term view. It's really been important.

Griffeth: You are now, to some extent, available to individual investors through Charles Schwab, for example, where the minimum investment for them is far lower than it is for your institutional accounts. Have you noticed a change in the cash flow of those funds, and do you manage that money a little differently because individuals are involved?

Gross: No. I think that one thing that helps is that the mutual funds we have are still about 70 percent institutionally oriented. In other words, we've got a $75 million minimum for institutions except for the ones that want to go into the mutual funds. So we get a lot of fives and tens and twenties going into those funds.

Griffeth: Fives, tens, and twenties?

Gross: Millions. So even though individuals might be a little more volatile, since 70 percent of those funds are small institutions as opposed to large institutions, you have some stability. And because what we've done with that longer term view has been so successful over 20 years, we figure that we are benefiting individuals with the same type of philosophy so that if they are willing to stick it out for a multi-year period of time, they are going to benefit in the long run. And it seems to have worked very well.

Measuring Success

Griffeth: How do you measure success? On the equity side, fund managers will pick an index to compete against, such as the Standard & Poor's 500.

Gross: Well, we do the same. The Standard & Poor's 500 for the bond market is either the Lehman Aggregate or the Salomon Broad Index. Those two indexes include all governments, all corporates and all mortgage passthroughs. Everything but international bonds.

Our objective is always to beat the Lehman Aggregate or the Salomon Broad by at least 1 percent, or 100 basis points, a year. Now that doesn't sound like a lot, but in Bondland 1 percent a year, without taking any additional risk from the standpoint of credit quality, is a lot of money. On a base of $55 billion in total assets, 1 percent outperformance per year is $550 million. So our responsibility here as we start January 1st every year is to basically take $550 million out of the market and put it into our clients' hands. And that's not an easy thing to do. That's a lot of money in terms of outsmarting the competition, but we've been able to do that for twenty years.

Actually, our record is about 150 basis points over the market place, and the mutual funds' performance has probably been about 2 percent, or 200 basis points over during the past five years. It's actually an awesome amount of money when you start talking about the 1 and 2 percents applied to billions upon billions of dollars.

Griffeth: Is it more cumbersome to achieve those kinds of return in huge accounts or funds, compared to a smaller fund?

Gross: Sure. If we only managed $5 million, I guess we could pick our little sweetheart deals and enhance our performance.

On the other hand, not many brokers are going to call if you are only a $5 million fund, and as a result you may never be offered the sweethearts to put in a fund.

But the markets have pretty well grown up with us in terms of liquidity. The financial futures market has been enormous in terms of its contribution. The mortgage market is enormous in terms of its size and liquidity.

Plus, we're a fairly big factor in the market. With $55 billion, we are probably more than 1 percent of the total pension and individual market combined, so it's a pretty significant sum. But, still, from a liquidity standpoint we've been able to move when we wanted to move.

How to Buy a Bond

Griffeth: I want to get a sense of how you evaluate a bond. Now there are different kinds of bonds, obviously, with Treasuries and corporates and munis and whatever. Are there general criteria you use to buy or sell a bond, or do we have to discuss each type of bond?

Gross: There are general criteria. All bonds have a number of characteristics that are similar: 1) Each has a maturity date. 2) Each comes from a particular sector. It could be a corporate, a mortgage, a government, and it could be international. 3) Each has a certain coupon. In other words, it may pay 7 percent annually or 9 percent or 6. And it could either be what is known as a discount coupon or what they call a premium coupon. And 4) each has a perceived level of quality, whether it's Triple A, or B Double A [which are the ratings used by companies like Moody's and Standard & Poor's], or it's in the junk category. So selecting bonds is a delicate mix of combining all those characteristics into what you consider to be the proper mix on a risk basis relative to reward.

Now, the most important of all these characteristics is the maturity, because the maturity dominates the field in terms of price performance as interest rates change. If interest rates move up or down by 1 percent, say from 7 percent to 8 percent, a 30-year bond will do much worse than an overnight investment and anything in between. In other words, 5-year, 10-year, or

20-year bonds will perform differently because of their maturity relative to that interest rate change.

So that's the number one criterion when you come down the list of all these propositions. You first have to ask yourself how "long" you want to be. Do you want to be in intermediate bonds, or do you want to be in long-term bonds because their price change will differ based upon where you think rates are going.

The second most important characteristic would probably be the sector, whether it's governments or corporates, or whatever.

Griffeth: Do you determine that based on what the economy is doing, or where you're finding values?

Gross: Both, actually. It is something like the stock market. When economic times are good, if you are a stocks investor you probably want to run with cyclical stocks. It's the same thing on the bond side. When economic times are good, corporate bonds do very well as a whole because investors perceive less risk during those times. If corporations are doing well and profits are coming to the bottom line very rapidly, then the ability of a corporate bond to pay interest and to pay principal down the road is enhanced.

So corporate bonds do better, price-wise, during recoveries and they do much worse during recessions. If you think we are headed into a slow growth period, or into recession, you would want to dump your corporates and own governments and some mortgage passthroughs.

So a lot of this business has to do with being one-third economist, one-third mathematician, and one-third horse trader. It's a delicate combination of all those things.

Prices Go Down, Rates Go Up

Griffeth: Let's use a specific example that we can all recall. When the Federal Reserve started to raise interest rates in February of 1994, obviously that ended a long period of declining interest rates. How did you react? Did it cause an overnight shift in your portfolios?

Gross: Well, it's not an overnight thing, because that's not the way we work. Nonetheless, a move by the Fed in the opposite direction such as in February 1994 certainly rings a bell and puts you on alert as to a change in market direction.

I can remember talking about this on your show when it happened. And I said I thought it was the beginning of at least a 12- to 18-month succession of Fed increases in interest rates. It was the end of a declining interest rate cycle and the beginning of the tightening based on a strengthening economy and upon potentially higher inflation. It automatically shifts your mind into a defensive mode, because as interest rates go up prices go down. It's a phenomenon that I guess a lot of individuals don't quite understand. I know I try to convince my wife as to this teeter totter concept of rates going up and prices going down, and in the same way most individuals find that hard to conceive of. Nonetheless, that's the way it works.

Griffeth: [Laughing] Listen, as long as you understand how it works, I'm comfortable with it! [also Gross laughs] But at that time the prevailing wisdom was that if the Fed did start to raise rates, it would calm the market for 30-year bonds because it would tell bond traders that the Fed was on the inflation watch. Instead, the first time the Fed increased its Federal Funds rate [which is the rate banks charge each other for overnight loans] bonds sold off quite sharply. Is that because people like Bill Gross said, "Okay, it's time to become defensive," and you started to shorten your maturities by selling bonds?

Gross: Yes, that's part of the process. It depends on how long you expect the rate increases to continue and how high you expect the rates to go. I mean, if the Fed was only going to go from 3 to 4 percent, there wouldn't be too much to worry about. You have to wait to see how the economy digests the increase, whether it slows down, and whether inflationary fears are reduced. And that's just not an overnight proposition.

But when the Fed does start to raise rates, it certainly puts you on notice. And investors such as myself start to sell bonds in order to reduce the average maturity of their portfolio. Let's say your portfolio has an average maturity of eight years. When interest rates start to go up, you probably want to bring it down closer to cash in order to protect prices and principal. Now, you might say, "Why don't you just go completely to cash if you want to protect principal?" Well, there is always the constant problem of what cash returns. For instance, we could have sold the entire portfolio and moved into 3-1/2 percent commercial paper. But in February of 1994 3-1/2 percent commercial paper still looked very unattractive relative to the 6 percent or 6-1/2 percent 30-year bonds were paying or the 5-1/2 or 6 percent 10-year treasuries were paying. So you sacrifice yield in order to become defensive, or to protect principal.

That's always the rub a bond portfolio manager has: how much yield is he willing to sacrifice by going into cash in order to protect potential principal erosion as interest rates rise? That was our dilemma in February of 1994. We did sell bonds, and we did reduce maturity, but God knows in retrospect we didn't do enough of it. We weren't expecting the 2 percent, or 200 basis point, rise [in short-term rates] that we've had.

Bonds in a Retirement Portfolio

Griffeth: There is a theory in portfolio management that says when it comes to saving for retirement the younger you are the more you should be invested in equities. And the theory says you don't start thinking about bonds until you are getting close to retirement. Give me your reaction to that as a bond person. I mean, are we overemphasizing equities or overlooking bonds as a viable portion of a portfolio?

Gross: I would agree completely with your first adage that the younger you are the higher percentage of equities you need in your portfolio. That doesn't, however, suggest that you need 100 percent equities. I know you didn't say that, but to my way of thinking it doesn't mean that you need a complete portfolio of equities even if you are only 20 years old. By the same token, it also doesn't mean you need a lot more bonds in your portfolio when you hit age 60 or 65.

Equities have a higher risk element than bonds. They are more volatile, and they are dependent on a company's earnings growth. And because of that their prices are discounted to reflect a higher return than bonds provide. If the next 50 years are like the last 150 in the United States, stocks should do better than bonds. I'm 50 years old myself, and I still don't have many bonds in my personal portfolio. I have a lot more equities. So I guess I'm an example of what you just suggested.

Griffeth: You don't try to manage your own account?

Gross: Actually I don't. My own funds are in mutual funds.

But a young person's goal should be to assemble a diversified portfolio that will protect against substantial volatility. One of the beauties of being young is that you can weather volatile storms like the crash in 1987. You know, five or ten years down the road you barely remember what happened because you have had the time to recover.

Nonetheless, even when you are young, a substantial bear market or a crash can have a very negative influence and end up forcing individuals out of markets at the wrong time. So it pays to diversify a portfolio.

Thinking About Shareholders

Griffeth: This might be an unfair question to ask somebody who manages so much institutional money, but do you ever think about all of the individual shareholders behind the money you are managing?

Gross: Oh, I think about them all the time. As a matter of fact, I get letters from them, and I try to answer every one of them. Don't forget, even the institutional money we manage is comprised of millions upon millions of individuals.

Griffeth: True.

Gross:: In fact, that reminds me of a funny story. When I first started in this business, my idea of building a franchise was to stick an index card on the bulletin board in the local Albertson's supermarket right next to the Leisure World here where the retired people are and to advertise my bond expertise to them for a fee. It was just a handwritten thing. It wasn't even printed, for God's sake! And it didn't elicit a single response.

At least I was thinking about individuals, and that has stayed with me all along. The minute you lose sight of who's behind the money you're managing, I think you can get carried away in terms of taking too much risk or in terms of being too complacent.

Gross on Derivatives

Griffeth: Let's talk about derivatives. What's your take on their impact on the markets right now?

Gross: Well, to put it simply, there are a number of derivatives. There are financial futures and options and collateralized obligations and a substantial number of derivatives in the mortgage market. There are what they call IOs ["interest only" mortgage-backed derivatives] and POs ["principal only" mortgage-backed derivatives] where they slice and dice a market in a thousand different ways. And you get different principal streams and different interest streams.

There is nothing really wrong with derivatives. The real problem is in making sure you know how they work. Some of the problems these money market funds have gotten into in the past 12 months or so has been that they didn't really know what they had in terms of a derivative. In other words, if they were managing money market funds that supposedly were to have three to six months of average maturity and very little principal risk, what they reached for on the derivative side was a piece of paper that could change its character or change its maturity very rapidly if interest rates changed. And all of the sudden, instead of a three-month piece of paper, they wound up with a 10- to 15-year piece of paper that declined in price to 85 or 80 cents on the dollar.

> *"There is nothing really wrong with derivatives. The real problem is in making sure you know how they work."*

That was the real problem. Managers didn't realize what they had purchased, and I think this has been the responsibility of Wall Street. The brokers who sold to the managers made a lot of money marketing these derivatives, and they have confused the buyer because they have sliced and diced and used the Vegematic approach on these mortgage loans to such a great extent that you really need a computer to analyze these things. That's why they call some of them kitchen sink types of bonds.

Griffeth: I find it scary that that many professional money managers could buy instruments that they really didn't understand. How much of that do we lay to the tremendous competition in the industry for the extra amount of yield that they can use for marketing purposes?

Gross: It's a very competitive business. If you establish a good track record, you can bring in a lot of money, and therefore you can make a lot of money. There is no doubt that Wall Street bears some responsibility for the derivatives fiasco this year, but there is also no doubt that money managers bear responsibility for taking on too much risk.

And that combination has given derivatives a bad name. But you know, a derivative is just a piece of a bond. So if you don't like derivatives, you're really saying you don't like bonds. Because if you could take all the derivatives combined and reconstitute them, you would just come up with a mortgage loan.

Griffeth: A high profile fund that got into trouble because of derivatives was the Paine Webber U.S. Government Fund, of which you ended up taking over management. For marketing reasons, did you have to make it known that you were cleaning out all the derivatives in the fund even if you didn't want to?

Gross: Yes, that was a part of the initial process in order to induce confidence in the remaining shareholders. We had to let them know that this fund would be run as a money market fund, not as a fund that took on any additional risk.

That was definitely one of our first objectives: to calm shareholders down and to basically tell them that things were going to be run differently in the future.

Griffeth: Do you use derivatives in any of your funds, or do you have to shy away from them now?

Gross: Actually, we've been using derivatives in some of our institutional portfolios for about 14 years now. But these derivatives would not have a place in a money market fund like Paine Webber's. I mean, the purpose of a money market fund is to run a high-quality portfolio with a three-month average maturity, and you can't utilize financial futures to meet that objective.

We have used futures, not as leveraged vehicles but as substitutes for treasury bonds. You can buy a U.S. treasury bond future as a substitute, so to speak, and back it with 100 percent commercial paper, and you pick up liquidity in return.

Just a quick statistic: the clients who have used financial futures with us have managed to return about a half a percent more, or about 50 basis points more per year, than those who decided not to use futures. It's a pretty good testimonial, I think, over time that we've been real successful [with derivatives]. At the same time the volatility of the portfolios has been just the same as those that chose not to use derivative or financial futures. So it has worked out pretty well.

"It Weighs on Me Some Nights"

Griffeth: You hit 50 this year. Any thought that maybe you will eventually get to trade equities? [Laughter] Or are you going to stick with fixed income?

Gross: [Also laughing] Oh, gosh, no. Actually, up until about seven or eight years ago, I had thought that maybe I would try equities. We have a small equity operation here, and I always thought that as I retired from one area I could slip into another. But I really think my personality is best suited to the bond side.

When you think about it, an equity manager is more of an optimist and more of a "glass half full" type of person. A bond manager, on the other hand, is more of a pessimist, a "glass half empty" type of person. It's all because bonds do best when the economy is going bad, and stocks do best when the economy is super strong. And my personality either began that way, or else over time it has become that way. And I think it would be a pretty hard adjustment to all of a sudden start hoping as opposed to start being pessimistic.

There is enough action and enough excitement on the bond side to fill anybody's day. I don't know in reality how much more fun bonds are than stocks, but to me they are a lot more fun. So I guess I can give up on that dream of ever trading equities and stick with the bond market with good conscience and with a full heart.

Griffeth: Do you ever feel the enormity of overseeing $55 billion of other people's money?

Gross: Sometimes I do. As our company grew, and the asset base grew, I used to say that the game was always the same, it was just the color of the chips that changed. You know, in Vegas a green chip is a five-dollar chip, and a black chip is a hundred-dollar chip. And you can play the same game with either color.

I said that for about 10 or 15 years. But then it got to a point, when we got up to around $10 billion or $20 billion, that I started thinking about the sheer enormity of the amount of money and all of the individuals that were behind it. I think about the awesome responsibility and it weighs on me some nights.

Now, I'm not making excuses, nor am I complaining because it's a very, very well-paying job, and it's a lot of fun. It's like a professional basketball player hitting the hard court. They would probably do it for five dollars a day, and that's about how I am. But it has some awesome responsibility to it, and I've felt it over the past five years or so.

G. KENNETH HEEBNER

Birth Date: September 27, 1940

Education: B.A. from Amherst College, Harvard M.B.A.

Hobbies: Sailing

Alternate Career: Trial Lawyer

*I*n the investment world, Ken Heebner is known as the Mad Bomber. He doesn't exactly endorse its use, but, as you'll see in our interview, he does seem to secretly relish what it symbolizes. It refers to his style of trading. Heebner is a momentum oriented growth investor, and there are times when he deems it necessary to exit his position in a stock in a hurry, hence the nickname. And usually when he sells out a position that quickly, he is way ahead of the crowd.

Heebner is highly competitive and very much a loner. He left Loomis Sayles in 1990 and started Capital Growth Management (CGM) in Boston because he felt too many of the other fund managers at Loomis were using his investment ideas to enrich their returns.

Indeed, Heebner is almost legendary for providing his shareholders with a consistently high return. His CGM Capital Development Fund was among the top 1 percent of all mutual funds, in terms of performance, over a 15-year period, according to Morningstar. He also manages the CGM Mutual Fund, which is a balanced fund. And in the spring of 1994, he introduced the CGM Realty Fund. The Capital Development Fund has been closed to new investors since 1969, and when Heebner is asked if he has plans to open it again, he usually answers with a terse "No."

I interviewed Heebner in the Green Room at CNBC a few hours before he appeared as my guest on Mutual Fund Investor. During our interview, he described in detail how his momentum style of investing works, and we discussed where his competitive nature came from and why real estate is his new investment passion.

July 5, 1994

Economics Lessons

Bill Griffeth: Tell me about your early career.

Kenneth Heebner: When I graduated from Amherst, I went into the General Electric Business Training Program for nine months, then six months into the Coast Guard to fulfill a military obligation, then to Harvard Business School. Then, after graduating from Harvard Business School, I was an economist for four years without a degree [in economics]. No degree, no M.A., no nothing! [laughing] The other economists that I dealt with always reminded me of the fact that I was practicing without a license.

I went to work for Kroeger & Co. What we did is, we collected orders from companies all around the country. We then put together a weekly index. And I wrote reports on interest rates and capital spending. I forecasted those and I forecast the GNP.

Griffeth: Did that hone your forecasting skills for the market?

Heebner: Well, it gave me the background on how the economy works. We had a corporate client who invested aggressively in the stock market, and I worked with him on that. He introduced me to new issues, flipping new issues. He had clout with a broker, and we would make something like $3,000.00 on $500.00 worth of capital. In other words, we made a lot of money for his account.

◆

"You always push these five-year forecasts, but no one is going to remember what we said five years ago."

◆

So he was a very smart guy. He sat on the board of a lot of companies, and I saw the process of investing. All the raw materials of it were sitting there right in front of me.

Now a couple things came through from my experience at Kroeger. One, it became apparent to me that economists are marketers. I said to him one time, "You always push these five-year forecasts, but no one is going to remember what we said five years ago." And he said, "That's the point." [laughing]

Next, I was forecasting recession in 1967, and he says to me, "Get out that chart of industrial production over the last 30 years." Well, the chart showed that it had gone up 90 percent of the time. So he says, "What percentage of your recession forecasts have been right?"

The point is, as smart as he was he wasn't interested in trying to be right. He was creating an impression of knowledge and ability for which U.S. Steel paid him, for which Alcoa paid him. He was collecting big fees from major U.S. corporations for nothing more than a song and dance. I learned something about economics, but it's not what I thought I was going to learn. [laughing]

Griffeth: So, you had wanted to be an economist?

Heebner: No, I was interested in learning how to invest. But in the process, I learned a lot about economists. And what he [Bud Kroeger] taught was economists don't know anything about investing. So where that leads, in terms of how I currently invest money, is I'm my own economist. I'm not always right, but I'm not going to follow that herd down the wrong road every time!

Griffeth: You're not selling yourself a bill of goods with your own forecast.

Heebner: Right. One thing it taught me was, don't listen to them. Do your own work, which I do.

Investment Lessons

Griffeth: When you left there, is that when you went to Scudder?

Heebner: Yes.

Griffeth: Tell us about that.

Heebner: I went to Scudder in 1969, because they were devoted to research. We were also at a bull market peak, and a lot of people employed concept investing methods. It reminds me a little bit of recent periods.

So at Scudder I got right in. I was a conglomerate analyst, and as a conglomerate analyst I had all these multi-divisional companies to look at.

Griffeth: There were a lot of conglomerates at that time.

Heebner: That's right, and I dissected them. I got original documents. I found all the divisions, and I went out and called on the divisions. So I really focused on what makes a company work.

Then I was an oil analyst. Then they made me a photography analyst. And then they made me assistant portfolio manager of the Scudder Development fund, one of the few small cap emerging growth stock funds at that time. And they gave me 70 stocks [to keep an eye on], and I learned as the fund went from $40 million [in assets] to $10 million, with no redemptions in the 1973–1974 bear market.

So I learned how you lose money big. And one of the ways you lose money big is you average down in a situation where the market is looking further ahead than you are. In other words you're seeing stocks today where everything's fine, but prices keep eroding. Well, the market can see that two years from now there is going to be a disappointment.

Averaging Down

Griffeth: I want to talk about that. You say that one of the lessons you learned from that is don't average down.

Heebner: If you do, really be sure that you are right.

Griffeth: All right, but a fellow like John Templeton will tell an individual investor that, over a longer period of time, the odds are that the market is going to go higher. And if you have been averaging down when the market declines—through dollar cost averaging—in the long run, chances are you're going to make money.

Is averaging down not a good idea for the professional money manager who has short-term performance to think about, where it might be a different story for a long-term investor?

Heebner: As a professional money manager, I can say that I'm not going to average down for the next two years, whereas maybe the individual investor should take a longer term view.

But all I can tell you is how I operate. The further you go out in time the less you know about the world and the less you know about a company. For instance, if I showed you a list of the growth stocks from 1972, you would not recognize it. They wouldn't be on today's list, because everything keeps changing. So my strategy is I want to look out maybe a year or two, because that's when I have my best shot at being right. I'm not going to say, "Well, this stock is starting down, but in the next five years this company is going to be in a very different position." I don't take that long term a view. The person who I think probably does that very well is John Neff. [*see page 169 for an interview with John Neff, who manages the Vanguard Windsor fund.*] I think what John Neff probably does is, he buys into something that has been going down for a while, maybe a year and a half. All the brokers have given up on it, and no one is even following it. Now I've done that type of investing, but I don't call that averaging down. I call that moving into a bottom area.

Griffeth: What's the difference? Does it depend on your outlook for the company?

Heebner: The difference is you can satisfy yourself that there is protracted and widespread capitulation. Now, you don't get that when a $70.00 stock goes to $60.00. You get that when a $70.00 stock goes down to $20.00 and it doesn't have any earnings. But every situation is different.

Griffeth: You're willing to follow a stock down if you're still convinced that the reason you bought that stock to begin with is still valid.

Heebner: Right.

Griffeth: Your earnings momentum is still with this company but you're willing to follow the stock down to a point, I would imagine, if you feel that the street is misreading this company's earnings.

Heebner: Well, let's look at that. Every situation is different now.

Griffeth: I understand.

Heebner: It's so complex.

Griffeth: Yes, but yet you're willing to make the blanket statement that you never average down. See what I'm saying?

Heebner: I generally don't average down. There will be occasions where I do. For example, I think we're in a situation right now [in 1994] where growth stocks are entering a period of disillusionment. In my judgment they are going to be under increasing pressure for the next two years because of higher interest rates. Then if I average down in a growth stock the whole multiple structure of growth stocks in two years is going to be a lot lower than it is today, in my judgment. I'm going to lose money by doing that. So I wouldn't do that today.

When would I do it? In 1991 when money was coming into growth stocks when the percentage ratios were going up. Then, sure because the wind is at my back. It's going to pay me to do that. So everything is very conditional.

Griffeth: So you've made the case for a technique which could be considered averaging down but in the long run as long as it works itself out, you haven't averaged down.

Heebner: I bought Ford Motor Company in 1981. Everybody thought the company was going out of business; the stock had been going down for a couple years. Most Wall Street analysts didn't follow it, you could call that averaging down. I say it was more like jumping into what looked to me like a bottoming area. And I had my reasons. I thought the economy was going to turn around. The world at that point was heading downward, and I said the economy is going to turn back. This company's got $5 billion in cash, it's got the staying power to rise out of this. And even if I'm wrong on my timing, this company is going to be in business for several years with its cash position and a highly profitable European operation, so I'm going to buy that.

So that's what I'll do. And that's sort of a Neff type of thing. In other words, Neff obviously knows how to do that. I've heard where Neff has really borrowed in to some companies, and they were already really pounded. And I think it works for him, because if even one of these works you can triple your money. You can go out and buy 15 of them, and a couple of them will keep going down. But the ones that work pay you off so well that it's worth the risk.

The Mad Bomber

Griffeth: You have to be a nimble enough trader so that when it does go against you, you have to know when to get out.

Heebner: That's always true. And I'm very aggressive about selling when something's wrong.

Griffeth: Let's talk about that

Heebner: The Mad Bomber thing! [laughing]

Griffeth: [Also laughing] You're known as the Mad Bomber because of the way you sell a stock.

Heebner: Let me tell you something. My competitors say I'm the Mad Bomber. And there are two reasons why they say that. One is I think there have been a number of occasions where something went wrong with a stock, and I got out ahead of them.

Let me put it this way: the XYZ [mutual fund] Company is a structured organization. It runs $20 billion. And within the organization, there is an analyst who reports to a money manager who in turn reports to a committee. Okay, so something happens to a company they are invested in. Well, a decision isn't rendered for three days. But I'm right there at the trading desk, and I've got 30 years' experience. I can decide sometimes in 15 minutes that this is a sell. So, am I going to wait for these other elephants? No. I'll just bang out. Now that's not typical, but it has happened.

> ◆
>
> *"I can decide sometimes in 15 minutes that this is a sell. So, am I going to wait for these other elephants? No. I'll just bang out."*
>
> ◆

And there is another aspect to this. Sometimes when a stock is down four points, they'll say, "The Mad Bomber is selling it." And I've seen this happen to stocks I've never heard of. Now I could call up the media and say, "Look, gentleman, I've never owned this." But then I think, "Wait a minute, my competitors think I'm in this stock now."

Griffeth: [laughs]: It works to your advantage.

Heebner: Yes.

Griffeth: But you got your nickname because you are a momentum investor. When you see a company's earnings momentum decline, you get out.

Heebner: That's right.

Griffeth: And even if you have a large position in the company, you sell that position, period. I mean, you don't feed the market.

Heebner: Well, every situation is different.

Griffeth: Okay.

Heebner: I mean, if something goes wrong and I have reason to believe it's going to look worse in a month, and I also have reason to believe that more people are going to be selling two weeks from now, then, sure, I begin a very aggressive sell program. But you don't have to do it that way.

If my judgment is that this isn't the greatest news in the world but I think the rest of these guys are going to be slow to react, then I've got time to start feeding. My strategy is always: how am I going to get the best price here. Now, in a roaring frothy bull kind of market, they'll be lined up to buy your stock when it's down a point. And so you've just got to beat it out. Every situation is different. But, as I say, I've deliberately sold that way.

Now, you won't tell the world this, right?

Griffeth: [laughing] No, it's between you and me, Ken!

Heebner: Let them laugh at me, because I think it's best . . .

Griffeth: That's just your style.

Heebner: It's a very competitive business, and a lot of information flows. You know, I'm sure than Salomon and Goldman and Merrill really don't like it when their traders talk [about buying or selling positions on Heebner's behalf], but they can't stop it. It's human nature. People breach confidences.

How Momentum Investing Works

Griffeth: The momentum strategy you use. Is it the result of what you learned at Kroeger and at Scudder and at Loomis

Sayles? Or was it something you brought to the party to begin with? Or where did it come from?

Heebner: It came from experience and what works. Momentum to me is where you are investing in a company where the earnings are going to surprise on the upside over time. And that means the earnings estimates are going to be going up, and then you look at the valuation. And if it looks like the valuation is low relative to what I think the earnings estimates are going to be a year from now, then I buy it. Because as the good news comes out, more and more people come aboard. And the big opportunity there is that the stock moves up with the earnings, but very often as that higher growth rate of earnings becomes apparent it gets a multiple re-valuation. You then get the double whammy of higher earnings and higher multiples. [*In other words, Heebner is saying the stock's price is rising because 1) the company's earnings are currently rising, and 2) analysts are increasing their estimates for future earnings.*]

Now, I'm not doing that in this market because I see a pull back on the relative price earnings ratios of growth stocks. I see money moving from growth stocks into cyclicals.

Griffeth: So do you change your momentum barometer before you invest in one of those growth stocks? In other words, do you accept less momentum in this market climate?

Heebner: What I need now is far more momentum to get me into that kind of stock.

Griffeth: Okay, relative momentum?

Heebner: Yes. I need far more, because when you're in an environment where everybody likes growth stocks (like they did in 1993), more and more flaky companies get called growth companies. And out of 100 stocks this cadre of portfolio managers have in their portfolios, maybe forty of them aren't even going to grow for two years. And as these frenzies start to roll, leaving their "growth stocks" behind, these managers start to get shaky and lose confidence. And they're suddenly not as aggressive, so they are not going to bid up what I own. They are not going to come in behind me anymore. They're shattered. They're looking for some new strategy, see.

So you have to make sense of where you are in the market. If you look at the period 1990–1993, I was a very aggressive investor. But today [in the summer of 1994] if you look at the Capital Development Fund portfolio, or better yet, if you take the balanced fund, the [CGM] mutual fund, 21 percent of it is invested in bank stocks. I mean I own Citicorp at six times its earnings. Same thing with Chemical Bank. I own Telefonos de Mexico at 8 times earnings. My "aggressive" play right now is Xerox.

Griffeth: What you're saying is you usually will go for higher price-to-earning ratios when you think the market will meet those expectations.

Heebner: Right.

Griffeth: But right now what you're saying is that you're investing in lower price to earnings ratios.

Heebner: Because of current market conditions. I believe short rates are going to keep going up. And I don't know about tomorrow, but I think that for the next two years short rates are going higher. I hope long rates don't go up. Short rates are going up, I think, because we are in the midst of a global economic boom. (I'm putting my economist hat on now.) I think that under those conditions, market forces and the Fed are going to push short rates higher and flatten the yield curve. In a few years T-bills will probably be at 7-1/2 percent.
[NOTE: T-bills were yielding between 4 and 5 percent when this interview was recorded.] I don't think that's a good environment for growth stocks. And while that happens, you are going to see several companies with blowout earnings, just much bigger than anybody thinks. And my judgment is that's where the opportunity lies. Now when I have a fund with an income objective, like the CGM mutual fund, then I turn around and say well, Bethlehem Steel doesn't pay a dividend. But Money Center Banks pay nice dividends, or Xerox pays a nice dividend. So you have to consider the fund's objective.

And then I saw these REITs (real estate investment trusts) where you get a 7 percent yield, and the dividend's going to grow 15 percent a year? I said, wow, that beats anything I can find. The bond gives me 7 percent, and then I'm at the mercy of interest rates. But at least with this REIT I've got this rising income stream coming up underneath my valuation.

At any rate, what I'm really saying is that as an investor, I look at everything to determine what my strategy is going to be. And it's going to shift over time.

Griffeth: So while we're in this period right now in 1994 where it's unclear how much higher short-term interest rates are going to go, you're saying you can't play the momentum game the way you normally would.

"... as an investor, I look at everything to determine what my strategy is going to be. And it's going to shift over time."

Heebner: Right.

Griffeth: But you want to stay fully invested.

Heebner: Yes. I'm investing in earning surprises. LTV is a big position. LTV, and Wheeling Pittsburgh, and British Steel. And every one of these is very cheap for what its earning power is going to be because of the steel shortage globally. So that is earnings momentum in a sense. It's one thing to buy a company that's been growing at 15 percent before it accelerates to 20, and it's another to buy something that loses a lot of money one year, and then makes a lot of money the next year.

I mean, I'm trying to do with steel what I did with Ford in 1981. Same thing with the Money Center Banks. It's earnings that will drive these stocks. It isn't price to book, it isn't yield, it's an earnings surprise.

Griffeth: You are not known for being too patient. I mean, you'll give a stock a certain amount of time to meet your objectives and if it doesn't it's out. But in this current environment you've described, where you are not exactly a momentum player, do you give a stock more time to prove itself?

Heebner: I have to. As I said, I own LTV. The news from the steel industry is wonderful, but that stock has only gone from 14 to 15-1/2. Now I'm impatient about fundamental disappointment, but in this case stock prices aren't responding because this is a bad market. And, actually, owning any up-stock has been pretty good so far this year. So I'm patient on the price, not on the fundamentals.

To give you an example, I was in Bombay Company two years ago when it looked to me like there was a little deceleration creeping in. I sold it, and then it went way up from there. It was a case where all these people started piling into these growth stocks and they were just ignoring the facts. This is a company that had been selling little brick-a-bracks, which are inexpensively made, and they decided they were going to sell larger pieces that were also inexpensively made. Well, the big pieces fell apart and the little brick-a-bracks didn't so basically there was a perceived quality deterioration. But they were doubling the size of their stores and everybody was getting excited about it and I looked at it and said, no, there's a problem. I'm getting out of here. This company was transforming itself from a knick-knack seller into a Levitz Furniture, trying to operate out of a mall.

I went and bought one of their things and I had the experience of buying it and there was no way for them to deliver it to me. And then I got this really heavy box, and I opened it and it was obvious how cheap the stuff was. And I took it home and put it together, and I just leaned against it and it fell apart! [laughing]

Griffeth: [Also laughing] Time to sell the stock!

Heebner: Yes! And now, of course things are slipping [for the company].

So what I'm talking about is earnings, about how a company works, about why I think a company is going to have better earnings than anyone else thinks (or in the case of Bombay Company why everybody is getting excited and they shouldn't be). I just want to have a better view of the earnings outlook for all these companies than everyone else does, and that's what I try to do.

Staying Ahead of the Competition

Griffeth: How much professional knowledge do you need? I know that you are something of an expert on the drug industry, you have a firsthand knowledge of that area. You, as I understand it, read some rather eclectic magazines. For example, to get the latest price of scrap metal, you read a magazine called—

Heebner: American Metal Market.

Griffeth: Okay. Is that just Ken Heebner's quirky take on what it means to be a mutual fund manager? Or should a fund manager have that much internal knowledge about an industry before he or she commits dollars to it?

Heebner: I think you should have the internal knowledge, and I'll tell you why. Wall Street is on the phone to everybody. If the analyst at Goldman Sachs is writing a report with a lot of stuff in it, generally speaking, all the other money managers will have the same information. Very hard for you to have an independent viewpoint if you're getting information from Goldman Sachs. I get a lot information from Goldman Sachs but I'm looking at the raw data. You'd be amazed. I threw it away, but I should show you a report I just read on the steel industry. It was tremendous. Table after table, stuff like that. Now the analyst was saying buy this one and sell that one, but I didn't pay any attention to that. I looked at the raw data. It's data that can come from many different sources, but sometimes I get it from the back of brokerage reports. I just want to build the judgment about this company or this industry before Goldman Sachs picks up on it and tells all my competitors. This is a business where I don't know any dumb people that run money. My competition is very energetic and very intelligent, and so I just can't walk into the office at nine in the morning, get a phone call from Goldman Sachs and beat these guys. I've got to have an edge.

> ◆
>
> *"My competition is very energetic and very intelligent, and so I just can't walk into the office at nine in the morning, get a phone call from Goldman Sachs and beat these guys."*
>
> ◆

Griffeth: Speaking of maintaining an edge, let's talk about how you made it through the Gulf War. You put a map on your wall.

Heebner: Yes, of the Persian Gulf. I have maintained a 7 or 8 year relationship with sources in the international area which I think are far and above what I can find anywhere else. I'm not even talking about people who are talking about their contacts in Washington. You know, somebody who knows somebody who was briefed by the CIA and all that.

For example, we had a trustee on our funds who was being briefed by the CIA, and he was scared of the war. But I got up during a meeting before the Gulf War and I said, "Gentleman, I think we're going to have a war, and I think we're going to slam dunk these guys, and don't believe anything the press is going to say." And they just looked at me like I'd lost it. Because everyone else was seeing it different. But that was very important from an investment point of view. Because in the fall of 1990, when the market was bad, everybody was going for the hills, nobody was thinking that we were going to have big victory and that our allies were going to pay for it. I mean people were afraid of another Vietnam. They were thinking about body bags, bombing the Saudi oil fields, the price of oil was up around $40 a barrel. And it was all nothing. It went puff.

So that's when I became massively invested in expensive momentum oriented stocks because the next thing that's going to happen is rates are going to go down when all the fears of inflation, and oil shortages, and massive defense expenditures, and budget deficits go away. That's the insight my guys brought to me. They were saying don't worry about it. But even then I had to read it with a grain of salt. One of my guys is actually pro-Arab, and he was a little too negative on the scenario because he didn't want to see the war because it was negative for the Saudis.

Griffeth: You were absolutely convinced it would be a quick war and that the U.S. would prevail. In hindsight it makes for a great story but weren't there a couple of nights when you sat and wondered?

Heebner: Oh yes, there always are. But bear this in mind: these things had gotten cheaper. I was buying into disillusionment. There was a lot of negative sentiment at the time. But sure, it could have gone wrong. And I've been wrong. I've made these kinds of judgments and they've gone against me and they've cost me performance. You can't believe that you're going to be right every year. I know I'm not going to be right every year. But if sentiment is very negative, if the expectation is for American failure, and I think we're going to win, that means that if I'm right, big payoff. And if I'm wrong, a lot of the bad news is already in the price anyway, so the risk/reward isn't bad.

This is a very important point. I don't buy a single point. I always ask myself, what's the risk/reward in this stock. That's all I think about, because I know I don't know what's going to happen in the future. But I track the fundamentals very closely to see if it is all going my way. And when I feel that I can make a lot more than I'm going to lose, then I'm in. And with the Gulf War, I thought I had a very favorable risk/reward.

And that's where an REIT just comes right up front on the radar screen. I can make 20 percent there, and I don't see how I'm going to lose anything.

Investing in Real Estate

Griffeth: Let's talk about your real estate fund. As we speak here it's almost two months old. It came to market in a rising interest rate environment and fully six months after real estate investment trusts ceased to be a hot commodity, as far as initial public offerings go. What was your thinking in starting the fund at this time?

Heebner: My thinking is that you are going to get growth and dividends and a high current yield. So if we invest in something yielding 8 percent and the dividend grows at 10 or 15 percent a year, I don't think the price is going to go down. I'm going to get paid from current income. And I think the price is probably going to be driven higher, and three years from now if that dividend has grown 10 or 15 percent a year I think the yield will be 7 percent or 6 percent reflecting the [real estate] management's delivery. Then you say, "Why is that?" and the answer is we're at the bottom of a real estate cycle in many property types, rents are rising, occupancies are rising and a good operator is going to have rising cash flow from existing properties. And he is still able to go out there, depending on the various property types, and acquire them from the savings and loans and banks and insurance companies that foreclosed on them, but don't know how to run them and never wanted to own them in the first place. And he can also buy from the individual investors who lost money.

Take an apartment, for example. You know, if the rent goes up 7 percent, his cash flow will go up 10 [percent] and then if he acquires advantageously the dividend can grow, and the funds from operation of that thing can go up 10 percent a year. And although there were a lot of [real estate investment trust] IPOs in the market last year, I would say that the level of expectations for REITs is far less than it is elsewhere.

Now, I'm not saying that somebody who wants to go out and double their money by catching a spectacular growth story is going to find it here. But if you're thinking about income what you get is the ability to have rising income and a high current yield to start with. That's unique. I can't find that anywhere else.

And the next thing is the real estate developers have to come to the public market in the form of REITs in order to get long-term growth financing because the banks cut them off. You know: no more 30-year mortgages with no money down. So if [the real estate developers] want to grow, they have to come to us [the investment world] and sell us, and make us their partner. And so we [stock market investors] for the first time are being allowed to share the opportunities that have made the real estate people some of America's richest people. And that's the concept. You're at the right point in the cycle. I mean, it all fits. And then we [the CGM Realty Fund] are, what, the 13th [real estate investment trust] fund [to date]?

Griffeth: Something like that, yes.

Heebner: All 13 funds have a little more than a billion dollars. And there's $3 trillion in mutual funds right now. Is it $3 trillion?

Griffeth: It's over $2 trillion now.

Heebner: Okay, over $2 trillion. So a billion dollars is a lot of money, but compared to the whole industry it's just tiny. There are only 13 funds, which means that the mutual fund industry has not yet seized the opportunity, and I think the opportunity here is far in excess for income-oriented investors than it is in junk bonds or government bonds or money market funds with derivatives.

Griffeth: People looking for a decent income from the stock market used to turn to utilities stocks. But now some utilities are facing deregulation and competition, and their dividends are coming down. Are you saying that the new play for someone who is seeking a better than average return is now the real estate investment trust?

Heebner: That's right. I think the real estate investment trust offers a better balance between current income and capital appreciation than anything else that I'm aware of.

How Heebner Diversifies

Griffeth: As we speak, your CGM Mutual Fund is practically a real estate investment trust fund right now.

Heebner: Yes, 25 percent is in real estate.

Griffeth: 25 percent. Is that the maximum you could invest in a sector?

——— ◆ ———

"I think the real estate investment trust offers a better balance between current income and capital appreciation than anything else that I'm aware of."

——— ◆ ———

Heebner: That is the maximum I can actively cause the fund to get to. It can rise by appreciation above that but in terms of cause I have to own more than 25. That's it.

Griffeth: Would you go higher if you could?

Heebner: Oh, I don't know.

Griffeth: Have you ever taken that large a position in a sector before in that fund?

Heebner: Well you know, I've got 21 percent in banks.

Griffeth: Okay.

Heebner: It's been as high as, almost at 25.

Griffeth: Okay. So almost half your fund is in two sectors.

Heebner: Oh sure. Let me describe the mutual fund for you. It's four stocks. It owns REITs, it owns banks, it owns high-grade corporate bonds and the fourth stock is autos. And there's only 10 percent of the portfolio in that sector.

Griffeth: Is that a typical portfolio for CGM Mutual, or is it just reflective of your view of the market?

Heebner: It is more concentrated than usual, but not that much more. If I got out the growth portfolio, you would see 35 percent in metals and basic commodities, and you would see 25 percent in banks. I don't want to be in growth stocks so these groups take an awful lot of the capital. There are other industries like energy or utilities where I don't see any surprises coming. So I'm left with a small amount to work with. But it is typical for me to be much more concentrated than the rest.

Heebner the Competitor

Griffeth: Let me go back for a second and get a better sense of where the Ken Heebner trading style came from. You were fired at Scudder when the market went against you. And you had a less than happy experience at Loomis Sales because of a kind of competition with fellow fund managers there. Did it instill in you this competitive instinct to move against the herd? And perhaps a strong desire to show them that you could do what you could do.

Heebner: Let me tell you something. When I was five years old my father sent me to this school where everybody was an athlete. I'm a healthy person, but I'm uncoordinated. I couldn't compete, and yet I had to get a letter. So I had to be the water boy for the athletes. And so it was clear to me at the age of 6 or 7 or 8 that I had to use my brain. That's all I had, nothing else and I had to outsmart, that was it, I had to get grades because I couldn't do anything else. It was just instilled in me as a young man by the time I was 7 or 8 years old, so I've always been that way. So all my competitive instincts are focused intellectually because I've never been able to, I'm just guessing, that I've never been able to express it physically. So I think that's why I'm a very competitive individual, no question.

Griffeth: How much are you driven by performance numbers? I mean, you are known to be a driven guy, you focus on your investments, but how much of it is also the performance numbers?

Heebner: No, no, no. I'm not driven by that. I'm driven by capturing the opportunities that are out there. The thing I feel worst about is when a stock goes up without me that I should have been in.

I believe that you just can't be good every quarter and every year. There will be times when you either make a mistake or circumstances will take longer for what you are doing than you would like. I always feel I should be doing better, but I still think I've captured the best opportunities.

RICHARD HOEY

Birth Date: May 8, 1943

Education: Yale University, B.A. in Politics and Economics, M.B.A. from NYU

Hobbies: Computers

Alternate Career: Lawyer

*R*ichard Hoey is the chief economist at the Dreyfus Corporation, and he manages the Dreyfus Growth & Income fund. That makes him one of the few people on Wall Street who makes a living forecasting the future course of the economy and investing money based on those forecasts.*

Hoey has worked for a number of firms during his Wall Street career. He is probably best known for being part of the all-star team of analysts at Drexel Burnham Lambert when it went bankrupt during the junk bond market collapse in 1991. He was hired almost immediatly by Dreyfus.

At the time I interviewed him for this book, he had been managing the Growth & Income fund about 2-1/2 years, and with admirable success. In 1992, its first full year of existence, it returned an impressive 20 percent to shareholders, and in 1993 it returned another 18.59 percent, making it one of the top performing growth stock funds in the country.

During our interview, we discussed his long varied career on Wall Street, his unusual Top Down/Bottom Up approach to investing, and the stock market's ability to forecast the future of the economy.

JUNE 23, 1994
College Days

Bill Griffeth: Much was made back in December of 1991 when you took over the brand new Growth & Income fund at Dreyfus. You know, people were saying here's an economist suddenly taking over as a money manager. I guess they forget that you managed money in a previous life.

Richard Hoey: That's true. I started out in the business working in an investment counsel firm which managed money for substantial individuals. It was basically a two-man investment counsel firm.

Griffeth: Were you very successful?

Hoey: Well, yes, it was a reasonably successful business. I don't know whether I would say very successful. We had a pretty decent performance back then, although you didn't have the emphasis on performance the way you do now.

Griffeth: What years were those?

Hoey: Actually, I started before sophomore and junior year when I was at Yale. I commuted down several times a week to New York.

Griffeth: So you were managing money in college.

Hoey: Yes.

Griffeth: That would have been what, the mid-1960s?

Hoey: Yes, I went there in the summer of 1963 and then in 1964 and 1965 I was commuting down from Yale a couple of days a week. I had one of those majors that met from 2 to 5 P.M. on Wednesdays, and then you had to read 100 books. That type of thing.

Griffeth: Were you getting credits for managing the money?

Hoey: No, no, I was getting credits for reading the books. [laughing] I was getting money to finance my weekends.

Griffeth: The investment philosophy you learned, or developed, there. Did you take that to Dreyfus Growth & Income?

Hoey: Sure. Basically the man whose firm it was kind of taught me the business. He had been a portfolio manager at Calvin Bullock which was an old mutual fund firm. And I worked for him for about eight years managing balanced accounts of stocks, convertibles and bonds for individuals with accounts of several million dollars each.

Griffeth: So, let me be clear. When the opportunity came up for you to manage the Dreyfus Growth & Income fund, did the investment philosophy you learned in college fit that particular fund?

Hoey: There are several aspects. One is that there are certain things you learn in terms of investment philosophy that are accumulated from the mistakes you make. In other words, I'll make new and creative mistakes this year, but I'll try not to make the same mistakes next year. So there's a learning process when you are involved in running portfolios.

Now in the 1960s, we had a blow-off type of bull market in the 1966 through 1968 period.

Griffeth: The Go-Go years.

Hoey: Yes, it was just an explosive bull market, especially for secondary and lower quality stocks. And then we had a pretty tough bear market after that. So that was kind of my learning curve. I rate portfolio managers by how many bear markets they've lived through, and I've lived through the one that was linked to the credit crunch of 1966, the one that went down because of the credit crunch of 1970, the one that went down as the credit crunch of 1974, the one that went down as the credit crunch of 1980, and then the one in 1982 and then 1987, if you count that as a bear market, which I think you should.

> ◆
> *". . . there are certain things you learn in terms of investment philosophy that are accumulated from the mistakes you make."*
> ◆

Griffeth: So let's see. With that many stripes, does that make you a sergeant or a lieutenant?

Hoey: [laughing] I don't know. I think that makes me at least a colonel. But you do learn through the alternation of the bull and bear markets. As I say, I define portfolio managers by the number of bear markets they've lived through.

Griffeth: So are you a money manager who became an economist or an economist who decided to manage money as well?

Hoey: Well, it was kind of both. I took my graduate work in economics while I was working as a portfolio manager. Then I went to NYU Graduate School and took economics, got my MBA, and then I did course work for the doctorate. I didn't do my dissertation, so I'm not Dr. Hoey, but I did the economics course work in graduate school. So, therefore, I was mixing the economics from the academic side with the practical experience of managing money right from the beginning.

Double Duty

Griffeth: When you worked at Pru-Bache, Becker, and Drexel you were the chief economist and many times you also served on the investment policy committee, didn't you?

Hoey: Yes, in some portion, and I was also serving on the stock selection committee which is not that common for the chief economist. Usually you have the chief economist serving on the investment policy committee, but it's fairly uncommon to have the chief economist sitting on the stock selection committee.

Griffeth: Because sometimes the duties are at odds, aren't they?

Hoey: It depends. If they are two different people, sometimes they're at odds.

Griffeth: But in terms of job description, your travel schedule, and what you have to focus on to do your job, sometimes they get in the way, don't they?

Hoey: I don't sense that. It's just a time commitment issue. During several portions of that time I was the investment strategist as well as the chief economist of the firm. That was true when I was at W.E. Hutton, not E.F. but W.E. That was true when I was at Thomson McKinnon, it was true a portion of the time when I was at Bache. I think I'm the only fool who has ever been both the chief economist and investment strategist of a major firm simultaneously. That was at Bache.

Griffeth: Why?

Hoey: I found it interesting. At least we didn't have too much disagreement about how the economic outlook fit the investment strategy. [laughing] The left side of our brain was consistent with the right side of our brain.

Griffeth: And now you're able to do that again with Dreyfus. How did that start?

Hoey: I came over here in July of 1991, and I joined as chief economist. Part of my objective was to end up running a mutual fund and see whether it would succeed. It wasn't promised to me but it was a possibility, and so when the new fund opened up, they offered to let me do it.

Griffeth: And I guess there were no qualms on your part?

Hoey: No, no. Having run money before I was interested in doing it, and also—being at Dreyfus—I had more time because I wasn't a "sell side economist" trying to get on the I.I. list.

Griffeth: The I.I. list?

Hoey: Institutional Investor, which is a ranking for economic strategists. [*NOTE: A Wall Street economist's year-end bonus will often be tied to his or her ranking on the annual I.I. list*] You do an awful lot of traveling as a sell side economist, and I don't have nearly the same travel schedule at Dreyfus as I did when I was working for the brokerage firms.

Hoey's Investment Philosophy

Griffeth: So they brought this fund to you to manage. Did the prospectus dictate the investment philosophy you had to use, or were you able to mold the fund with your own philosophy?

Hoey: The investment philosophy in the prospectus was broad enough that I was able to pretty much use my own to put the portfolio together.

Griffeth: And what is that philosophy?

Hoey: My philosophy is basically what's known in pension fund circles as "top down, bottom up" which is to say you start with a top down view of the world economy, the U.S. economy, interest rates, market outlook, sector outlook and then mix that with the bottom up approach of finding individual stocks that fit your macro-view.

In addition, I believe in switching among sectors very aggressively in terms of being substantially underweighted in certain sectors and substantially overweighted in others. I don't believe in what's called in the business "closet indexing," which is making very minor deviations from the index you're competing against.

Griffeth: Do you manage the amount of risk in your portfolio based on your top down view of the markets?

Hoey: I try to manage the level of risk. But what I'm most focused on is managing the total portfolio risk, which is the weighted sum of the risk of the individual securities. Therefore I'm willing to mix low-risk and high-risk securities.

Griffeth: How do you measure risk?

Hoey: There are a lot of different ways of doing it. You can look at betas, you can look at quality ratings, you can look at the nature of the businesses they're in.

Griffeth: All of that is what you look at?

Hoey: Yes, I look at those characteristics. I don't do it by mathematical summation. What happens is, there are periods when I choose to raise the risk level by buying high-risk, high-potential securities, and then there are periods when I sell out the high-risk securities and move toward higher grade securities. But I'm not managing to a number.

Griffeth: I assume you change the risk level based on your view of the overall risk in the markets at that time.

Hoey: That's right. Overall risk and potential reward, because even if you think the risk level is unchanged, if the potential reward is down, you may shift toward less risky assets.

Managing the Fund

Griffeth: Your record so far has been commendable, to say the least. Not to belittle it or to second guess it, I would think any economist worth his or her salt would have found success managing money during the obvious and dramatic bond rally we experienced the past few years.

Hoey: I don't know. I don't think any of these things are necessarily no-brainers. Certainly when you look backwards, any situation becomes clearer. But at the time you're going through it you are subject to a lot more uncertainties. So I wouldn't say this has been a particularly easier time to make good decisions.

Griffeth: So let me ask you then, as we sit here in June of 1994, to what do you attribute your good performance in the fund the past 2-1/2 years?

Hoey: Some of it was avoiding areas of danger, getting out of the way of an oncoming freight train. When I started managing the fund at the end of 1991, looking into early 1992, I very quickly came to the conclusion that the consumer nondurable and drug companies were vulnerable, that their earnings momentum was decelerating, and especially that their earnings momentum relative to more cyclical stocks was decelerating. And so I pretty aggressively underweighted investments in food, tobacco, beverages, drug stocks, etc. And that decision was a very, very important one in terms of generating relative performance. And then during the period I also made some swings back and forth between interest sensitive and cyclical stocks as the outlook looked better or worse. I also had some period when I was participating in the small cap stock market, and then I sold it back substantially after rallies. One of the things that I've been able to do is capture the profits by being in some areas when they were performing but getting out before they gave it back. And that first occurred in terms of getting in and out of smaller cap stocks.

Then back in the fourth quarter of 1993 I sold off a large portion of the information superhighway-related communications stocks that I had, because while that had been a very profitable investment it got insanely overdone.

Griffeth: You also started selling off portions of your interest-sensitive utilities, figuring that interest rates would start to rise.

Hoey: Yes, I had sold them off early; I didn't catch the highs. I was out of them before we actually made the absolute highs in the bond market and the lows in interest rates. So it wasn't like I caught the rise and got out of the way of the decline, but I was out of the way early enough so that I didn't catch the big negative impact of the decline in the bond market.

At the end of 1993, we also had a blow-off in the emerging market stocks, so I started to sell them in December and continued to sell them in early 1994. Now a lot of these emerging market stocks that I owned had generated good gains, and in some cases I gave back a portion of the gains, but I got a lot of this money back out before the full decline set in.

> "I would tend to buy some areas with the intention of holding them for three years, and then if they ran to excessive levels I was forced by prudence to cut back."

Griffeth: So you try to be a pretty nimble trader.

Hoey: Well, I didn't start out intending to do that, but what I found was that the behavior of the speculative fervor in the market place was such that stock prices were much more volatile than their underlying fundamentals. I would tend to buy some areas with the intention of holding them for three years, and then if they ran to excessive levels I was forced by prudence to cut back.

Top Down / Bottom Up

Griffeth: Now let's talk about the bottom up portion of your investment style. After you have identified an economic trend and the industry groups that will benefit from that trend, how do you choose the stocks within those groups for your portfolio?

Hoey: Let me answer that by pointing out that in terms of the macro top down view, I'm using a multi-scenario approach. I don't come at it saying I can see one scenario or one outcome, and therefore I can pick just the portfolio that will work for that. I don't, because I can't see the future.

Instead, what I try to do is say there's a most likely scenario, a next most likely scenario, and a third most likely scenario. And given the probabilities of these outcomes, what kind of portfolio can I build that will have the best risk reward within that context. In other words, I'm trying to rationally evaluate different possible outcomes that can occur in kind of a multiple scenario top down frame work.

Griffeth: Okay, then take us to the next stage.

Hoey: So then after I have developed a world outlook on the global economy, interest rates, and currencies and an outlook on the domestic economy, interest rates, the stock market, and various sectors, I say, "These are the industries that seem to make sense." Then I look at the specific companies in those industries. I talk to our own analysts to see what ideas are coming up from them. I try to talk to company managements to see whether my conclusions from the top down point of view are in fact validated by the information that's coming up from the individual companies. Sometimes it's consistent and sometimes it's inconsistent because of some specific characteristic of the company. Or sometimes it's inconsistent because my top down conclusion is wrong. And so you need the information from the individual companies, a) to find out whether they fit the theme, or b) as a check and balance to tell you whether or not your theme is right to begin with. Often, the bottom up information will tell you that your top down theme is wrong. In other words, you've got a wonderful theory but they're telling you it's just not happening out there in the real world.

Griffeth: Then what do you do?

Hoey: Then you try to figure out what is going on. In other words, what is the cause of that. One of the things I've concluded is that in the process of forecasting for 20 years, the big mistakes are not mistakes about facts. The big mistakes are mistakes about the cause-and-effect linkages.

> " . . . the big mistakes are not mistakes about facts. The big mistakes are mistakes about the cause-and-effect linkages."

Griffeth: Do you have a for instance?

Hoey: You get a situation where you have a conclusion that the economy is fairly strong and you start to get information up from companies that their orders are fading away on you.

Griffeth: Do you then change your economic scenario?

Hoey: Yes, I go back to re-examine it and modify the scenario in terms of probabilities, taking into account the additional information I am receiving. And so what you've got is a daily process of changing the probabilities of different scenarios.

Let's say you have developed a scenario that says there's going to be a lot of inflation because oil prices are going to go up. Then you meet with the oil companies, and they tell you that the supply and demand they are currently experiencing doesn't support your scenario. Then you have to decide whether they just haven't seen it yet and it's in the macro background or whether you're just wrong.

Griffeth: It's a great argument for bringing some economists out of their proverbial ivory towers.

Hoey: Well, yes. I think there is a kind of generic economics taught that's a little bit like teaching doctors medicine for the healthy patient. Instead, in order to really understand how the system really works, you have to see how it reacts when the normal processes don't work that well. You have to examine what's actually going on.

Now I use different schools of economics to monitor business cycle indications, but one of them is institutional economics which is used to understand how the financial system actually works as opposed to how it's suppose to work in theory. I have a peculiar characteristic which is that I've been on the scene for most of the financial crises of the last 25 years. And so I understand the way the system works, especially when it's under stress. Back in 1970 when I was managing money at John B. Braine Inc., we owned the bonds of the Penn Central Company. Penn Central went bankrupt when the commercial paper couldn't be sold by Goldman Sachs. Well, that was a learning experience as to how the financial system works.

In 1974 I was at W.E. Hutton and I made a forecast that we'd have big trouble in the Eurodollar market and that some brokerage firms would go out of business. Unfortunately, about four months later it was my own brokerage firm that went out of business!

In 1980 I was chief economist of Bache when Bunker Hunt ended up with too much silver. He had borrowed twice the net worth of Bache to be in the silver market, and Bache nearly went bankrupt.

And then in 1990 I was chief economist of Drexel Burnham when the junk bond market collapsed, and they went bankrupt.

Griffeth: And Dreyfus hired you anyway!

Hoey: [laughing] Dreyfus hired me anyway! It goes to show, only a certain number of companies have a strong enough balance sheet to take the risk of hiring me! But I accumulated through the process of being on the scene of these financial crises kind of an institutional economics understanding of the way the financial system, and the stock market, and the bond market, work under stress.

Griffeth: But let me be clear on the actual stock selection for your fund. You rely, I think I heard you say, on your research department to give you some good anecdotal evidence of companies that would fit your scenario.

Hoey: Analysts in our department as well as some on Wall Street or other portfolio managers either here or in other firms. So I don't restrict myself only to stocks covered by our portfolio managers.

Griffeth: Some fund managers will go out and actually meet company executives. Given your dual role at Dreyfus, do you have time to do that, or do you rely more on research?

Hoey: I do a fair amount of the leg work, because your sense of corporate dynamics is much better if you meet the management. They can give you that sense of micro economic supply and demand in force. So I gather information for my top down perspective from the corporate managements, and I use the knowledge that they have within the business in which they are actually operating.

And often company managements come in here to Dreyfus. We're centrally located here, so we get an awful lot of managements coming through.

Stock Market as Economic Forecaster

Griffeth: Let me ask you this, since you are an economist who manages money or a money manager who is also an economist. The stock market, it is said, forecasts the economy six to nine months down the road. I can think of an instance in 1982 when we were still in recession and the stock market started to rally. Those who didn't understand the relationship between the stock market and the economy were scratching their heads. How could the stock market be rallying while we were still in recession? The question to you is, if you have a particular economic forecast in mind and the market seems to be discounting a different scenario, which way do you go? Does the money manager in you go with the market trend, or does the economist in you stick with your own forecast?

Hoey: First of all I think the consensus logic about the issue that you just raised is wrong.

Griffeth: In other words, you don't believe the stock market is that much of a forecasting tool?

Hoey: Well, let's put it this way: that characteristic is an accidental side effect of something else. What I believe is that the stock market and the economy are joint effects of the same cause. One operates with a short lag and the other with a long lag. And the cause is financial liquidity within the system. And so what you don't want to do is make a forecast for the economy and then come back from that to your forecast for the stock market based on the hope that your forecast on the economy is right. What you want to do is look at the core driving force for both the stock market and for the economy, which is the financial liquidity in the system.

Griffeth: Let's go back to my example and put it in English. What was happening in 1982 when the economy was still mired in recession and the stock market was taking off?

Hoey: Well, it is very traditional late in recessions for the stock market to rise. Bear markets end in mid to late recession and bull markets start. So what we had was an absolutely classic type pattern where your low in the stock market in the summer of 1982 preceded the low in the economy a few months later. Same thing happened in 1974 and 1975. You had a double bottom in the stock market in October 1974 and again in December 1974, and you really didn't come out of the recession until the spring of 1975.

The interesting instance, I think, is 1990, because in 1990 you went into recession in an environment where few people forecast that you would go into a recession or bear market. The reason was that they had a model in their head that high inflation causes a rising Fed Funds rate which causes a recession. So since the Fed didn't have a big inflation that caused it to raise the Fed Funds rate a lot, the conclusion that most forecasters had was we wouldn't have a recession.

I had a forecast that we would go into recession. Why? Because we had financial illiquidity of a different sort. The correct model was that financial illiquidity causes recessions, and financial illiquidity causes bear markets. We had financial illiquidity linked to the meltdown of the savings and loans, the meltdown of the junk bond market, and the problems in real estate. And the people who argued we couldn't have a recession because the Fed hadn't tightened aggressively had the wrong understanding of what was actually going on in terms of the system.

So you have to get the causal linkages right. You could have all the facts right but if you misunderstand the way the system is really working, you're going to come to the wrong conclusion. The 1990 recession was the real test. Basically, most economists were dead wrong. They did not forecast it because they used a model that wasn't checked in with the real world. Now I had an intellectual advantage at the time because I was working at Drexel Burnham, and I could see the financial illiquidity collapsing on the scene.

> "... when people say the stock market forecasts the economy, what they are saying is it forecasts the economy the way a temperature gauge reflects the heat inside a boiler."

So what I'm getting at is when people say the stock market forecasts the economy, what they are saying is it forecasts the economy the way a temperature gauge reflects the heat inside a boiler. The temperature gauge doesn't cause the heat in a boiler to go up, it merely measures it.

Griffeth: So the market is sensitive enough to sense a recovery or slow down before it becomes evident in the government numbers.

Hoey: Yes, and it isn't even psychological sensitivity. It's merely a reflection of the residual liquidity in the system. People often buy stocks because they have excess liquidity.

The Growth of Mutual Funds

Griffeth: You have had a tremendous amount of liquidity moving into the mutual fund industry the last few years. From an economic standpoint what does that mean, and from a business standpoint for mutual funds, how do you read it?

Hoey: Well there are two different things going on, and they have different consequences for both the economy and the mutual fund business. This is a classic case where a single explanation won't cover it, but there are two main explanations.

Explanation number one is a longer term demographic phenomenon, which is that as the baby boomers came into their jobs and started to invest they initially faced in the 1980s an exceptional period where real yields—that is to say, long-term bond yields minus inflation or short-term T-bill yields minus inflation—were very high, so they didn't need to bother to invest in the stock market that much because they had real yields with not much risk. That was an unusual occasion. We had a period of a decade there where the yields available in excess of inflation were way above the norm. That was associated with the aggressive use of credit by the baby boomers as they bought their houses and went through the phase of their life cycle when they had the desire to use a lot of credit.

What has happened now is we no longer have these very, very high interest rates. And when that happened, you started to see the baby boomers—who are now thinking about retirement—shifting their assets toward more permanent investments, including stock mutual funds.

I think the other side of it is that what you had was an excess investment in very short-term money market instruments—like CDs, etc.—where when the short-term interest rates dropped down to 3 percent, way below where the prevailing level had been for the past decade, then people raced away from the short term money market type investments and bought bonds and bond funds, and stocks and stock funds. And in some cases, as often happens, you go from undershooting to overshooting. So there were some cases of people who ended up taking on more risk than they probably should have for their financial circumstance.

So what you have now is the combined effect of these two phenomena. A longer term sustainable phenomenon of the need for permanent retirement savings by the baby boomers, which is an underlying positive for the money management business and for the market, as well as some overinvestment by people who were driven into more volatile investments by the extremely low yields they were getting from short-term paper. You've got the combination of both of those.

Griffeth: So give me the forecast. How will it play itself out? I mean, the theory is that at some point when the market becomes serious in terms of a correction or bear market or whatever, the hot money from your overinvestors will be quick to leave and the baby boomers will become disenchanted with the risk they found themselves taking, and the market's decline is exaggerated.

Hoey: What I'm saying is that this is likely to be partially correct and partially incorrect.

Griffeth: [laughing] Spoken like a true economist!

Hoey: No, I think that's correct. In other words, some of the excessive swing from underinvestment in stock and bond type investments to overinvestment will be reversed, but as that occurs you're still going to have a substantial portion of money in the markets which will have a permanent investment compo-nent. What will tend to happen, I think, is that the psychology will shift somewhat more toward investment grade vehicles and away from the more speculative investments.

Griffeth: From a business standpoint, a number of young people have started their own mutual funds, not nearly as highly capi-talized as the Dreyfus Corporation or Fidelity or a Vanguard in terms of the amount that they are managing. Are those the people who are washed out if we do get enough of a correction from the markets?

Hoey: No question that the mutual fund business is going through a cycle that starts with high profits, then there is an influx of new entrants, then an excess of suppliers, and then a weakening of the business and a rationalization and contraction in the numbers of suppliers. And this is a cycle that goes on in most businesses you can think of out there.

You know, the investment business has seen cycle after cycle after cycle of building up and contracting and building up and contracting and building up and contracting. And one perfectly well can raise the question of whether in fact there should be more mutual funds than there are stocks listed on the New York Stock Exchange without thinking that it's the end of the world. There are economies of scale, and what you have is a bunch of people getting into the business who figure they will experience the same rapid growth most everyone else has. Well, not all of them will. Some will, but some won't. Chances are those who build a good solid business will experience strong growth. But those that don't won't experience it, just as in any other industry which attracts a lot of new entrants.

Hoey's Choice

Griffeth: Last question. If you had to choose between just managing money, or just being an economist, which one would it be now?

Hoey: I enjoy managing money. I guess my choice would be to be a portfolio manager, but the real test for that choice is what you say after a period of bad performance rather than a period when it has worked. That's the real test. I mean, everybody enjoys the honeymoon, and then everybody goes into a dry patch at some point. Everybody has a period of a batting slump. We'll see how I feel about it then.

I enjoy doing the combined job and carrying it down to actually being a portfolio manager. One of the reasons is that there's no other job I know of with as immediate and objective a feedback about how you're doing. I get my grade every morning in the paper when I look at my fund's performance. I don't need to depend upon the scowl or frown of someone in the office to know how I'm doing. I have a very objective feedback loop which is nearly instantaneous. And with technology moving the way it is, I'm sure we'll soon be able to get a performance measurement on a minute-by-minute basis during the trading day for those of us who want instant feedback.

J. MARK MOBIUS

Birth Date: August 17, 1936

Education: Boston University, B.A. and M.A. in fine arts. MIT, Ph.D. in Economics/Political Science

Hobbies: "Work!"

Alternate Career: Health club owner, or physical education instructor

*M*ark Mobius is the dean of all emerging market mutual fund managers. He probably knows more about the world's developing countries than anyone else on earth, simply because he has visited each of them many, many times.

Mobius is a true citizen of the world. He literally lives on the road. Witness the incredible two-month itinerary I have included here from the summer of 1994. He has been keeping this schedule year-round since 1987 when he became director and executive vice president of Templeton Worldwide Inc.

At Templeton, Mobius really has two jobs. First, he oversees management of more than $6 billion in 24 different privately managed accounts and mutual funds. Four of the funds are available to investors in the United States: one open-end fund, Templeton Developing Markets, and three closed-end funds, Templeton Emerging Markets, Templeton China World, and Templeton Vietnam. (By the time you read this, there no doubt will be more.) And his efforts have won him some professional recognition. In 1992, for example, The Sunday Telegraph in the United Kingdom named him "Investment Trust Manager of the Year," and here in the United States, Morningstar named him "Closed-End Fund Manager of the Year" in 1994.

The other reason Mobius travels so much is he is busy setting up a global network of offices for parent company Franklin/Templeton, preparing for the day when every investor will have direct access to every stock around the world.

Gaining access to Mark for this book was not easy. His secretary in Singapore, Zita Ng, and I targeted my interview with him for sometime during a six-day period in September of 1994 when he was

in the United States Monday he was in California. Tuesday he was in Chicago. Wednesday he was in New York. Thursday morning he had a breakfast meeting at the New York Stock Exchange for the launch of the Templeton Vietnam Fund, and then he flew to Florida that afternoon. That Thursday evening, Jim Rogers and I interviewed him on CNBC via satellite. Friday he attended a Templeton board meeting. Saturday he flew back to New York to spend a few short hours with his brother's family. That Saturday evening, he and I finally sat down to talk before a car whisked him off to the airport for a late night flight to Russia on his private corporate jet.

Despite the pace he maintains, Mark Mobius is a surprisingly calm person. The number of times I have met and spoken with him, I have never known him to be in a hurry. It is the result of unwavering physical and mental discipline. As you will read, he maintains a rigorous exercise regimen and watches his diet very carefully. (What would you expect from someone who earned a Ph.D. in economics from MIT?)

During our interview, we talked about his diverse career, his investment philosophy, the dangers of investing in the emerging markets, and the five countries where he sees the greatest long-term investment opportunities.

SEPTEMBER 17, 1994

About That Schedule

Bill Griffeth: How in the world do you maintain your schedule?

Mark Mobius: Well, I think one of the things is that I'm highly motivated because I love what I do. I love the work, and I find it interesting. I think that's very important. Second, I'm very careful to keep in good health, and I exercise as much as I can. In fact, if exercising is a hobby, then that's probably a hobby for me. I like to jog, I like to go to the gym and work out, that sort of thing. Health is very, very important.

Griffeth: But with the very tight schedule you keep, where do you even find the time to exercise?

Mobius: I make the time. Whenever I'm in a city, I make sure that I can find a health club. One of the requirements of any hotel I choose is that it has a health club or something like that.

Extract From Mark Mobius's Itinerary—1994

June 22:	Athens, Greece
June 26:	Budapest, Hungary
June 28:	Prague, Czech Republic
June 30:	Warsaw, Poland
July 3:	Krakow, Poland
July 5:	Moscow, Russia
July 9:	St. Petersburg, Russia
July 11:	Novosibirsk, Russia
July 13:	Vladivostok, Russia
July 14:	Tokyo, Japan
July 16:	Singapore
July 20:	Bangkok, Thailand
July 21:	Kuala Lumpur, Malaysia
July 22:	Jakarta, Indonesia
July 23:	Bandung, Indonesia
July 24:	Tokyo, Japan
July 27:	Hong Kong
July 30:	Hanoi, Vietnam
Aug 2:	Danang, Vietnam
Aug 3:	Ho Chi Minh City, Vietnam
Aug 6:	Manila, Philippines
Aug 11:	Subic Bay, Philippines
Aug 11:	Singapore
Aug 14:	Bangkok, Thailand
Aug 18:	Yangon, Myanmar
Aug 21:	Singapore
Aug 22:	Hong Kong
Aug 24:	Guangzhou, China
Aug 25:	Beijing, China

Zita, my secretary, even gets lists of the kind of equipment hotels have. And I try to jog as much as I can, wherever I am. There is always time.

The great thing about those two ways of staying healthy is that you can do them on your own time, and you can do them in a relatively short period of time. With golf, for example, you need other people to play with, you have to make appointments, and it's an all-day or half-day deal. But with jogging or weight training you don't need anyone else to be around. You can do it anytime, and it can be done in a very short period of time with very good results.

Griffeth: Given the fact that you've lived in the Far East as long as you have, I could picture you also practicing Tai Chi or some other form of meditation.

Mobius: Well, I do practice some Judo and Tang Soo Do, which is Korean, but I have found that weight training is probably the best. The combination of weight training and jogging is the best, because you are getting your internal organs jiggled around a little bit when you jog and then your skeletal muscles are being trained when you are doing weight training.

Griffeth: Don't you ever get jet lag?

Mobius: Oh, yes. But I have less and less jet lag now than I did before. The more traveling you do, I think intuitively you begin to restrain yourself from eating too much and doing things that will accentuate the jet lag. So I tend not to drink alcohol at all on planes, and then I don't eat very much before, during, or after a flight.

A lot of the jet lag problem is psychological. It is tied to your ability to sleep when you have to, and I can do that. Like tonight, I'll get on the plane and I'll put on a video or something and then go to sleep.

Griffeth: We've talked about how you maintain this schedule. But why do you do it, Mark?

Mobius: Because I find that in our style of investing it's so important to meet the people we are putting money with. I look at each company we invest in as a little fund manager for us. Basically, the management of that company is handling our money as a shareholder of their company. We are entrusting money with them, so the better I know them the stronger my commitment to them will be.

Very often, I buy a stock and it goes down. And the only way I'm going to make money at the end of the day is by buying more shares until I hit the bottom of the price cycle, and then I ride it back up again. Now, I wouldn't do that if I didn't have confidence in the company. So I meet with each company to gain that confidence.

The second reason I travel so much is I find when I'm doing research on a company, the more I read its balance sheet and profit and loss statements, the more I realize how little I actually know about the company. And the only way I can complete the picture is by going to see them and asking them directly. You can do some of it by phone or by correspondence, but often the direct visit is most effective.

"My Job Is to Pick Stocks"

Griffeth: The obvious question, then, is: where do you find the time to manage mutual funds?

Mobius: Yes, I am often asked that question. Some people picture a fund manager as someone sitting at a big desk with a computer, and he's punching numbers into that computer and miraculously he gets a great performing portfolio.

> "My job is to pick stocks, and I can pick stocks better when I'm traveling than when I'm in the office because I'm getting a broader view of the world."

But that's not the way it works. My job is to pick stocks, and I can pick stocks better when I'm traveling than when I'm in the office because I'm getting a broader view of the world. I'm uncovering things that no one sitting in his office is able to uncover.

Griffeth: I'm not trying to take away from your abilities, but couldn't you assign one person to cover, say, Europe, another to cover the Far East, another to cover Latin America, and so forth?

Mobius: Oh, we do. We have people covering one group of countries, and we have consultants covering another group of countries. But at the end of the day I've got to crack the whip, so to speak, and make sure these people are performing. And that means I have to go and see things for myself.

And then, if you get two people looking at something you can get a better result. Because very often one person may be too close to the situation. So if a guy from Hong Kong comes over and looks at a Portuguese company, or a Polish company, he will get a view that the analyst on the spot will not get. So it's very important.

Griffeth: I can understand that, but I want to know how you handle the logistics of managing your funds. I mean, you visit a country, you visit a group of companies in that country, you decide you want to buy or sell shares in those companies, and then what happens?

Mobius: I should point out that a lot of the stuff I do is opening new markets. Diversification is essential to a global portfolio. The more diversification you have, the more choice you have, the better your performance will be.

So, for example, the purpose of my trip to Russia tonight is simply to open that market. I want to find out how we can get in, what the custodial problems are, what the research problems are, hire staff on the ground, that sort of thing.

Once that's done, we will do a scan of the entire market. We will create a list of companies in which we can invest, and we will assign the companies to an individual analyst. Then the analyst will take over. He becomes the portfolio manager, in essence, because he selects those companies which he finds to be the best bargains, and I don't second guess him.

Griffeth: Does that mean a stock you don't like could go into one of your funds, or must each stock have your blessing?

Mobius: Theoretically, yes, a stock can go in without my blessing. It's my job to ensure that the reasoning behind a stock going into the portfolio is sound. In other words, it has to meet the criteria we've set out for the entire portfolio. It has to have some characteristic that makes it a bargain, like not being at the top of its price. You know, we very seldom want to buy a stock that is at the peak of its price, although we do buy stocks like that from time to time when there is a good reason. But at least there is someone there who questions that kind of selection.

So, yes, there have been stocks where an analyst said, "I think this is a great thing," and I said, "Well, I don't, but I'm going to put it in because you've looked at it."

Griffeth: It had better work. [Laughing]

Mobius: Yes, it had better work. [Also laughing] Your salary might be in it!

By the way, that's one of the big problems in this business, providing the proper incentive to the analyst. On the one hand, you don't want to have the analyst look at the short-term performance of a fund. But on the other hand, if you're incentivising him on that basis you tend to get that kind of thinking. So we are constantly struggling with how to compensate our analysts who are, in essence, our portfolio managers.

Griffeth: When you find a stock you like, how do you decide which fund or institutional portfolio to put it in? I mean, sometimes it obviously depends on a particular fund's investment objective. But you manage over 24 different funds and institutional portfolios. How do you allocate shares to each portfolio?

Mobius: Well, we allocate according to how much cash the different portfolios have in percentage terms, and also—as you suggested—the specific requirements of each portfolio. Some portfolios have restrictions on various kinds of things that we can't buy. So we have computer programs that spit out all of the weightings, because we are watched very carefully by clients, and the SEC, and others to make sure that we are treating each fund fairly.

Bargains

Griffeth: Let's talk about your investment philosophy. Are you a value investor or a growth investor?

Mobius: We look for bargains. In other words, we look for things that are intrinsically cheap relative to a number of criteria. The criteria we use differ according to the country, but let's say, for example, that a particular company usually trades at a price-to-earnings ratio of 15 times. And then suddenly—either because its earnings go up or because the price goes down—it's selling at seven times earnings because it's out of favor, or because people think the outlook is not so good. Whatever the reason may be. That constitutes a bargain.

We will also look at a company if it is cheap relative to other companies in its own market. You'll see many markets where the index is going up, the big cap stocks are going up, but many companies within that market are actually going down in price for one reason or another. We will zero in on those companies.

Or a company may be cheap relative to its counterparts in other parts of the world. For example, let's say a particular cement company has a market cap to capacity price of, say $25. We know that cement companies normally sell at $100 per ton. So that company is a bargain.

Those are the kinds of things we will examine very carefully. And after we've done the analysis we may find that a company is cheap for a good reason. But many times we find a stock is cheap because of things that don't make sense. Emotional reasons. Outlook reasons. So very often we look at this discrepancy between reality and outlook.

> "The perception of risk is very, very important in finding bargains, because if people think something is risky we could find a bargain."

One of the reasons the Hong Kong market is cheap right now is because many people fear the outlook for 1997 in Hong Kong [when control of Hong Kong reverts to mainland China]. Well, that presents an opportunity, and of course when you see an opportunity there is always a risk. So, in essence, what we are looking for is risk. The perception of risk is very, very important in finding bargains, because if people think something is risky we could find a bargain.

Griffeth: In other words, the markets in some countries are underdeveloped enough that you're able to find these wide discrepancies in value?

Mobius: Exactly. But, you know, even in the United States you'll find some stocks that are out of favor. I mean, what a great opportunity there was when IBM was in big trouble. Remember that?

Griffeth: Sure.

Mobius: The price was down, nobody liked it, the company was going bust, blah, blah, blah. But for those who looked at it more carefully and were willing to take a risk, they've already made, what, 60 percent, 70 percent?

Griffeth: So far.

Mobius: So you know, that kind of opportunity is always there.

Griffeth: But can you use that analytical fine tooth comb in some countries where the accounting practices are not as sophisticated as in the United States, and where the markets are not nearly as developed as they are elsewhere?

Mobius: Yes you can, and with good results because a lot of times people are not looking at the same things that we are looking at. They are looking at things emotionally, or they are just gambling in the market, or taking bets on the market, and under those conditions of course the value investor can do very well if he is patient.

Griffeth: Let's use Vietnam as an example. Your closed-end Vietnam fund just opened a couple of days ago. Can you use the same methods of valuation in a country where the market is not as developed as the others in Southeast Asia?

Mobius: Yes, definitely. We will look, for example, at the banks which are our stock holding companies. And we'll ask the question, "How do these banks stack up to their counterparts in other countries?" Even if they don't have the same kind of an account that we see with Citibank or with Chase, how do they stack up against those companies?

Then we will watch carefully as this market moves from a command economy to a market economy, and we will decide what these banks are going to do in the future and how perception of value will change among investors in that country.

And this is also one of the opportunities, by the way, that we are seeing in the former Soviet Union and in China. The perception of value is undergoing tremendous change.

Griffeth: You feel the Russian market has developed enough to justify investing there?

Mobius: Yes.

Griffeth: I mean there are plenty of people who can't wait to invest there, but they don't think all the economic pain has been felt yet.

Mobius: The problem for us in Russia is that our custodial banks are not ready for us. This is a perennial problem we have in breaking into new markets. The custodians are not ready, and that's one of the reasons I have to go over there and see if I can push that along.

Top Down or Bottom Up

Griffeth: Other emerging market fund managers have told me that when they invest in the lesser developed countries, they choose companies using the traditional top down approach. In other words, they go with the big infrastructure plays, for example. And then as the country's economy becomes more developed, they can more closely scrutinize individual companies using the so-called bottom up approach.

Mobius: Oh, I think it is just the opposite.

Griffeth: Is that right?

Mobius: Yes, in fact, the bottom up approach to me makes eminent sense to the emerging market for one very simple reason. Information about the macroeconomic political environment in these emerging countries is very, very difficult to get. And whatever you do get is often inaccurate and late, so by focusing on a bottom up approach we often learn more about what's happening in the country than by trying to look at the macro statistics, if you know what I mean.

If you are on the ground, you are talking to people who are actually living and suffering from the pain of the environment. This is true in Brazil, by the way. When we were looking at Brazil many years ago when they had the tremendous inflation that they're now beginning to lick, we got many, many more insights by talking to the companies than by talking to the government.

Griffeth: You know, the more "traditional" play, if you will, is when a market opens up you go to the companies that are going to build the infrastructure for that nation, and you go with the banks that will be lending those companies the money to build the infrastructure. Then you call it a day and wait for that country to develop.

But apparently you go in and start looking for smaller companies right away.

Mobius: Exactly, because the banks may or may not be the best bet for that particular country. It depends on what's happening on the ground.

Emerging Markets Cycle

Griffeth: Investing in the emerging markets for most Americans began in the mid- to late-1980s. How far along would you say we are in that cycle?

Mobius: I would say we're probably at the high end of a cycle right now.

Griffeth: We're reaching the peak, then?

Mobius: I think there will be several peaks along the way. I mean, certainly 1993 was one peak, but we had our correction in 1994, and now we're moving into another phase.

The problem, though, is that it is very difficult to generalize because each market has had its individual peaks and crises and busts at different times. Turkey is a good example. While Hong Kong was moving from strength to strength, Turkey was bombing out.

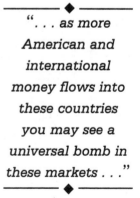

" . . . as more American and international money flows into these countries you may see a universal bomb in these markets . . ."

Now, as more American and international money flows into these countries you may see a universal bomb in these markets, but I think it will be very short lived. Because at the end of the day, in each of these markets, the local investor is the one who determines what's going to happen, not the foreign investor. There are a few very small markets where you might see the foreigners dominate.

I think you could see a sell-off like we had in 1987 when the American funds pulled money out of foreign countries in reaction to what was happening here. But then immediately after that the locals took over, and the foreign markets took on lives of their own.

Griffeth: Would you say that, for the most part, U.S. investors are still underinvested in international markets?

Mobius: Oh, yes, by a long shot. The vast majority of American investors don't have a clue about what's happening internationally. And they are certainly not invested internationally, because they don't trust the international markets. They still fear them.

Griffeth: Shouldn't they?

Mobius: No, they shouldn't. Japan is the best example in our lifetime. If an American had put all of his savings in Japan in 1960 or 1970, he'd be sitting pretty now.

Griffeth: Then let me ask you: as we sit here in 1994, Mark, where should someone who is still 10 or 20 years from retirement put their money? Is there another Japan out there waiting?

Mobius: Yes, I think there are many Japans out there waiting. The problem is we don't know which one! [Laughing] And that is why we opt for globally diversified portfolios. I mean, we'd like to think that China or India or Brazil or any of these countries will become the tremendous success that we've seen in Japan, but there is still no way of knowing.

There was no way of knowing when I was living in Japan in 1960 that Japan would be where it is today. You read the writings of people at that time who were making predictions about Japan. They all said, "This country is hopeless, it will never go anywhere, it has too many problems," blah, blah, blah.

Griffeth: Those were the days when the words "Made in Japan" were almost a joke. Remember?

Mobius: Exactly. That's a good example of what people were thinking about the Japanese in those days. Meanwhile, the Japanese were in the United States taking pictures of every piece of equipment we ever had. [Laughing]

And you see a similar pattern now with the Chinese, of course. From the American perspective, China is not a very safe place to be with all your money. Now, I'm not saying that a majority of your money should be in China, but if you look around that country you see more ambitious people, more clever people. I mean, you just have to look at how the United States is being taken to the cleaners in the trade negotiations with China, and you realize that you've got to bet on the winning side on this game. [Laughing]

These are the things any American saving long term for retirement should be thinking about. It is very, very important.

Who Is Mark Mobius?

Griffeth: Let's talk about you for a minute. You grew up in New York.

Mobius: Yes, I grew up in Long Island, New York of a German father. I carry a German passport, by the way.

Griffeth: As a youngster were you interested in investing at all?

Mobius: No, not at all. I had no concept. I was more interested in psychology. I wanted to become a psychologist, and I eventually gravitated to social psychology and then to mass communications. I got interested in survey research work.

In fact, one of my first jobs after I graduated was with International Research Associates. They do a lot of survey research work. And one thing led to another, and I got interested in economics. That's what led me to MIT.

Griffeth: How did you end up in Japan and Hong Kong?

Mobius: I got a scholarship to study in Japan when I was at the University of Wisconsin. In those days if you asked me to locate Japan on the map I, like most Americans, wouldn't have been able to do it. [Laughing]

Griffeth: What year was that?

Mobius: That was in 1960. I got this Carnegie Foundation scholarship. First I studied the language at Syracuse University for a few months, and then I went over to Japan. I studied with an interesting group of scholars, different people from different fields. There were doctors and lawyers, and so forth, and each of us did a project in our particular field. Each of us lived with a Japanese family. It was a great program.

That sort of hooked me. I said, "Hey, I'm going to get back to this part of the world." So I did. The first job I got was with the Institute for International Research working in Korea on troop community relations. You know, at that time, the Eighth Army was in Korea, and they had all kinds of problems with the troops and the various villages where they were located. So we tried to figure out how to make the situation better by doing surveys of the local population. I spent a year in Korea doing that. Then I spent a year in Thailand doing the same thing.

Then I went to Hong Kong and worked for Monsanto's new enterprise division. I don't know whether they still have it. At that time I think their biggest business was fabrics or fibers, and they wanted to diversify away from that. So we worked on things like astro turf and all these products that the Monsanto scientists came up with.

I remember working on a soybean milk project. You know, in those days everybody thought that the whole world was going to starve because of overpopulation. It's interesting that 30 years later the so-called experts are still talking about over-population and starvation. They don't realize that, in fact, this problem is being solved by science and by the natural behavior of people. Just as the so-called food crisis is being solved, it turns out that people's birthrates are going down.

Anyway, back to the soy milk project. It's an interesting story. We had a joint venture with a company called Hong Kong Soybean. (Which, by the way, is a great stock. It's listed on the Hong Kong Stock Exchange.) We were trying to produce a soybean milk product that would be accepted globally. It was an interesting case of complete cultural misunderstandings.

First of all, we tried to change the flavor because to the guys at Monsanto in St. Louis, soybeans were something you feed to pigs. They didn't think it had a very appealing smell or taste. But for the Chinese, it's something they've had all their life and they like the taste. But that was unacceptable to the Monsanto people, so we tried to hide the flavor and taste. So we did taste tests and everything, and it was awful. I remember taking it down to Singapore and forcing it down the throats of some kids, and they got sick to their stomachs. So that was over pretty fast.

Griffeth: [Laughing] End of soy milk story!

Mobius: Yes, so Monsanto wanted me to come back to St. Louis. I said, "No thanks, this is not my cup of tea." And I started my own company.

Griffeth: Doing?

Mobius: Research, because that was the only thing I knew. I had always been a professional student. So I started on this little adventure in 1968, and I struggled going door to door trying to get jobs from different companies. Finally, after a year or two I started to get clients. In those days the business was very small, so I would get a job, do the research, and then start looking for another one. So I learned the hard way how to do this kind of business.

I traveled a great deal even then, because I was always going to Indonesia or Malaysia or wherever. I would do all kinds of projects. I did projects for Volvo. They had a dumper and loader division that did heavy equipment, and I did a study for them all over Asia on how to introduce their equipment. I also did a study for the Hong Kong Bank on how they could improve their market share in Japan. And I did a study in Indonesia for the National Renderers Association. Have you ever heard of them?

Griffeth: The National Renderers Association?

Mobius: Yes. You know, rendering is a euphemism for collecting all the bones and fat from slaughter houses and rendering them into tallow or bone meal. The tallow, of course, is used not only in animal feed to increase the calorie count but also in soap and in food.

At that time, palm oil prices were higher than tallow prices. So my clients thought it would be smart to export the palm oil at the higher price and then, in turn, import the tallow made from the palm oil at the lower price. So we did some research and found that the Muslims were concerned that pig fat would be mixed up with beef fat. So we asked whether the renderers could guarantee that it wouldn't happen, which they couldn't, so that was the end of that project.

Griffeth: [Laughing] Another one bites the dust!

Mobius: [Also laughing] Yes, I killed a lot of projects!

Griffeth: But it occurs to me, Mark, listening to all of these diverse experiences, all the traveling, learning the cultural differences, it was the perfect training for your current job.

Mobius: Exactly. It was the perfect background for what I am doing now.

Griffeth: How did you end up at Templeton?

Mobius: After about 10 years of being on my own, I made some money for myself and one of my clients asked me to do a study of the stock market. That got me hooked. I initially did technical analysis of the stock market, and I started investing my own money.

I met somebody from Vickers da Costa, which was one of the big British firms at that time, and I learned that they needed somebody to do all their research in Asia. At that time my own company had been transformed into more of a distribution oriented firm, because one of my largest clients owned the distribution rights for Snoopy and the other "Peanuts" character merchandise. We started distributing in Asia for them, because I gave her the idea that there were a lot of potential consumers in Asia.

So I sold my business, and joined Vickers da Costa. Then after a few years in Hong Kong they asked me to set up an office in Taipei, which I did. In the meantime Vickers and some other brokerages had formed a joint venture with Taiwan Banks to create the very first Taiwan fund. I sat on the board of the fund as a representative from Vickers. When the fellow who was managing it left, the other board members asked me to take over management of it. So I became head of this joint venture, which was called the International Investment Trust.

During that period, I occasionally gave speeches at various Templeton client conferences. So at one point, Templeton came along and said, "Look, we are starting a new emerging markets fund. It's going to be a global fund, and we think you can run it."

Even though I had a tremendous job in Taipei and enjoyed what I was doing, I realized that this was going to be a great opportunity, so I left the International Investment Trust and started Templeton's emerging market fund in 1987.

Griffeth: And you've been traveling ever since.

Mobius: Yes, I've been traveling ever since.

Griffeth: Someone once told me that you don't actually live anywhere. Is that true?

Mobius: Not really. I have an apartment in Hong Kong and an apartment in Singapore.

Griffeth: How much time do you spend time there?

Mobius: No more than a few weeks a year. I'm in and out more than anything else. So even though Hong Kong is really our emerging markets base, I'm in and out of there. I fly in for a few days and go out again.

Global Investment Network

Griffeth: What are your goals at this point? Where is all of this traveling leading you?

Mobius: Well, the goal is to open a global network of offices including countries like Brazil and Vietnam. We're expanding all over the place. And basically my goal now is to make Franklin/Templeton the leader in emerging markets investing. That's really what I'm working towards.

Initially, we will open all these offices in order to widen our investment base and to bring in more analysts with different points of views. But then the next step will be to start bringing in domestic investors in each one of these markets. Of course, that is going to be a long time in coming, but it will come. And actually it's already happening. We have a joint venture in Sri Lanka, for example. It's a very small thing, but it's the beginning of that sort of thing.

Griffeth: For many U.S. investors, the only entree they have to certain markets is through a mutual fund like yours. They can't always pick up the phone and say, "Get me x number of shares of XYZ Company in Turkey," or wherever. Do you think we will ever be able to trade all international stocks directly?

Mobius: Oh, yes, definitely. That's coming sooner than you think. Don't forget, when I move overseas there's usually a broker there before me. The Merrill Lynches and Nomuras of this world are fast becoming global companies with offices all over. The British, of course, are leading the way. The Barings and the James Capells, for example, are all offshore companies.

At Franklin/Templeton, we in the emerging markets unit are based in Hong Kong, and we've become a significant profit center. So, more and more, these companies are going to become global companies in the true sense of the word. It's the only way they are going to be able to survive. Unless you create profit centers all over the world and utilize the energy and talents from people from all over the world there is no way you can survive.

The thing that made America successful was that it utilized the talents and abilities of people from all over the world, the immigrants who came to America. Now these management companies are beginning to realize that they must do the same thing. They've got to use the talents of people all over the world to increase their profits and to grow.

Long-Term Investment Opportunities

Griffeth: I can't let you go without getting a long-term forecast from you. Where do you see the greatest opportunities among the emerging markets?

Mobius: Well, China would be number one. That, I think, is very, very clear. Then Russia would be number two, Brazil number three, South Africa number four, and India number five.

Griffeth: But they will all go at their own pace.

Mobius: They will, indeed, all go at their own pace. And all will have enormous problems and upheavals, but at the end of the day I find it difficult to imagine that somebody who is really interested in their future security can avoid being invested in those countries.

The biggest challenge we face today is that things are happening so fast, because technology is moving so fast. Information is moving so fast that the past is no longer prologue. We may not have to wait as long for some countries to develop the way we used to, because technology is changing everything. I remember John Templeton saying that the most expensive words in the world are "It's different this time," but, you know, it is different this time because of technology.

> "We may not have to wait as long for some countries to develop the way we used to, because technology is changing everything."

In each country, there are certain patterns of development that are the same, but at the end of the day it is different because the technology is making the difference. The way people are communicating with each other is so different.

So we are seeing an acceleration of development in many countries, which on one hand is a great opportunity, but on the other hand is very dangerous. That's why when people ask me, "Are the emerging markets dangerous? Are they risky?" I say, "Absolutely yes."

We are living in very, very, very explosive times, because everybody's political and economic and social ego is being challenged by these changes that are upon us. And that's all the more reason why we've got to be diversified, because we don't know where the next problem is going to crop up. It all happens so fast that we'll be on top of it before we realize it.

JOHN NEFF

Birth Date: September 19, 1931

Education: University of Toledo, B.B.A.
Case Western Reserve, M.B.A.

Hobbies: Golf, tennis, history

Alternate Career: "That's a good question."

J ohn Neff is a giant in the mutual fund industry. He manages the huge Vanguard Windsor fund, which has roughly $11 billion in assets. (He also manages a closed-end fund called Gemini II.) When I interviewed him in June of 1994, he had just celebrated his 30th year of managing the Windsor Fund, which was founded in 1958. Besides a job with a bank in Cleveland in the 1950s, managing Windsor is the only job Neff has ever had. And, to say the least, he has performed admirably. His average annual return to shareholders over those 30 years is 14 percent, which means an investment made in the fund in 1964 would have increased roughly 45 times over those 30 years. That kind of consistent long-term performance puts Neff in the legend category.

Indeed, a number of fund managers in the industry have based their investment style on his. Neff is the ultimate value investor. He is constantly in search of beaten down, out of favor companies that still pay a relatively high dividend.

Despite the seeming enormity of his task, Neff takes a very relaxed, almost whimsical, view of it all. During our interview for this book, we talked about the unique way the Vanguard Group pays him to manage its flagship fund, about how he chooses stocks for the fund, when (or if) he will ever open it to new investors again, and how Windsor might change when Neff decides to retire.

JUNE 15, 1994

The Early Windsor Days

Bill Griffeth: How did you come to manage Windsor?

John Neff: Well, I'd worked at a bank in Cleveland for almost nine years. And I'd gotten great groundings, if you will, in a diversity of industries as one of six or seven in-house analysts covering everything from chemicals to drugs to banks to autos. Pretty much everything out there.

Then I became manager of security analysts. So I'd caught on to some broader responsibility, and it struck me that if I had anything extraordinary to contribute I probably wasn't going to find it out in the structured environment of a bank. So I decided that I was going to strike out and make a major change, and I happened upon Wellington Management in my travels. There were only two funds there: a great big monolithic balanced fund that had been around since the 1920s called Wellington. It had about $2 billion [in assets]. And there was a somewhat difficult fund of $75 million called Windsor that had been hatched in 1958. (I came in 1963.) The company was quite sales-driven and that had not worked out well for this fund. As a matter of fact, it had manifested all that was wrong in the market in 1961 and 1962.

Griffeth: How so?

Neff: It emphasized investment in small alleged growth companies. They developed very high multiples in 1961, and they got killed in 1962. So this fund was hitting behind the ball, and so I said to myself, "I would like to manage that." And a year after I came to the company, I did.

Griffeth: Was your investment style already developed by that time or did it evolve? I mean, you're known as a value investor who looks for cheap stocks with a dividend. Was that style already in place when you took over the fund?

Neff: Kind of. I'd obviously come from a prudent man background [at the bank] and within that environment there never seemed to be much of an opportunity to use your imagination or stick your neck out a little bit to take some risks. Particularly when the reward was commensurate with the risk. It just wasn't the bank's style, so I did kind of come with that prudent man background but also with a wish, an opportunity, a desire to maybe make the fund 1) a little more flexible and 2) a little more risk-taking.

Griffeth: How did you do the first couple of years?

Neff: Well, actually pretty well versus the averages. But that was the period of "the adrenaline stocks," (as I called them) in the late 1960s.

Griffeth: The Go-Go years.

Neff: Exactly. So we were kind of buried a bit by that. That type of fund [that invested in "adrenaline stocks," which Windsor did not] was more saleable. As a matter of fact, we merged with Ivest, TDP and Thorndike, Doran, Payne & Lewis in the 1966–1967 period, and one of the reasons was to give the wholesalers something to sell. Remember, I said the company was sales driven. The wholesalers are the missionary salesmen who knock on the office of the RRs [registered representatives, or brokers] and try to get them to sell your funds. One of the efforts of that merger was to give the wholesaling staff a more saleable fund in Windsor.

Griffeth: How?

Neff: Ivest was more saleable then, because it was the exemplification of that period.

Griffeth: Right.

Neff: But then, of course, that period ended and lots of funds had a difficult time after that. But Windsor kind of, as the wholesalers would have a tendency to say, sticks to your ribs. And eventually we kind of—the hard way, but the good way— won them over, and eventually Windsor became quite saleable in its own right.

Founding Vanguard

Griffeth: When did you come under the Vanguard umbrella?

Neff: Well, Jack Bogle was the CEO of Wellington Management.

Griffeth: Right.

Neff: And about 20 years ago he was dismissed by the board of Wellington Management Company, and immediately the independent funds [in the group] hired him as their CEO, and that was the precursor of today's Vanguard.

Griffeth: So there was a mutiny of sorts?

Neff: I think you could call it that. We've referred to it as The Great Schism. The fund board kept him on, and he became the CEO of those funds. And so for the first time you really had a structure where the funds were generally independent. You know, the board of funds is always supposed to represent the funds. Well, in this case it was genuinely independent and there was no tie to the management company. Back in the old days, almost all management companies maintained a majority of the board members on their own funds so you had this incestuous relationship. And then the SEC said, "You shall no longer have on the fund board a majority of so-called affiliated directors." So you can see there's been a real evolution. It has been slow moving in some cases, but in the case of the now-Vanguard Funds, former Wellington Funds, it's become genuinely independent.

Griffeth: Certainly in the old days it stood for everything that Jack Bogle doesn't stand for today.

Neff: Exactly.

Griffeth: He is the champion of the small investor and of no-load mutual funds. So let me be clear about this: at one time the Windsor Fund was a load fund.

Neff: Yes, and actually it did not evolve to its present no-load status until Vanguard took over the distribution of the funds as well.

Griffeth: When was that?

Neff: Oh, maybe fifteen, sixteen years ago. And so immediately it became no-load at that point in time. But previously it had been dealer distributed, and the distribution was another function of the management company.

Load vs. No-Load

Griffeth: So you are one of the few managers who has been on both sides of the issue. You managed a fund that was a load fund and then it became a no-load fund.

Neff: Yes.

Griffeth: When you changed from load to no-load, did you also change the way you managed the fund?

Neff: No. No, we've always managed the fund for shareholders, and I don't mean to say that other people don't. We've always felt we represented a shareholder who obviously wanted to make a nickel, but he also didn't want to lose his tail or expose himself inordinately. We try to manage for somebody who wants to stick his neck out a bit and take a risk and kind of grind it out the hard way. But he also doesn't want to get killed by an unfortunate turn of events.

> ◆
>
> *"We've always felt we represented a shareholder who obviously wanted to make a nickel, but he also didn't want to lose his tail or expose himself inordinately."*
>
> ◆

Griffeth: Back in 1993 Mr. Bogle and I sat together in an audience at the Investment Company Institute convention and heard a Harvard professor speak about the price competition in the mutual fund industry. It was this professor's contention that eventually load funds would go by the wayside because of this price competition. I thought Mr. Bogle would jump out of his chair he was so elated to hear it. Do you agree with that? Do you think that someday we will see all no-load funds?

Neff: Well, I don't know whether you'll see all no-load, but certainly there has been a pressure and a competitive tug that has made the commission of lesser significance. In other words you've got partial loads or semi-loads or even reduced loads.

But you know, that's not totally unlike the evolution you've seen in some other industries. One that comes to mind is the auto and homeowners insurance industry. You know in the olden days you had to be sold [insurance] and as a result there was a pretty big commission attached to it. But when it became part of the public landscape, if you will, with a knowledgeable buyer and all, why eventually that commission structure changed as the Sears and State Farms and those kind of people came to the fore.

Much the same thing has happened in the mutual fund industry where the buyer has become more informed and doesn't need all that advice. There isn't as much pressure to sell the fund by a commissioned sales staff. In other words, the Vanguard kids on the phone are really providing information, not a sales pitch.

Griffeth: Sounds like a pretty good argument to do away with load funds, though.

Neff: Well, they have certainly become the lesser factor in the industry. But you know, as long as you have a typical brokerage company type of network, why, there is going to be some sale of load funds, very simply because some people have to be sold who are not informed.

How Neff Is Paid

Griffeth: You have a rather unusual relationship with Vanguard in the way you are compensated for managing Windsor. There are times when you get a piece of the profits you are able to achieve. But you can also be docked. And, in fact, you have been docked in the past when your performance didn't come up to predetermined standards. How does that work?

Neff: Well all incentive/penalty schemes, to use the British word, have to be symmetrical as a result of an SEC edict. [In other words, the size of the potential incentive has to match the size of the potential penalty.] And not very many funds are on that type of arrangement, which I've always wondered a little bit about.

We get, in effect, 16 basis points [which is .16 percent of the fund's total assets per year] just for the investment management. In other words, we get 16 basis points for an average performance. Now if we do well (and that's defined as 12 percentage points better than the S&P 500 during the previous 3 years, which would be 400 basis points a year) we get another 10 basis points. Conversely, and symmetrically, if we underperform the S&P by the same amount over the same period of time, we get 10 basis points less. So our compensation for investment management ranges from .06 to .26 depending on how well we do for the shareholder.

Griffeth: And you received the .06 in, when, 1989?

Neff: Yes. We've been doing this close to 20 years. And during that time, we've gotten the maximum incentive about half the time. But in, oh, in 1989, 1990, 1991, 1992 we suffered the maximum penalty.

Griffeth: Whose idea was it, yours or Jack Bogle's?

Neff: Actually it goes way back to when we were both employees of Wellington Management Company, and I convinced him. And he became an enthusiast expressing come confidence in me, I think.

Griffeth: That's a great story.

Neff: Incidentally, Vanguard has always stood ready to offer others the same deal but not very many takers have come forth. But now they are kind of insisting—well, insisting is strong— they are very aggressively suggesting to other managers that they should be in some kind of incentive/penalty program.

Griffeth: You mean of the other Vanguard funds.

Neff: Exactly.

Griffeth: Is Windsor the only fund that has that?

Neff: There are others that we manage that have it, but until lately I don't think hardly anybody else had it. Some are starting to now, but you'd want to get that song and dance from them.

Regulating Fund Managers

Griffeth: While we are sort of on the subject, let me get your take on the relationship of a fund manager to his or her fund. I'm thinking about the rules the Investment Company Institute issued in 1994 that placed restrictions on fund managers when it comes to trading for their own account. In essence, they discouraged managers from trading side by side with their fund. What did you think about all that?

Neff: Well, none of the ICI's new yardsticks were alien to anything we've got inside our company except that short-term one.

Griffeth: Where they require a fund manager to hold a security in his or her own account for at least four months.

Neff: Yes, I guess that would be the only one. And we don't have any problem with adopting that. In fact, I've carried that a bit further. I don't own anything that's owned in the funds until the funds have taken full positions. In other words, I don't buy anything while the funds are still buying it. I wait for them to take their full position. I come last.

And it's the same way on the south side [when the fund begins to sell a stock]. I don't sell anything until the fund is completely disposed of its full position. And it is our style to assume rather large positions [in some stocks], as you know.

> ◆
> "*I think you have a right, if you are turning your future wherewithal over to somebody to manage, to know how he stands personally.*"
> ◆

Also, I don't own anything that's not owned by the funds. You might say that sounds kind of crazy, but the thought there is that essentially my time belongs to the fund. And you know that as cheap as I am I wouldn't buy anything myself unless I spent some time on it. And that time belongs to the fund.

Griffeth: Should that be a part of the disclosure of a mutual fund, of how a fund manager manages his or her own money as well?

Neff: That's a good thought. In other words, a kind of personal disclosure?

Griffeth: Sure.

Neff: I think it has some merit. I think you have a right, if you are turning your future wherewithal over to somebody to manage, to know how he stands personally. So it certainly would not bother me.

Why Mutual Funds Are Popular

Griffeth: Let's talk about the mutual fund business and the tremendous growth it has experienced, especially over the past three or four years. There are two schools of thought on this. One school says it is the direct result of people who exited CDs in search of a higher yield. So they headed for higher yielding equities without understanding the risk they were assuming. And the moment stocks start to fall, they will redeem their shares in a hurry.

The other school of thought says no, this is a group of people who are finally thinking about investing for retirement, and they are in it for the long term. Which school are you in?

Neff: Well, like most everything in life, I'm somewhere in between. Obviously it's a medium that makes an awful lot of sense for an awful lot of people. On the other hand it has bursts of enthusiasm just as the whole market place does, so the industry's sales are guaranteed to fluctuate. Now they haven't fluctuated much lately so I would think we'll see that enthusiasm ebb, because mutual funds are not going to be as popular, maybe forever, as they are right now. But I think it's a very useful medium for people to plan for their financial future and there are so many different shadings and so many different security types and all, well, you can pretty well build a program if you are decently investment literate.

Griffeth: People who are concerned about the growth see the industry setting itself up for a big decline if it doesn't educate shareholders enough about the risks involved. There was that SEC survey in 1993 that showed a lot of people who bought funds from banks thought that they were insured the way a bank deposit account is. That kind of anecdotal evidence leads some people to believe that shareholders are in for a big surprise when they realize there isn't that safety net and mutual funds are not guaranteed.

Neff: Well there is certainly some risk out there. You can't forget that.

Griffeth: I mean there are an awful lot of so-called boutique funds that are small and certainly not as liquid as the Windsor

Fund. And they might run into redemption problems either because of a lack of experience on the part of the fund manager or the lack of liquidity in the fund itself.

Neff: Well, you can never forget that the mutual fund investor has the opportunity to get instant gratification in terms of being liquefied as of that day. And if enough people decide to do it, not unlike taking your money out of the bank en masse, why, it would present problems.

The small investor usually doesn't run for the exits at the bottom, you know. He'll hang in and if he's disillusioned he won't sell at the bottom. He'll sell at some kind of recovery point. So there's some obvious evidence historically to support the fact that any [large number of redemptions] would be orderly. But hell, you never know, it could be disorderly.

You know, we've already seen some manifestation of that in some segments. Like junk bonds two or three years back. As a matter of fact, Vanguard, in 1990, maybe in 1991, lost something like 20 percent of the value of its junk bond fund in one month. (We manage that one, by the way.) A lot of it came back in subsequent months, but that doesn't make the management job any easier.

Neff as Shareholder Advocate

Griffeth: Let's talk about shareholder as advocate, and I think of you in your capacity as manager of Windsor when you take a large position in a company you will often have a say in how the company is run.

Neff: Try to have a say.

Griffeth: Well, you let your views be known. One year you let it be known that you felt Iacocca should let the world know that Robert Lutz should be his heir apparent at Chrysler. At IBM, Lou Gerstner called you and some others in one time to get your opinion on what he should do about the dividend, among other things. You said, "Don't cut it," but he did anyway. And in 1994 there was the employee buyout at UAL, which you publicly opposed.

Talk about that. You know, a lot of funds won't take the large positions that you do. They will diversify more. They will buy a lot more stocks and take smaller positions. But you do it the other way around.

Neff: Well, I think it's somewhat a manifestation of, very simply, when you do take these large positions that you can't entirely vote with your feet. Obviously you can in any small period of time, and you can't when the wolf's at the door or when the market is looking at the fundamentals particularly adversely. So you become, if you will, more married to the company. So one of the additional arrows in your quiver is to be able to voice an opinion if you think management's on the wrong track.

No, it's kind of unusual that we do it that way. We do agitate a bit and even write letters to the board, and that type of thing, thinking they are our representatives in respect to dividend policy, or merger terms, or the sale of stock. We do get their attention at least. We are not only representing ourselves but we are representing a lot of small shareholders who don't have the ability to either assess or certainly to voice an opinion that's going to be listened to.

And so we've never been shy on that. We don't ordinarily get into these things in the newspaper largely because we don't seek that, but I'd be less than candid if I didn't say occasionally knowing that we'd get some kind of platform there we do go public.

Griffeth: I'm not putting you in the same category as a George Soros in the terms of advocacy but he made it clear in 1993 when he wrote an article for the *Times* of London advocating a lower deuschemark. And, in fact, it became a self-fulfilling prophecy. He acknowledged that later in an interview that that was his whole point, was to go public with it to move that market because he had a large position and he wanted to see it move in the direction he was after.

You know, you could either call it a matter of prudent management of your holdings when you publicly voice your opinion, or you could call it unnecessary intervention in the markets. I wonder how people view John Neff on those occasions when you do publicly voice your opinion on a stock that you hold.

Neff: Well, you raise some good points. As I said earlier, I try not to wear it on my sleeve. It's only rewarding or viable if it enhances the shareholders' pocket. But in the case of the UAL buyout I just finally decided they had gone too far, and that I would make my opinion known. And if that emboldened anybody else to have the same opinion, fine, but I didn't contact any other shareholders. I just don't really have the time for that if I'm going to be doing what I'm supposed to be doing, which is managing other people's money. So in that case, at least, I offered up my opinion and that was it.

Griffeth: You would not try to oust any board members over an issue?

Neff: Well, I might vote against them, but I wouldn't lead any fight or proxy battle, or that type of thing. Because, very simply, 1) I don't think that's what the Lord has put me here for, and 2) that becomes fiercely time consuming and I would argue actually with the public funds' stances on a lot of corporate issues where they spend an awful lot of their time to try to manage the company, get involved in managing the company, even getting on the board in some cases. Well, I just don't believe in that from several standpoints. I don't think that really we have an awful lot of expertise other than the investment area specifically, and it's a considerable dedication of time and I think we are able, if we lose confidence in management, to still sell our stock so we can fight the good battle. But, you know, it is not written that I have to keep UAL.

Griffeth: Do members of management cringe when they see John Neff coming, or do they welcome your thoughts? I mentioned before about how Lou Gerstner called you first, but what about others?

Neff: I think they are usually pretty receptive. Again, we don't spend a lot of time going out rattling or haranguing management. It's only at some of these inflection points that we are heard from at all. But, you know, you have a responsibility to protect your shareholders' investments.

In other words, when we entered the fray a little on Chrysler, it was a very critical hour where that company could have gone belly up with the wrong combination of circumstances.

We felt that the company was dividing in the Lutz camp and the Iacocca camp and that just isn't good when you are fighting GM and Ford and the Japanese as well as, as that point in time, onerous industry conditions. And we wanted, one, to survive, and two, be of a single mind to fight the good fight. And Iacocca was not, at that point in time, that dedicated to business, yet he still wanted to stay CEO. It just wasn't a good situation as best as we could view it, and that was the view of the public.

Griffeth: How much influence did you have do you think in that decision of Robert Lutz becoming the head of Chrysler?

Neff: Well, he didn't become the head of Chrysler. We lost that part of it.

Griffeth: I know. And that's partly my point. What impact do you think your opinion had on the process?

Neff: Well, I think we might have been—and I'm just guessing—part of the process that convinced the board members that they had to get off their rear ends and make a decision as to the new CEO. As it turned out, they went outside. But nicely enough, or interestingly enough, or gratifyingly enough, when [Robert] Eaton came in from General Motors [to become the new CEO of Chrysler], he was smart enough and collegial enough to realize you don't run a company all by yourself. So he included Lutz [in the new management team]. And Lutz is still there, so it kind of worked out. As a matter of fact I talked to him [Lutz] recently, and he said he has been very pleased.

How Windsor Picks Stocks

Griffeth: What is John Neff's typical day like? I mean, one man does not run an $11 billion fund all by himself. How does the decision making process work when you choose stocks? And how involved do you get in the day-to-day trading? Give me a sense of what your day is like.

Neff: Well, obviously you are quite right, I don't do it by myself. On the other hand, I don't need an army, because if you have an army you relegate yourself to an administrative position. And 1) I'm probably not a very good administrator, and 2) my skills, if anything, are assessing undervalued securities and acting therein.

But I have three people who work very close with me. Chuck Freeman has been with me for 25 years, and he likely will be my successor. And two other fellows have been with us for nine years. I call them The Double Jims, Jim Mordy and Jim Averill. And essentially what we do together is chase companies. And companies that we own, or are about to own, or are thinking of owning, we pretend to know as well as almost anybody on the Street. Oftentimes they are overlooked, misunderstood, forgotten, wobegone kinds of companies.

Griffeth: Do you meet daily, weekly? Do you fight over some stock? How does that work?

Neff: We don't have much in the way of formal meetings. There is a formal meeting each day within the company, the total [Wellington Management] company. But our group [that manages Windsor] doesn't do much of that. Of course, we are in daily contact and our offices are all together, and we exchange comments. They sometimes call on the companies that we own, and sometimes I will. We are in the business of constantly assessing whether our model of expectation is on track or not.

Griffeth: How do you decide how much of a position to take in a company?

Neff: That is limited by the size of the company. We cannot own, compliments of the SEC, any more than 9.9 percent of a company's [market capitalization]. But we get up around that in several cases, depending on just how far we are willing to stick our neck out with any confidence. And then, don't forget that no more than 5 percent of the fund can be invested in a single company. So it's a combination of those two.

Griffeth: If there is a dispute on whether or not to take a position or the size of the position, are you the final arbiter or have you taken positions in companies that even you did not want to do?

Neff: No, I have to want to do it. I refer to it somewhat glibly as a benevolent despot–type of management. In other words, you have to have somebody, by my standards at least, who's responsible for the final decision. But they are all a very eminent part of it and we talk about it, and I bounce things off of them and they express opinions, sometimes adverse to mine. But in that final quiet hour, I make the decision myself.

Griffeth: $11 billion is a lot of money to manage. Do you sleep at night?

Neff: Sure.

Griffeth: Yeah?

Neff: You do the best you can and you can't do much better than that.

Griffeth: Have there been times when you haven't slept nights?

Neff: Not really.

◆

"I bounce things off of them and they express opinions, sometimes adverse to mine. But in that final quiet hour, I make the decision myself."

◆

Griffeth: Even over the last 30 years when the market went against you. There were a few years when your value stocks did not do as well as the growth stocks. You were still able to sleep nights?

Neff: Right. Sometimes [laughing] it was because I was so tired. You know, there are going to be some dry spells. In the past 30 years there have been three or four of them. You try not to get too dejected just like you don't get too high when you are doing well. You just keep your equilibrium, and you give it your best shot. It doesn't do you any good to stay awake at night. As a matter of fact, if anything, it's counterproductive. So I go to bed satisfied I've given it my best, and I don't have any trouble going to sleep at night.

Windsor after Neff

Griffeth: You've only had two jobs in your career. Is there a third one in the offing sometime for you?

Neff: Well, I'm going to retire somewhere out there. I'm not going to stay beyond my time. I want to go out on the top of my game, and I still think I'm on top of my game. But I'll go sooner rather than later. Will there be something after that? Well, I think I'll write a book. I taught some, way back when I was in

Cleveland. I might teach a course at Penn. I might smell the roses a little more.

Griffeth: Play a little more tennis?

Neff: Well, I'm not sure my body will let me play more tennis, but I played four rounds of golf at my club last year at $900 a round. I might amortize that down a little bit.

Griffeth: That doesn't sound like a very good value to me!

Neff: [laughing] No, that's right! You know, they used to rib me about my Corvette. I had a Corvette for a long period of time, and that's hardly a "low P.E." car. But I said it's the cheapest of all those sports cars! Versus Lambourghini, it's low P.E.!

Griffeth: How about Windsor after Neff? I know you expect Freeman to be your heir. Will the fund change much?

Neff: Oh, as I mentioned earlier, we have kind of been in the crucible together with the likes of Chrysler and Citicorp and all, for twenty-five years. So he has certainly been subjected to some of those same ebbs and flows that I mentioned earlier. I think he'd do it kind of pretty much the same way with maybe two exceptions. He might not do the liquidity thing.

Griffeth: The liquidity thing?

Neff: Yes. Going to cash a bit as we have on the margin.

Griffeth: He's more inclined to want to stay fully invested.

Neff: Yes. We've gone to cash maybe four times in the last twenty years and of course our definition is no more than 20 percent. In other words, the investor has selected equity. You can do something with the margin, but you'd better have him at least 80 percent invested otherwise you just aren't being honest to your mandate. So I would guess that he might do less of that and maybe the positions wouldn't be quite as big but still very big. I'm just guessing.

Re-Opening the Windsor Fund

Griffeth: Finally, the question that all nonshareholders of Vanguard Windsor want to know: Will it ever be opened to new shareholders again?

Neff: I would guess not. But you know Ben Graham said, "Never say never." If you've got a really bad market, and there are all kinds of opportunities out there, goody wise, why, I could see maybe opening it up. But at this point I don't see a real bad market.

MARGARET PATEL

Birth Date: December 22

Education: B.A., University of Pittsburgh

Hobbies: Field hockey, jogging

Alternate Career: Journalist

*M*argaret Patel has been managing fixed income portfolios for almost twenty years. And she has held a number of positions in the investment community around the country. For example, she managed money in Pittsburgh for the United Mine Workers Pension, she managed money for the State of Maryland's pension, she managed funds for American Capital in Houston, and she worked for the Dreyfus funds in New York.

Since 1988, she has been director of fixed income at Boston Security Counselors in Boston. In that capacity, she has managed Advest's High Yield Bond Fund (which she no longer does) and its Government Securities Fund (which she still does).

During our interview she talked about her method of evaluating bonds as if they were stocks, about her longtime friend Michael Milken and his impact on the junk bond market, about why her gut is smarter than her brain when it comes to investing, and about why—if she could—she would start a mutual fund full of nothing but derivatives.

JUNE 30, 1994

"You Are Now the Bond Fund Manager"

Bill Griffeth: You have had a pretty varied career, and you moved around a lot. Tell me about that.

Margaret Patel: The reason I sort of jumped around in an illogical system has been as much as anything just because I was married. I followed my husband whenever he was transferred.

Griffeth: Why did you choose finance as your field of choice?

Patel: I had always been fascinated by it, but when I came out of school there really were not that many opportunities for women in a man's field like that. And I sort of had the idea that the academic road was the more noble one, so while I was in Washington, I started to work at the Brookings Institution with the idea that I would work there for a year and go get my Ph.D. in economics. But about a month later I realized how boring it was to do that. So I worked as an economic analyst for the government, and I was never really happy doing that because I would pick up the paper and read about what's going on in the world and I felt disconnected from it just looking at it as an academic.

So when my husband was transferred to New York, I was lucky enough to be hired by Dreyfus as a low level gofer/economic person because one of the guys there had this idea that he wanted to do economic stuff more in-house. And after about one day there I realized that this is what I had wanted to do, to be in the securities business, and more to the point to be a portfolio manager.

Griffeth: Were there any noticeable hurdles thrown at you as a woman?

Patel: No, not that I know of. Dreyfus at that time had started a joint venture with Marine Midland. At this time it was a trendy wave of the future to have mutual funds combining with banks to take advantage of the fact that banks could bring in the assets that had lousy performance and mutual funds could improve that performance.

One day, one of the managers said to me, "I don't know anything about bonds, and I don't want to know anything about bonds, so you are the bond manager." And that's how I became a bond manager.

A lot of the bonds in those portfolios were stuff that had gone sour from the late 1960s and early 1970s. So I went to a number of workout meetings, bankruptcy meetings, I went down to the bankruptcy court in New York City and looked through financial records to try to figure out what some of the stuff was worth. And at that same time I was doing some equity analysis too, so I really got an interest in bonds as an equity, you might say. Or, rather, I became interested in the value of bonds apart from just interest rates going up or down.

And as our unit grew I got to do all the bonds, and I became a bond specialist, but I always kept my interest in equities. And then since I had gone to so many workouts I got very interested in lower grade junk bond area.

Griffeth: Workouts. Do you want to explain that?

Patel: When a company goes bankrupt or can't meet its interest payments, the creditors get together to work out some sort of a payment plan to give some value back to the shareholders in case of a liquidation of the company.

Griffeth: I would imagine that the fellow who made you a bond manager, his feelings are pretty pervasive on Wall Street. Why is it that equities are so often front and center and bonds are secondary?

Patel: I think it's because, in general, except for junk bonds and secondarily convertible bonds, your rates of return are so much more limited and you have so little range to the rates of return.

Griffeth: But it's ironic that much more money is in the bond market than is invested in the stock market.

Patel: Oh yes, that's true. But I think it's a feeling that if you are investment grade there is no risk, and that there is little way to add value in the investment grade part of the bond, which I would basically agree with.

Treating Bonds like Stocks

Griffeth: Tell me about your process of evaluating bonds as if they were equities.

Patel: When I make an equity recommendation or analysis I still start from the industry trends and the biggest mistakes and the biggest wins I've had have been not because of the nitty gritty of analyzing earnings for the next quarter but because of a broad overview of the industry that they are operating in. That's where I've made and lost the most money. And I would lose money because I was blindsided when I did not understand the product cycle or pricing pressure or competition the company faced. I made money when I was lucky enough to say, "These are the factors that matter in this particular industry, and this company has caught the wave and it is where it should be, competitive-wise or cost-wise."

That's why I feel that sector orientation is so important. Even when I look at stocks, I give 50 percent of the weighting to the company—you know, the kind of widgets they make, and so forth—but at least 50 percent or more of the weighting is the industry they are in and whatever the fundamentals are that are driving that industry. That's so much more important, because you have to realize that companies can really control what their earnings are going to be on a short-term basis.

> ◆
> *"If you are in the right place when the market moves you are either lucky or smart, but it doesn't matter."*
> ◆

When I was with the United Mine Workers Pension Fund, it was interesting to see the variance you could have in bond managers' performance, depending on the sector they were in. I learned that geography is destiny. If you are in the right place when the market moves you are either lucky or smart, but it doesn't matter. Early positioning in the right sector is so much more important than the minutiae of next quarter's earnings, or whether the company is going to be upgraded or downgraded half a notch. It's just irrelevant. That is not where you make the big money. It's more in the big picture.

Griffeth: Let's quantify this management style you have of determining where the opportunities are and finding the right geography. How would you describe the style?

Patel: In jargonistic terms, I would call it a sector concentration style, or a sector rotation style. The way I find the best relative value is to look at what's out of favor and what's the cheapest. Logically speaking, if you look at what yields the most and what's out of favor you are more likely to find something cheap than if you look at what's clearly in vogue and widely held.

A good example would be the American auto industry when it was tremendously out of favor a few years ago. Chrysler is the perfect example of a company I would go after. When Chrysler was at the bottom of its cycle in, say, 1990–1991, if you talked to bond analysts all they would talk about was the company's unfunded pension fund liability, about how Chrysler makes lousy cars and about how the economy is really bad. But I said, "Well, what about these new cars they are bringing out?"

These bond analysts could recite the company's numbers chapter and verse down to the dollar, but they had never seen the new cars. "Have you read the reviews in the car magazines?" I would ask, and the answer was, "Well, no, bond analysts don't do that." They were just plugging away at the numbers and saying, you know, "They'll have a negative cash flow with x dollars this quarter, and their health costs will be this much next year." They couldn't rise up to the level of acknowledging that this was a company that was producing products people wanted to buy. They missed the whole big wave of the fact that car sales were going to explode upward. They just didn't get the big picture.

Now, sure I could recite whatever the figures were, too. You know, $4 billion in pension fund liability. But I mean, it was irrelevant. The numbers were horrible, but guess what, the numbers didn't matter. They didn't matter because the whole car cycle was picking up for the industry and for Chrysler in particular. They had lowered their costs, and they brought out new cars that people wanted to buy, and that was the whole story.

And when Chrysler's bonds were [trading] in the 1960s, I couldn't find a bond analyst who had anything good to say. And then after it was clear the cycle had turned, everybody looked very positive on Chrysler and it got around par or above. So that's a prime example where the minutiae of numbers are not going to make you or lose you a lot of money.

Griffeth: In other words, you have to keep your head up.

Patel: Yes. Here's a good analogy. Have you ever done any sailboat racing or sailing?

Griffeth: No.

Patel: And you're from California?

Griffeth: Amazing, I know.

Patel: [laughing] Anyway, when you go out on a sailboat there are a hundred variables when you go around the course. Now, I've always been a crew member, not a captain, but there are all these variables. You know, the wind, the tide, the current, all this stuff. Inevitably, the people who win the race decided what really mattered that day was, you know, the offshore breeze, or the tide, or whatever. And they decided ahead of time how they were going to chart a course by sailing toward land and away from land.

Now the other people who finished in the middle of the pack or at the end of the pack were fiddling around with all the minutiae of making minor adjustments to the course, constantly changing the tension on the sails, changing the lines, and all this stuff. But those weren't the variables that mattered.

It's the same thing with investing, whether it is in stocks or bonds. There are thousands of variables, but guess what? Only two or three variables really matter, and those are the big ones that will determine the course of the company. That's what you have to figure out, and you can't figure it out by starting at the minutia level. You have to start at the top level.

Patel on Milken

Griffeth: Let's talk about Michael Milken. What were your impressions of him as a human being? I've heard he was highly intelligent, very aggressive, all the usual things you hear about somebody who becomes as successful as he did.

Patel: Having met Mike when he was basically nobody and I was basically nobody (so it didn't matter how he treated me), I found him to be of extremely high integrity. And I know that on more than one occasion way back then—we're talking 20 years ago—he had had his feelings hurt because people had stolen his ideas, or had tried to trade behind his back, or had taken advantage of some situation. So I think that, certainly at that time, his ethics were the same as yours or mine. You know, when you are a big public figure, you have to control your behavior more than when you are a little nobody. I think you're able to see the real person when they are nobody.

Even today, I can call him and I know he'd pick up the phone because we've always had a friendly relationship. I've never seen the guy do drugs, he's never abused alcohol, he's never run around with other women, he's been married to the same woman from day one, and, you know, he's a good father. I respect him a lot as a person.

It seemed to me, though, that Mike got to a point where he wanted to trade all the bonds. His goal was to buy all the cheap bonds, and to punish the people who were "bad" (i.e., stupid about financial matters). So I always sort of think of him as this avenging angel in a sense.

And I think he probably became too immersed in such a narrow sector of life (i.e., the junk bond business), that I think he lost perspective of how outsiders might view some of his activities. You know, a lot of the worst stuff that he [allegedly] did a) is still unproven, and b) occurred in gray areas or silent areas of securities legislation. Maybe if they had been equities it would have been more black and white. But in the case of bonds it was sort of gray.

> "... I think he [Milken] probably became too immersed in such a narrow sector of life, that I think he lost perspective of how outsiders might view some of his activities."

Griffeth: Talk about Milken's legacy in helping to create a role for junk bonds in financing corporate America.

Patel: If you think back, initially, junk bond investing (up until the Disney takeover) was really about investing in fallen angels. There really weren't that many new junk deals. Yes, there was MCI, but basically it was investing in unpopular fallen angels and buying bankrupt paper, obscure paper that other people were forced to dump or didn't want to bother with. And that really was Mike's stock in trade.

And it wasn't until the Disney deal in the early 1980s when Saul Steinberg made a run at it—and then the Bass brothers got involved—that junk bonds changed into takeover vehicles. And, again, up until that time you were really investing in the fallen angels that traded far below their intrinsic investment value. And statistics absolutely showed that you were well paid for the risk you took.

What's changed now is you have flooded the market with junk bonds and securities, and you've got a supply and demand imbalance because people have developed a tremendous appetite for junk bonds due to these historic performance figures. What they're ignoring is the fact that they've artificially created a supply of junk bonds that lack a lot of the underlying quality the fallen angel type junk bonds had.

Griffeth: What you seem to be saying is Milken was nothing more than a victim of circumstances, when in fact the charge against him was that he misrepresented the risk involved in these instruments.

Patel: Well, again, look at the historical numbers. You look over the last 50 or 100 years, wherever you get the data from, up to the mid-1980s, it's absolutely true, there's no doubt about it, people were paid handsomely for the risk they took.

Then you got in the period where you had this proliferation of junk bond issues where truly junky companies were handed $200 million to basically throw away, and then they would file for bankruptcy.

And you had the ever growing daisy chain effect when Mike would bring people into the circle who would issue bonds and then as sort of a tit for tat they would buy junk bonds from other issuers to keep it all afloat.

Griffeth: So was the junk bond market's downfall in 1991 the result of economic conditions or just a flaw in the system that he had put together?

Patel: I don't think you can put very much of that burden on Mike because many of the biggest deals were non-Drexel deals.

Number one, the thing that really killed the junk bond market was the extreme credit crunch in the banking system. You can find company after company where the banks pulled the plug because the regulators were breathing down their necks. And that's really what I think caused most of the high default rates in 1990–1991. The banks wouldn't give any forbearance to a lot of junk companies. If you talked to companies then, they told stories about how, you know, they would say, "We had a banking relationship for 10 or 20 years, and all we needed was a six-month forbearance and they wouldn't give it to us. Or they arbitrarily, you know, put very burdensome requirements on whatever line we did have outstanding."

If this had been a more normal market climate, some of these companies might have been able to just skate through, but because of all the changes in the banking regulations you had extreme duress on the system which forced a lot of companies into a liquidity crisis.

And then the RTC came in and took over a lot of S&Ls that held a lot of junk paper, and they put our tax dollars to work liquidating securities without regard to fundamentals. Without regard to what the bonds might be worth if they just held on to them for six months or a year. So if you were there at the bottom of the market buying all this stuff, people made obscene amounts of money buying from the RTC in the early days of the first S&L bailout. And then with Mike there began, again, a religious crusade where he was the epitome of everything that was evil and corrupt and awful about the 1980s. It was like a Greek tragedy where you could see it wouldn't stop until the guy was ruined. So in the spring of 1990, I said to myself, it's over. You know, the market has to bottom out because they have killed the dragon.

A Fabulous Buying Opportunity

Griffeth: You were managing a high yield bond fund at that time. How did you navigate those waters? Did you see that period as a buying opportunity for junk bonds?

Patel: You mean in 1989, 1990, 1991?

Griffeth: Yes.

Patel: That was such a fabulous buying opportunity that if I had said that this isn't the time to buy junk bonds I should just have left the business and done something else.

Because, for example, the RTC was selling all this property owned by seized S&Ls, not because they knew this company was going bankrupt. They were just selling it to get rid of it. Plus, you had this moral stigma that junk bonds were wrong and if you bought junk bonds you were a little suspect yourself. And so you just had to say, there has to be value here because anything so negative has to have some gold in it.

And also, a lot of these companies that were trading at 60, 70, 80 cents on the dollar were buying back their own debt. So you had to say, gee, if this company has enough money to buy back its own debt, why shouldn't I buy it too?

I tried to buy the lowest dollar priced bond I could because then you can capture more on the upside. And in fact at the bottom of the market, my high yield fund had an average cost basis of 67.

Griffeth: You no longer manage the high yield fund but today, as we speak here in mid-1994 high yield bonds are no longer really referred to as junk bonds. Are they evolving into something with more respectability?

Patel: What's happened in junk has been very interesting. We've had default rates which have been zip, below 1 percent. Totally risk free investment. Whereas you had huge losses in stock, annuities, and tax frees. Junk, ironically, has been the safe harbor of 1994.

Griffeth: Has the pendulum swung all the way in the junk market's favor?

Patel: Well, this year [1994] so far long treasuries are down 10 percent and junk is off 2 percent. And so money has been slowing into junk funds because it's the only safe investment that people know. Plus you have this great experience from the last few years. It has outperformed many other fixed income sectors. But this is why the market is so cruel. Ironically at a time when the market is entering a period 1) of great uncertainty, and 2) when investor risk premiums are going to widen out, people have gone to junk.

So you ask yourself logically, is that the way the world works? The safest place to invest money is the riskiest place at a time when risk in other sectors is being punished, whether it is stocks, foreign currencies, or long maturity stuff.

Today, if someone said, "I have some money and I'm nervous about the market," the market is saying back, "Oh, junk bonds, what a great safe place to put money into." And, as a matter of fact, I do happen to think junk is okay here for a while, because, again, going back to the big picture, you have an underlying upswing in inflation, an underlying upswing in the economy, and an easing of bank lending. You know, banks are much more amenable to lending money now. So I don't think that you'll have any severe supply and demand imbalances. And you are not going to have any real default problems until perhaps 1995 or 1996. So junk is probably okay for now.

Problems with Government Securities

Griffeth: You have said that when you started managing money for Advest, you first had to straighten out the Government Securities fund. Not to knock the previous managers, but how does one mismanage a government securities fund?

Patel: Well, that is a mystery for the ages. They introduced these funds back in 1986. And, if you remember back then, all the government funds were these "Government Plus" funds where they could magically write covered calls. You know, sell options on the bonds.

Griffeth: Right. We should point out that the word "plus" in the name of a fund is a signal to investors that there is some option writing allowed in that fund.

Patel: Yes. The idea was that these government funds would give you virtually the same yield as the long bond using this wizardry of futures trading, and you would only have 40 percent of the volatility of the 30-year Treasury bond. What could be better than that?

". . . you could manage billions and billions with basically one person and a couple of clerical types. It was the most wonderful fund that was ever created."

They also had high payouts to the brokers who sold them and a very high income management fee for themselves. So it was going to be perfect. The investor gets a huge return with no volatility, the broker gets rich selling it, and the management company gets rich managing it. And you could manage billions and billions with basically one person and a couple of clerical types. It was the most wonderful fund that was ever created.

So they started the government fund here and basically promised what was not possible, because they started this fund in 1986, close to the very day the long end of the market bottomed out. So then as rates went up, the prices went down, and they simply couldn't produce what they thought they could. So they started trading frantically. In 1987 and 1988, the turnover rate on the fund was about 450 percent, and the guy who was managing it couldn't stand up to the brokers who were selling the fund. They were complaining about the performance. But, you know, you have to be very tough with the brokers, because if they smell fear they'll eat you alive.

This guy was running backwards and trying everything to make it work, and he just didn't get it. He was clueless. He didn't have a strategy of what he was going to do with the big picture. He kept market timing, and that didn't work. And then he would try to up the dividend by creating income from writing calls, and that didn't work. So they were just trying to achieve the unachievable instead of saying, "We can't do this."

Griffeth: So you took over in September of 1988?

Patel: Actually, in November.

Griffeth: And what did you do?

Patel: Well, first of all I said, "The cost structure of this fund is too high." I mean they had a cost structure at that time of about 2 percent. [*NOTE: In other words, two percent of the fund's total assets each year were used to pay for sales and management.*] I don't care what rates do or how magical I am, I said that with this cost structure the best we could do over time would be to finish in the [bottom] 16th or 17th percentile [of all government securities funds]. Because in a bond fund where your income is going to determine 90 percent of your return over a long period of time, if you have a high cost structure you are not going to be able to compete with a no-load with a total cost of 70 basis points [where .7% of the fund's assets go to marketing and management]. So you could see that with our cost basis at 2 percent, or 200 basis points, that no-load fund would probably yield 130 basis points more than my fund. So they lowered the payoff to the brokers, they lowered the management fee, and that saved maybe 70 basis points. I really give the company credit for stepping up to the plate on that one.

Number two, what the fund needed was a rest. You know, it had had something like a 500 percent turnover rate. You cannot make money that way. So it just needed whatever we had bought to be held for a while. So what I did was put the fund in Ginnie Maes which then were a terrific value compared to treasuries. In a market that basically flipped and flopped, Ginnies produced more returns. So that restored the value of the fund.

And then when we got to 1992, I began to get concerned about prepayments and rates falling, so at that point I started selling the Ginnies, and put the portfolio into Treasuries.

The Super Bond Bull

Griffeth: Yes, much was made in the financial press at that time about how aggressively you went into long Treasuries in that period, and about how it was exactly the right play. Is that your normal method—to be that aggressive—or was it just the market conditions?

Patel: The only way to really achieve incremental value is to move into a cheap sector in a big way. If I had bought long Treasuries for only 10 percent of the portfolio it would have just caused little ripples.

Griffeth: The problem is you perhaps stayed a little too long at the Treasury party in 1994.

Patel: Well, I did. As you may know, I had accepted another job, and I wasn't sure I was going to stay here. So mentally I sort of shut everything down in November of 1993.

So in other words at the time when I needed my wits about me, my wits were orbiting Mars. I had basically given my notice, I said I had accepted another position, and they had hired my replacement. But when I got up to the altar with the other firm I said, "This is not a good move for me." Luckily, Advest was very anxious to get me back. But, in the meantime, mentally I had sort of said, "The end."

Looking back, after having quit and everything, maybe I should have just made a fresh start somewhere else and, you know, taken some time off. But I didn't, and unfortunately the market kept trading every day. (All of this, by the way, is just an explanation. It's not a rationalization, not a justification. It's just basically what happened.) You know, sometimes it's hard to ignore what's going on with your personal life. I was definitely mentally distracted at that time, and then the market went against me. My old theory wasn't working. So I said, "Well, why isn't my theory working? What am I missing here?" And it really took me until February [of 1994]. I finally said, "All right, I'm going to stay here, and I'm going to fix things now that I've broken them." And it took me a month or so to kind of refigure the universe in a way that made the facts work. And once I did that I changed the portfolio out of Treasuries back into Ginnies.

Yes, the fund took some real pain in that six-month period, but my three-year numbers were still great and my five-year numbers were still great. And my relative strength is already picking up. So I'll make a fearless prediction that, even though I am close to the bottom of the pack year to date, I predict to you I will finish the year in the top half of the pack.

"My Gut Is Still Smarter Than My Brain"

Griffeth: I've always said that I could never manage other people's money, because I wouldn't be able to sleep nights with all that responsibility.

Patel: When I feel my instincts about the market are right, it doesn't really bother me when the market goes against me. But let me tell you something I've learned: My brain intellectually can do all the numbers, but my gut is still smarter than my brain. And when I go against my gut feeling, that's when I've made mistakes. Your guts are everything you've learned in your whole life. And that includes things that you don't know you've learned, or things you may have forgotten.

So when the market goes against me, I can intellectualize the whole thing and ask myself, "Is my theory still working?" And if I feel I'm right, I sleep well. But I must say when I don't sleep well, that tells me I'm wrong. I may be holding an individual bond that I just know I'm right about. But why is it the last thing I think of when I go to bed? I say that is a clear sell signal, because my subconscious knows something my very smart brain hasn't learned yet, and I'll find out later. So I basically never go against my instincts.

Griffeth: Do you ever worry about individual shareholders when the market goes against you?

Patel: No, because I would say I probably have met more of my shareholders than any other portfolio manager you'll talk to. They come up to me and say, "We have our whole retirement fund with you," or, "We have $10,000 or $100,000." I'm a shareholder, too. When I started managing the government fund, I switched out of high yield funds and put my money in the government fund. I'm normally a risk taker, but I said, "I'll put my money where my mouth is." You know, I'm not going to ask them to feel pain if I don't feel it, too.

By the way, I welcome people calling me up. It's amazing how people actually have that perseverance to try to call the manager. Whenever anybody calls I always talk to them. You know, it's their money.

But people should also realize that you can't be right every single day in the market and be right in the long term. If I'm bearish and the market jumps a point, I say, "So what? That's just one day." I try to look at the long term.

Griffeth: You said something earlier about how the previous manager of the Government Securities Fund didn't have the personality or the makeup to be a fund manager. Describe what you think the proper personality is.

Patel: Well, I think you have to have a vision of what you are trying to do, how you are going to do it, and what your fund is about. With any fund I've ever managed, I can tell you in 15 seconds what the fund is trying to do. Period. And I can tell you what my approach is. It's very simple.

It's just like when you are at sea. You know, when you're in a sailboat near these big waves. When you are on the bottom of a big wave, you can't see anything. You're clueless. You don't know which way the shore is, and so you have to have this internal mental compass to tell you where the shore is or what your goal is. And then you have to realize that you are going to get buffeted and say, "Well, I can see my goal mentally so I'm not going to worry if I get a little jostled."

The Magic Derivatives Fund

Griffeth: I want to spend a moment on derivatives; What do you think of them?

Patel: I have never used derivatives; I think they're lousy investments. The reason I don't use derivatives is I've always felt they were too costly. The yield was too low for the advantage I was supposed to gain by using the derivative. In other words, you have less volatility with a packed CMO [collateralized mortgage obligation]. Well fine, but you give up eight basis points in yield by purchasing the derivative. I would rather have the volatility and have the extra eight points. So it never seemed like a bargain to me for the benefits that you supposedly got.

Griffeth: If an investor finds that a particular fund uses derivatives, should he or she run the other way?

Patel: Actually, it's interesting. If I could create a magic fund, I would like to have some money to put into derivatives. Not today, but three months or six months from now because you are building to a crescendo in the same type of morality play that we saw with junk bonds. You know, derivatives are evil right now. So I can see that they are going to have a terrible supply and demand imbalance where everybody who owns certain types will be forced either to sell them or they're not going to buy nearly as many as they did last year. Certainly not when the big boss comes down the hall and says, "You don't own any derivatives, do you?"

So I would like to buy derivatives in three to six months. I could buy 20, and I would get wiped out in three of them. But I would quintuple my money in a handful, and I would make 20 percent in some of the others.

I just think you'll eventually see a selling climax in derivatives creating a terrific buying opportunity.

SUSAN G. PEABODY

Birth Date: February 28, 1957

Education: B.A. from U.C. Berkeley, with a degree in Renaissance and Medieval History

Hobbies: Heli-skiing, sailboat racing

Alternate Career: Architect

Susan Peabody is the senior vice president at Alliance Capital in New York, where she oversees $5 billion of municipal bonds for 25 separate mutual funds and institutional accounts. The mutual funds include a national municipal bond fund that invests in munis issued in various states, and she also oversees management of a number of single state muni bond funds, which provide residents of those states with income that is exempt from both federal and state taxes.

Because the income investors receive from municipal bonds is generally tax exempt, the yield on munis tends to be less than taxable bond yields. So muni bond investors are always looking for higher yields without too much risk.

Peabody apparently likes to take risks. Her hobbies include heli-skiing, which involves jumping out of a helicopter and skiing down treacherously high, snowy mountain peaks. Does she also take risks in the municipal bond market? Consider her investment in the bonds issued by the city of Denver, CO to pay for construction of its new airport. Major glitches in its highly touted high-tech baggage handling system delayed the airport's opening a number of times and depressed the airport's bond prices. But Peabody didn't blink. At the time I interviewed her for this book, the airport's opening date was still in question, but she was convinced her investment was still a sound one.

During our interview, we also discussed her investment style, the evolution of the municipal bond fund business, and what she thought would happen to it if the federal government ever removed its highly coveted tax-exempt status.

JULY 7, 1994

The Denver Airport Fiasco

Bill Griffeth: You're known as a risk taker. I mean, it's obvious from your hobbies that you are. And it seems to be the case in the way you invest in some municipal bonds. Have you always been that way?

Susan Peabody: I actually think that the kind of risk taking that I do is pretty conservative in the sense that we look for the things that are out of favor that have the least amount of downside and the greatest amount of upside. What I try and do is just dig in when I see an opportunity which is generally created by price. And a lot of that is driven by the press. So when we see a situation like Denver Airport or New York City general obligations we start doing our homework and try and figure out, number one, if the debt can be paid back. So it's pretty basic and, again, I would argue that I'm more of an opportunist than a risk taker.

Griffeth: You don't consider it higher than normal risk than any other manager takes.

Peabody: No, I don't. Take the Denver Airport, for example. We know the airport's built, we know the baggage system problem will eventually be resolved, and our feeling is the bond is at depressed prices to create value and opportunity for our shareholders.

Griffeth: Let's talk about Denver Airport for a moment. You got in early and had people scratching their heads.

Peabody: Right. Early on, the risk was whether or not they were going to be able to get the thing off the ground. We actually bought in in the middle phases. We did not buy in at the first financing opportunity. If you recall, I believe in 1990 they did the original bond issue. It was roughly a billion dollars. They knew they needed between $3 and $4 billion for the project. The second phase of financing was really the tricky part of it in terms of whether or not the deal was going to fly, to coin a phrase. [laughing]

That was when people were becoming skeptical. If you recall, it was at that point that Continental Airlines had filed for chapter 11 bankruptcy protection. Enplanements were down, the economy in Denver wasn't very good. United had not signed on. Basically United was fairly outspoken in terms of being opposed to a new airport at that time. I mean, they knew eventually they'd be in a new airport, but they didn't want to have to come up with the money to do it then.

Griffeth: What year was this?

Peabody: 1991.

Griffeth: And this presented a perfect investment opportunity, as you saw it?

". . . everything we do in terms of the kind of risks that we take is driven by price, initially."

Peabody: Well, you know, at first I said, nah, I'm not interested. And then the price got a lot cheaper, the spreads were, if I recall, roughly 140–150 basis points above comparably rated Triple B bonds. And so at that point we said, well, I guess we're suppose to take a look here. We were at 9 percent on the airport bond when basically everything else on the market was between 7.50 [percent] and 7.75 [percent] for Triple B.

Griffeth: So you could justify getting in based on those valuations.

Peabody: So everything we do in terms of the kind of risks that we take is driven by price, initially.

Griffeth: But then things seemed to go from bad to worse on Denver Airport. By 1993 there were more delays. It became the stuff of jokes by guys like Jay Leno and David Letterman. At that point were you starting to sweat?

Peabody: No, we knew going into it that there would be this cloud hanging over it, so that was okay. We could deal with that. And I think the worst point in terms of the pricing was at the time of the financing. They really didn't get any cheaper than they were right before the second phase of the financing was done. We also knew that we were in good company, because at that point people who I have a lot of respect for in terms of their research effort also stepped up to the plate. People like Fidelity and Dreyfus. And this is of course after doing their due diligence. In general, large public infrastructure projects do take a certain amount of vision. Things like the George Washington Bridge [linking New York City to New Jersey] never would have been built, or the Triboro Bridge [in New York City] would never have been built unless somebody had a vision. This was the first new airport to be built in twenty years, and we knew that one of the big arguments against the facility was that it wasn't going to be competitive with other airports around the country because [Denver Airport's] costs would be higher per passenger enplanement. I do a lot of traveling, I'm sure you do too, and all you had to do in 1991 was go out to a place like Kennedy [Airport, outside New York City] and see that they were going to have to improve the facilities there. And they would have to borrow money to do that, which would kick up their cost per enplanement. So the higher costs at Denver didn't bother me.

Identifying Investment Opportunities

Griffeth: When things get rough as they did with Denver Airport, as the fund manager, are you . . .

Peabody: We don't really care.

Griffeth: Do you get pressure, though, from shareholders? Are you accountable to a committee of some kind? In other words, do you have to continue to justify the investment?

Peabody: Sure, I mean we get out there and we just tell our side of the story. I mean the bottom line is that it makes good news headlines. That's why Jay Leno and David Letterman are picking it up. So we think we're the experts and the press, the guys writing the articles, were not the experts. I mean, they're selling newspapers.

Griffeth: They're selling newspapers, and you're buying bonds.

Peabody: Exactly. [laughing] And actually I think it works to our benefit. You look at a situation like the city of New York back in 1989 and 1990 with people losing confidence in the Dinkins administration, the credit rating services had the city on credit watch and everybody was focused on the budget gaps and what have you. But that also was an opportunity for us. When you looked at it, that actually was a very stable situation as far as I'm concerned. Because New York is a city of 9 million people. The revenues to pay off the general obligation debt come from property tax, and unless a neutron bomb takes out all the tax payers . . .

Griffeth: If that happened, your funds wouldn't have to pay a dividend anyway. [laughing]

Peabody: [Also laughing] Exactly. The worst case that you have, particularly on general obligation debt, would be cash flow interruption like you had in the case of Philadelphia. It never actually happened, but there was concern that there could be. The city itself has some serious problems in terms of its revenue collection ability, which have to do with very wealthy outlying suburban areas and a poor urban area which needs a lot of services and doesn't have a lot of taxing ability.

Griffeth: The examples you're citing here are major cities, so they're not going anywhere. You're willing to be patient on those but are there others where things got bad enough that you lost your patience and you ended up selling?

Peabody: Yes, but they're related to things that are generally difficult for the public to understand. I mean, I think when you look at municipals that people don't really understand, the perceived risk is much greater than the actual risk. Remember, in order to qualify for tax exemption in the first place, a municipal bond issuer has to provide some public benefits. The Internal Revenue Service is very strict about that.

Griffeth: What's difficult to understand about that?

Peabody: For the public to understand it?

Griffeth: Yes.

Peabody: Most people don't have any idea how sewer bonds get paid for, for example. They don't think about the fact that it's an assessment on their property tax. People like to turn the lights on and flush the toilet, so those things will get paid for.

Griffeth: And when you do those things, you think about the bonds that are paying for them!

Peabody: That's right. More money for my shareholders! [laughing]

Peabody's Early Career

Griffeth: How did you get into munis to begin with?

Peabody: Well, I needed a job.

Griffeth: Good answer.

Peabody: I ended up getting a job on the trading desk at Smith Barney.

Griffeth: Was that out of college?

Peabody: Yes. I did a brief stint in the design world and decided that it was a lot of work and not very much compensation.

Griffeth: Did you do some designing?

Peabody: Not really, no. I was an apprentice. I would have had to go back to school. That was another reason to choose Wall Street, because I think at that point I thought that I wanted to move along. I was tired of being a poor student.

Griffeth: So you ended up at Smith Barney doing what?

Peabody: I was working in the marketing department there for a woman by the name of Toni Elliott. I think she's on the board of Smith Barney now. She was one tough boss, but she was a woman who had come up in the business back in the dark ages when the best a woman could do was to be an executive assistant for somebody. But she managed to work her way up, and she did extremely well. And, as I said, she was a very tough boss, but I think she was a good role model for me to have early on.

Griffeth: Did you find any glass ceilings or barriers of any kind?

Peabody: No, I was very fortunate. I did that job [in marketing] for just over a year, and then I was hired by a guy named George Davies who had been for a long time with a company that managed pension funds. Now this was in 1982 when, as you recall, interest rates were sky high . . .

Griffeth: They were rather high.

Peabody: Yes, they were rather high. And they had just developed this wonderful new product called money market funds and at that point, of course, you know a seasoned portfolio manager in his right mind—I say "his" because there weren't a lot of "hers" around then—wouldn't manage short-term assets. But these funds were seeing tremendous growth.

So the long and short of it is that Smith Barney had begun to expand in that area of the market, they had all this money and no managers, and George had identified me as cheap labor. He wanted somebody who was hungry and willing to work really hard and he didn't have to pay a whole lot.

Griffeth: What kind of fund did you manage to begin with?

Peabody: Well, I started off for the first six months working in the municipal marketing area. But I had interacted with the traders on the desk and all the institutional salespeople so I had some product knowledge in public finance as well. And so with my limited municipal background I think he [George Davies] had in mind that eventually he would put me on the municipal bond funds, but the first six months of the job I was really trained on the taxable side of the business with the taxable money market funds.

I worked with a 26-year-old, she was pretty ancient at the time (I was 25!). And the two of us would whip around billions of dollars. I thought it was really fun, you know, buying commercial paper and bankers acceptances and letters of credit.

Griffeth: You didn't feel the enormity of the job at all?

Peabody: Oh, absolutely! It was a total rush. But then I'd get my paycheck and I'd think, wait a minute, there's something wrong here. I was getting paid $12,000 a year! And she was probably getting paid $15,000 a year. Plus, we got a bonus of $1,000 that first year. It was a big deal.

Griffeth: Big money! So you decided to move on?

Peabody: No, what happened was in October of that year [1982], the woman who was running the tax exempt money market fund went on vacation, and so I was put on her fund to run it while she was on vacation. But when she came back—it was sort of a low move, and I had nothing to do with it—George pulled her into the office and said, "Lillian, I don't think this is working out," or something like that. I don't think she was doing a bad job. I think it was more of a personality issue. So then he said, "Susie, the job's yours!" And so from that day in October of 1982 I've been managing money.

The Developing Municipal Bond Market

Griffeth: How did you do initially?

Peabody: Well, it was a money market fund, so it was a pretty controlled environment. We'd get together with Mitch . . .

Griffeth: Mitchell Held, the chief economist at Smith Barney.

Peabody: Exactly. Our offices were at 8th Avenue and 34th Street and we would come up to the 1345 Avenue of the Americas' offices to have our weekly investment committee meetings, and Mitch would give us a presentation on the direction of interest rates. And then policy would be decided in terms of extending the average life of the portfolio or not. And then we would talk about credit issues in terms of new deals coming on the market.

> "... the municipal market is really a hybrid market because you don't have a natural product like you do with the money funds."

But the municipal market was so underdeveloped at that time. What was exciting for me is that we were actually in the process of trying to figure out the Investment Company Act of 1940, which regulates money market funds. I mean, the bankers knew that there was a lot of demand for products, but they didn't know how to make it money fund eligible. So I would spend my nights poring over the 1940 Act, highlighting various sections trying to figure out how to create a structure that would qualify investments.

In other words, the municipal market is really a hybrid market because you don't have a natural product like you do with the money funds. The money funds could choose from bank products and commercial paper products from corporations. But we didn't have that kind of variety on the municipal government level. For the most part, cities and counties are restricted in terms of their annual borrowing for cash flow purposes. Or if they do borrow they generally borrow for longer periods of time. You know, they borrow against future tax collections.

So anyway, we were trying to figure out what the Internal Revenue Service was going to accept. You know, the IRS at first was very much opposed to the proliferation of this new product in terms of passing through the tax exemption of the bonds to the money funds' shareholders.

Now, of course, the bankers have developed variable rate demand obligations which have become standard for the short-term tax exempt market. But at that time, the product didn't really exist. There was nothing in the short-term tax exempt world for fund managers to buy that would be the equivalent of say, doing a repo, or doing commercial paper or doing short-term investments. I mean, you need a lot of liquidity when you're running a fund.

So what I'm saying is that it was a really exciting time to be in the business because all this new product was being created for the very first time. Now we have daily demand notes, variable rate demand notes, and all sorts of new products that were created during that time.

And it was a lot of fun, because I would get to talk to these mid-level bankers with a lot more experience than I had, and we would hash out how to compose new products.

Griffeth: Interesting.

Peabody: Yes. So I think I had a very solid foundation in the business on the money fund side, and then I came to Alliance in April of 1984. At that time.we had $90 million, and they thought I was brilliant because I knew the mutual fund business. At that time Alliance was brand new to the mutual fund business. And since my boss at Smith Barney had insisted, again, that we read the 1940 Act and that we interact with the accounts people and legal people and really understand every aspect of managing a mutual fund, I had a very strong foundation.

Choosing Muni Bonds

Griffeth: So how do you evaluate a municipal bond? It is a rather difficult investment for a lot of people to understand. Give me the whys and wherefores of what you look at.

Peabody: Well, for the most part we're very much focused on finding products for our single state portfolios, and so we'll ask ourselves, "Do we need California paper, or do we need Pennsylvania paper?" And we also have diversification requirements. In other words, we have to keep a certain percentage of a fund's assets in housing bonds or student loan bonds or airport bonds.

Griffeth: That is required by your prospectus?

Peabody: By the prospectus, yes.

> *"... almost everything is driven off of trying to find the highest yield and the highest quality."*

Then, the second thing we do is, the bottom line is that this is an income-driven product. The benefit of owning municipal bonds is the tax-free nature of the dividend income. So almost everything is driven off of trying to find the highest yield and the highest quality. And high quality is important, too, because it's a market that is dominated by the individual investor; it's hard for them to understand the market in the first place. So what they do want to know is, they want to have some comfort in the fact that you're buying high-grade investments.

Griffeth: There are rating services that determine the "quality" of an issue, but what goes into that determination? How do they decide what's a better quality investment than another?

Peabody: By the ability to repay the debt and the risk associated with that.

Griffeth: But how difficult could it be to pay off a sewer bond? Or how difficult could it be to pay off a dormitory bond? Why would one necessarily have a higher credit rating than another one?

Peabody: Okay, let's say you're the city of Utica [New York], and you used to be a hot manufacturing center around the turn of the century. But since then things haven't been so hot and you're just losing population and you're having trouble attracting businesses. A lot of what we look at when we look at a bond deal is based on who the top ten taxpayers in the city are. The top ten taxpayers generally comprise the top ten employers.

Griffeth: So you're looking for a city with a strong income tax or property tax base.

Peabody: That's right and it depends on whether a city is in a growth situation or a contraction situation. You know, there's greater risk associated with a city like Bridgeport [Connecticut, which declared bankruptcy in the early 1990s] because basically they've got a lot of blue-collar workers. They're losing jobs in Connecticut right now to places like South Carolina. That means they are losing companies which provide the job base which provide the revenue base. And you get stuck with a bunch of people on welfare that you can't pay for, because you have a small base of people contributing revenues in terms of taxes.

Griffeth: So you're not buying Bridgeport bonds. You're buying South Carolina bonds.

Peabody: Well, fortunately I don't have a Connecticut fund so I don't need to worry about it.

Single State Funds

Griffeth: Speaking of which, when were single state muni bond funds created?

Peabody: That really started with New York and California in the mid 1980s. There was a huge boom in those markets during that period. That's when you saw a lot of money come out of money market funds into bond funds for the first time, and I think the marketing guys were thinking that we should try to create new product to attract as much money as possible. And that's when you started to see increased competition among single state portfolios. Managers were trying to create a new niche. They realized that there was an opportunity. Because if you're a resident of Minnesota it's nicer to have your income be 100 percent tax free instead of just federal tax free.

Griffeth: In other words, you get the double exemption from federal and state taxes.

Peabody: Yes, federal and state, right. And if, for example, you're a resident of New York City, you get a triple exemption from federal, state, and municipal taxes.

But the problem with single state portfolios is that they are driven by supply and demand. Benefits can be diluted if there is so much demand for paper that prices are so high and yields are so low. Sometimes, you're better off owning an out-of-state fund. Like, right now the national market for insured paper is at roughly 6-1/2 percent. And in Arizona, because there hasn't been a lot of new issuance, there's a tremendous amount of demand, so paper there is trading around 6 percent. It's a half a percent fuller in price and lower in yield. So oftentimes investors are better off being in a national fund instead of a single state portfolio. You just have to weigh the benefits.

In the case of New York, though, the northeast has been going through a period of economic contraction. And people have been worried about the state being able to balance its budgets, the city being able to balance its budget. So New York bonds have been trading at a cheaper price versus national names. It has actually been a very good investment to buy New York bonds as a result, even though we have some of the highest tax rates in the country.

I'll give you another example. In 1988 North Carolina funds were the best performing funds of all single state and national portfolios.

Griffeth: In terms of price?

Peabody: In terms of performance.

Griffeth: Total return you mean.

Peabody: Total return performance. North Carolina bonds had, by God, the strongest performance of any bond in any sector of the country back in 1988. Any guess why?

Griffeth: Let's see. All of the golf courses they have down there?

Peabody: Golf! [laughing] Good answer! I love it! No, it was the RJR Nabisco leveraged buyout. All those people [in North

Carolina, where RJ Reynolds is headquartered] who were paid off in the buyout bought municipal bonds.

Griffeth: That's wild!

Peabody: Those are the fun things that we get to deal with in our market.

Shaking the Muni Malaise

Griffeth: Before Bill Clinton was elected, the prevailing wisdom was that he would increase taxes. And when he did, people would rush to municipal bonds, thereby creating a demand that would push prices higher. But there was also an awful lot of supply coming to market at that time, offsetting the demand. As a result, people in your business keep saying that municipal bonds are undervalued. I've been hearing that for three years now.

Peabody: That's right.

Griffeth: What is it going to take to bring them out of their doldrums?

Peabody: Well, I think what it's going to take is a period when you see 1) a dramatic decline in new issues and 2) when people feel more confident about the stability of long-term interest rates. Especially if we see long-term interest rates declining. Then you will see a further gap between what taxable Treasuries are paying and what our tax-exempt municipals are paying. And it will make ours more attractive.

Griffeth: Insured versus uninsured. Does it matter?

Peabody: Well, I'll tell you, the benefit of insured [municipal] bonds is that they create a more generic security, and that's why I recommend them for people who are purchasing individual bonds as opposed to bond funds. Also, in our portfolios we like to use insured bonds for a couple different reasons. One is I told you earlier, this is a yield-driven market so you tend to get a lot of people willing to pay up to buy lower quality bonds. The spread between Triple A and Triple B has been very narrow.

Griffeth: So I'm not really taking on that much more risk if I'm buying an uninsured bond?

Peabody: If you're buying an investment grade bond, you're not. The problem is we have a very fragmented market. You have over 85,000 state and local government debt issuers. Last year alone we probably had, I don't know, 17,000, 18,000 issuers come to market. And the problem is a lot of these guys only come to market once every five or ten years. One of the issues that you do have from a credit standpoint in our market is that with state and local governments, there's no uniform financial reporting. They're trying to change that, but it's a long process.

Removing the Tax Exemption

Griffeth: Last issue. Every new president who comes in looks for new ways to raise revenues. And some have threatened to remove the tax-exempt status on municipal bonds. Will it ever happen?

> *"I don't envision sentiment in this country changing so that our representatives in Washington would really be willing to go along with eliminating the tax-exempt status of municipal bonds."*

Peabody: There are two issues here. The first is, if it were to be taken away would it threaten existing municipal debt and the answer is no, because the tax exempt status of municipal bonds is determined by Section 103 of the Internal Revenue Code. So they actually would have to go in and change the tax code, and they can't do that retroactively because it's unconstitutional.

Griffeth: So every single municipal bond that's out there right now will always be tax exempt?

Peabody: That's right. They'll all be grandfathered. Secondly, I don't envision sentiment in this country changing so that our representatives in Washington would really be willing to go along with eliminating the tax-exempt status of municipal bonds. The bottom line is that consumers have to pay for sewer systems and schools one way or the other and if they're not being subsidized, you know, vis-à-vis cheap borrowing in the tax exempt market, they'll pay for it through higher taxes.

Griffeth: But I would think that the nature of the demographic group that invests in municipal bonds would change drastically if the tax exemption went away.

Peabody: Oh, yes. But there will always be a municipal bond market because state and local governments have to have access for capital projects.

Griffeth: But how would they attract new investors?

Peabody: We would actually have a bigger market.

Griffeth: You think so?

Peabody: Sure, because right now people don't buy munis for their 401(K) plans, or for their pension funds.

Griffeth: Because of the tax exemption?

Peabody: Because the yields are lower.

Griffeth: So if the tax exemption were removed, yields on munis would simply rise.

Peabody: The way it works is the cost of borrowing would just be the equivalent of whatever they were paying in the corporate bond world. So they would just become another sector of the taxable fixed income market.

GARY PILGRIM

Birth Date: November 5, 1940

Education: B.S. in Business from Tulsa University, M.B.A. from Drexel University

Hobbies: Running, tennis, and mowing the lawn

Alternate Career: Jet pilot or aeronautical engineer

*G*ary Pilgrim is the president of Pilgrim, Baxter & Associates, based in Wayne, PA, and he is the manager of the PBHG Growth Fund.

Pilgrim started the fund in 1986, and he managed it in relative obscurity for seven years, turning in consistently solid gains for shareholders. Then he burst upon the scene in a Money magazine profile in August of 1993. That same year, he changed the fund from load to no-load, the fund's asset base went from $3 million to $183 million, and for reasons he explained during our interview, the fund's performance improved.

Gary is a growth investor who focuses on small companies. Unlike value investors who look for beaten down or undiscovered stocks, growth investors wait for a company's earnings to build up a head of steam before they are willing to commit.

During our interview for this book, Pilgrim addressed the growth vs. value investing issue. We also talked about why he converted PBHG Growth to no-load, and about why he doesn't pay much attention to what corporate executives have to say about their own companies.

JULY 20, 1994

Bill Griffeth: First of all, I want to hear about this hobby we have listed. Mowing the lawn?

Gary Pilgrim: [laughing] Where did you read that? It's true that I spend a lot of time mowing my lawn just because I have a big lawn, and everybody makes fun of me for mowing it myself. But I don't mind mowing it. It's a nice kind of mindless distraction after the kind of life I lead.

Griffeth: Rider or walker?

Pilgrim: It's a walker.

Pilgrim's Early Career

Griffeth: Fine. Now let's talk about your early career. Where did you get started?

Pilgrim: My first job in the investment business was Philadelphia National Bank.

Griffeth: Doing?

Pilgrim: I started at the bottom, came in as an analyst trainee in the Trust Department. Actually started at the bank as a regular old loan officer trainee. Having tried to get into the investment business and feeling that it was difficult to get into, I decided commercial banking was a close cousin, and as soon as something came up in the trust department, off I went to see about that. That's where it really started.

Griffeth: What was difficult about getting into the investment business to begin with?

Pilgrim: Well, I had a rather plain background and at that time going to work for an investment counseling firm required a little more of a pedigree than I had.

Griffeth: In other words you didn't just want to be a broker.

Pilgrim: I wanted to be a money manager. I wanted to do investment research, and so the next best thing was to find a large bank with a trust department and start there. So that's what I did. I moved to Philadelphia from Oklahoma in search of that first job in a big bank.

Griffeth: And then simultaneously got your MBA.

Pilgrim: I got the MBA at night, that's right.

Griffeth: How long did you stay at the bank?

Pilgrim: I was there for 15 years. It's the only other job I've had.

Griffeth: How did you and Baxter hook up?

Pilgrim: Technically, I hired him when I was in charge of the employee benefits area at the bank. I hired Harold away from Bankers Trust to see if he could take our regional bank growth stock management expertise into the national market. After about three years of trying that we both pronounced it a flop, because nobody wanted to hire a regional bank. People were busy hiring investment counselors at that point. So after trying to do something in that investment counseling mode with the bank we decided we would just go off on our own, and that's what we did.

Griffeth: What years were you at the bank?

Pilgrim: I was there 1967 through 1982.

Griffeth: So in that time you saw your share of both bull and bear markets.

Pilgrim: Oh yes.

Griffeth: Did you develop your momentum style of investing at the bank? Or did you develop it after you started your own firm?

Pilgrim: The only kind of investing I have ever done is growth stock investing. That's what the people at the bank did, and really everything since then has just been a refinement of technique. So I didn't really invent growth stock investing at the time. I grew up in the investment business liking growth companies, and once I left the bank and began my own firm I was able to further refine some of the strict momentum approaches to growth stock investing. I had this kind of compelling desire to see if I could bring a little more order to the process of finding a great growth company.

Griffeth: And how did you do that?

Pilgrim: Just from observing over time that most of the stocks that had great success always came from an extended period of accelerated momentum. And they not only grew very rapidly, but they always did a little better than people expected. So I wanted to build a model that measured and ranked stocks based on those observations. And that's what I spent the first few years of our firm developing.

Growth vs. Value

Griffeth: The two main disciplines, of course, among mutual fund managers are value investing and growth investing. You are a growth investor. What's wrong with the value approach?

Pilgrim: There's nothing wrong with it. I think it requires coming at the subject at a different point in time with a different set of bifocals on. You're just looking for different things. My attitude is there are really just about two basic approaches. People can focus on earnings, and people can focus on price. And then there's a whole bunch of people who aren't quite sure which they like more, so they try to focus on both. We focus strictly on business progress and when it begins to falter. But we're not interested in whether it's an undervalued or over-valued stock. The idea is stock price behavior comes from good things going on, or bad things going on, and we want good things.

> "... stock price behavior comes from good things going on, or bad things going on, and we want good things."

Griffeth: Value investors say they are looking for a company that hasn't been discovered yet by growth stock investors, that has the potential for strong growth, and they want to be on board early. You are saying that you want the stock to prove itself first before you are willing to get on board.

Pilgrim: I want the company to prove itself first, yes. And then I will operate on the assumption that as the company makes progress over time so will the stock price. And my bet is once a company gets on a fundamental roll and starts growing at exceptional rates it usually lasts longer than people expect. And that's more or less how you make money in the stock. It keeps going beyond the limits of the current price-to-earnings ratio. In other words, the company just kind of earns its way through the current valuation level and continues to sustain or enhance that valuation level as long as it is on this roll of growing rapidly and doing better than people think.

Griffeth: But we live in a time of instant access to information, and there is an awful lot of information. Almost information overload. How can a company develop the rate of earnings growth you're looking for and not have it already be reflected in the stock price, with all of the analysts and all of the information services and all of the mutual fund managers scrutinizing them?

Pilgrim: How is it that value investors can find some stocks that have a future different than the average person expects it to have? I mean, if you say growth stocks are efficient, don't you have to say that value stocks are efficient, that it's an efficient market? That everybody knows all that's knowable at some point in time about every company with all the analysts following them?

Griffeth: Well, but a value investor is looking at a company before it has developed a track record, or before everything is knowable about the company.

Pilgrim: The value investor makes his money only if, and when, the company asserts itself in a way differently than it is perceived at the time he makes his investment. And usually that means he sees a pickup in business or something coming that the world hasn't much thought about yet.

I'm saying with high growth rate companies what probably is the missing ingredient is that investors never pay enough for an extended period of growth. The typical investor's model is a vivid discount model where it is assumed that a company is decaying or that growth has to decay down to something like the market rate. And that's why high growth rate stocks always look kind of expensive, because nobody assumes that a company with a 50 percent growth rate is going to keep it up for very long. Even analysts don't assume it. They typically make estimates that call for a slowdown within a fairly short period of time. So our bet is that if we can identify those companies that grow faster and longer than people expect them to, we'll make our money that way.

Griffeth: Does a famous example spring to mind? Would a Home Depot, for example, qualify?

Pilgrim: Sure.

Griffeth: Or a Wal-Mart?

Pilgrim: Wal-Mart, I think, is the grand daddy of all the companies that always seemed high priced but continued to grow longer and stronger than people expected. And investors made something like 28 times on their money over a decade or so. As far as I'm concerned, that's heaven for the growth stock investor to find companies that do that. And it doesn't have to keep it up for 20 years. If a company that is perceived as a slow growth company suddenly perks up because its business conditions change or what have you, then it shows up on a growth stock investor's radar screen. You then see a couple of good quarters go by, and you figure, "Hey, if this can last forever, that's how long I want to hold it." But even if it only lasts for a couple years that's fine too, because it's long enough to exploit the opportunity.

Griffeth: Then you have to be a pretty nimble trader when it does start to slow down.

Pilgrim: Well, you do, but that's no different than a value guy saying, "I'll sell this stock when its value reaches my target." We want to move out of stocks as that exploitation cycle begins to mature. And sometimes it matures gracefully, which is not so bad. If a company has been growing at 70 percent and it slows down for a while to 60 percent or 40 percent or 50 percent or whatever, you can still make a lot of money on these very high growth rates continuing. But if a company runs into a wall and suddenly is having little or no growth and it starts falling short of estimates, that's the thing growth investors have to be the most careful to avoid. And sometimes it's hard to avoid. That's sometimes where you lose all the great returns you've made.

Griffeth: Once you've seen the earnings momentum slow, is it your style to exit your whole position as quickly as possible?

Pilgrim: It will depend to some extent on our analysis as to whether the slowing is material, whether it's transient, or whether it's meaningless. The basic problem with the strict approach to momentum investing is that companies don't grow in a straight line. Every quarter is a little different than the previous quarter. Sometimes they are picking up or slowing down, margins are going up or down or what have you, and you really have to be willing to analyze what's going on and make a judgment as to whether it's an important development or not. However, having said all that, the single most frequent reason that we sell is because "the inflection point" is perceived to be at hand. In other words, the company is slowing down, or it is about to.

> *". . . the single most frequent reason that we sell is because "the inflection point" is perceived to be at hand."*

Analysts, including ourselves, are about to have to lower our estimates for a company's future growth rate. Then the company's stock price has to adjust to that, and if you can get out of the way before it does you're ahead of the game. The problem, of course, is nobody knows very much about the future. So we think that it is particularly dangerous to assume that a high growth rate company is having a temporary problem. If it is having a temporary problem we'll sell it and buy it back when the problem is behind them.

Finding Good Information

Griffeth: Do you find you get better quality information in terms of earnings guidance from Wall Street, or does it come from the company itself?

Pilgrim: A lot of information comes just from looking at the trend in sales and earnings and margins. Then you have to make an educated guess as to whether the trends are solidly in place, whether they are getting better, or whether they may even be deteriorating. And I think you can do this without listening to any analysts. Analysts are of marginal value to us because most of the Wall Street community reports rely pretty much on what the company is saying about its own future. And analysts who spend their whole life following a few companies seem to be as surprised about changes in earnings growth about as often as people who take a slightly more superficial approach.

In other words, it's hard to see around the corner, and I think often the best guide is just to be a very careful student of the present trend. If you simply assume that, for the most part, trends will continue, that a body in motion stays in motion, you'll be right more often than if you try to guess when it's going to change based on a lot of assumptions.

Griffeth: I take it you don't visit too many companies if you really don't value their information.

Pilgrim: I don't find analysts or companies terribly helpful, and that's not to say that they are dishonest or not smart or any of those things. I just find that they are always telling me the good story right up until it becomes a bad story. It's kind of hard to get any incremental negative nuances from the typical company. You know, the glass is half full until you wake up one morning and it's completely empty!

Griffeth: Did you learn that through the school of hard knocks?

Pilgrim: Oh, of course.

Griffeth: Do you have examples that you can think of from the past where you were misguided?

Pilgrim: Every bad stock I've had in my career I could probably associate with guidance from management that turned out to be wrong. Just the other day we had a company in here telling us this, that, or the other thing, and literally two or three weeks later the company made an announcement that exactly contradicted the substance of what they had told us. And this is not that unusual. Now, do business conditions change that dramatically, or is it really that companies just keep talking positive until the very last minute, hoping that things will turn out differently? I think it's more of the latter. There are plenty of people out there who, I'm sure, work to deceive the investor because there is a certain advantage in doing that. But my experience for the most part has been that it is nothing more than wishful thinking on the part of business people who are optimistic that they are going to make the quarter. And they always think things will be fine if they just had one more day they could actually get that order they need to make the quarter.

Griffeth: But, to be fair, you do focus on the smaller companies that presumably do have their best years ahead of them. And they typically will have a little hope mixed in with whatever they tell the analysts.

Pilgrim: Oh, absolutely, you are right. This is the entrepreneurial crowd down here in the small capital world. These are the companies that are dependent on their enthusiasm and ingenuity and resourcefulness and optimism, and so forth.

A New Economic Revolution?

Griffeth: Some economists equate the period we are in right now, in the mid-1990s, with the Industrial Revolution of the 1890s, when there was such a tremendous explosion of growth. If that's true, it would seem to me that this is kind of a sweet spot for the area of the markets that you invest in. I mean, there are a tremendous number of industries that do have perhaps their best years ahead of them. Would you agree?

Pilgrim: There is certainly something to what you are saying. The only hesitation I have is I don't know how new change is. I mean a growth investor is always finding change around him and companies that are gaining and losing. Is this anymore a productive period than 10 or 20, or even 50 years ago? I think you always feel as though it is, and as we look at the universe of companies that we think make up today's great American growth companies, about 40 percent of them are in the broadly defined area of technology. So that area is certainly a prolific producer of great growth companies. So is health care. It's not the big drug companies showing the fastest growth anymore. It's companies solving cost problems in health care. And [in the retail sector] it's not K-Mart [with the fastest growth rate] anymore it's much smaller companies like Bombay and Gymboree and Sunglass Hut. These are companies that exploit changing fads and tastes of consumerism, and because they are small they can jump on an opportunity and exploit it sometimes before the big guys know it's there.

We just try to get involved with as many growth companies as we can get comfortable with. And, as I say, a lot of them tend to be in those traditional kind of areas like consumer, technology, and health care services. But I can't say for sure how that has changed over the last 10 or 15 years.

The PBHG Growth Fund

Griffeth: Let's talk about the fund. Your firm, Pilgrim Baxter, was in operation for three years before you started the PBHG growth fund?

Pilgrim: The first full year of the fund was 1986, and the first full year of our firm was 1983.

Griffeth: How did you decide to start the fund?

Pilgrim: We had a pension customer that had a financial services and small mutual fund operation and they wanted to add a growth fund and so they hired us as a manager. This was a load group to begin with and after a few years, most of the life had gone out of the fund; there was very little growth in it, and so we decided to take the load off of it and see what would happen. We and our former partner parted ways at that point because they didn't see how they could have a no-load fund in a load fund family.

Griffeth: I was just looking at the net assets of your first few years. $20 million the first year, $27 million the next year, $24 million, $22 million, $12 million, down to $8 million, down to $3 million. What happened there?

Pilgrim: Well, the misleading part is that it was never actually $20 or $30 million. The fund never had any retail distribution at all, it was pretty much occupied by a few institutional type accounts. We had a bank up in New York using it in their mutual fund family, and they offered it to their trust customers. We had a local pension customer who wanted to use it for clients. So when it was a load fund, there were probably never more than 400 or 500 shareholders.

Griffeth: And then when you became a no-load fund, what happened? Some of them pulled out?

Pilgrim: Yes. And then the other thing that happened was this financial services company I described had some insurance companies who put maybe $10 million or $15 million worth of seed money in there to start the fund, and over time they gradually took their money out. The bank trust department gradually stopped doing this program they were doing and then one of our institutional pension plans said, "Well, gee, I can't be in this fund, it's too small." So he left, and we were left with 400 or 500 friends, family and other accounts with $3 or $4 million in the fund.

Griffeth: And when you became a no-load the next year, in 1993, you suddenly had $183 million.

Pilgrim: And a year after that we are up to $460 million.

Griffeth: That is astounding. Is that all just because you became a no-load fund?

Pilgrim: The whole thing started with a *Money* magazine article. I believe it was the August edition of last year [1993]. We were about to take the load off, and that's what really made it a story. And it has been nonstop publicity since then.

Griffeth: I find it interesting, and I haven't crunched the numbers totally, but just looking at the Morningstar figures, it looks as though you also turned in your best performance to date in 1993 after the load came off. Is that just a coincidence?

Pilgrim: I think it's a fortunate coincidence that 1993 was a good year for small cap growth investing and it was the best year we had relative to our peer group. We were number one in the capital appreciation fund category last year [in 1993]. But the thing I'm even more proud of as a manager is that if you look at the Morningstar report you will see seven out of the eight years we've been at or above the norm for all capital appreciation funds.

Now there will always be a certain number of investors who chase after a fund when it has had a good hot year, but it's that longevity of doing pretty well most years that gives us credibility and sets the stage for the good press we have.

Griffeth: How much of it also, perhaps, was Gary Pilgrim saying, "Now I've really got to work to prove myself, because I don't have a built-in set of investors anymore. Now I've got to go out and find them, and maybe work a little harder"?

Pilgrim: I would say this. We manage a lot of other people's money outside this fund, and the main difference between the performance of the regular accounts and the mutual funds had to do with IPOs [initial public offerings, when companies issue stock to the public for the first time]. The fund was small enough to use IPOs, and it had a risk profile that was more aggressive and we were willing to do that. And if you look at that 47 percent return [the fund achieved in 1993], I would guess 16 or 17 percent of that came from flipping IPOs [*NOTE: A stock's price will often rise shortly after it is first issued to the public. "Flipping" refers to a system of buying a portion of an initial public offering, and then selling it soon after it comes to market.*] So to get back around to your question, if you want to say that I was motivated to do that because I wanted the fund to have a good record, I say no, not really. But the fund was in the opportune place to use that available condition in the market-place.

Thoughts on Mutual Funds

Griffeth: What do you think of this explosion of mutual fund business the last few years?

Pilgrim: I think it's great, not from a selfish standpoint, but I truly think mutual funds are a wonderful investment vehicle for a lifetime accumulation of wealth.

Griffeth: Will we eventually see load funds go by the wayside because of the tremendous competition out there?

Pilgrim: I think so. I think it is ridiculous for anybody who is willing to spend a little bit of time educating himself to pay a load. It's just ridiculous.

Griffeth: Even for people who don't have the time?

Pilgrim: I think I would just as soon throw a dart at a list of mutual funds as to listen to a broker tell me about his "favorite" fund that's got a load on it. I just think there is an inherent kind of a problem going to a broker for investment advice. They tend to be drawn to higher profit products and since they don't have a particularly compelling motive to find the most appropriate mutual fund for their client, they tend to be vulnerable to the lure of the incremental profit and whoever markets the product to them. A lot of people market to brokers in a very high-powered way, and they are just like the rest of us. You'll buy a product if someone sells hard enough to you.

I think that if you are going to invest you should educate yourself and at least do a minimal amount of research. Don't depend—well, let me rephrase that—don't pay somebody a fee to figure it out for you. Don't go to brokers.

Griffeth: With all the money coming in, have you thought about closing the fund to new investors?

Pilgrim: The circumstances that would lead to our closing the fund would have to do with the way money comes to us. If it comes to us in buckets because of market conditions there might be times that we'll feel that we should close the fund to manage our affairs in a more orderly fashion.

Griffeth: You don't have a capitalization target?

Pilgrim: No, no. We think that we can manage a lot more money in this small cap sector if we can do it in an orderly, systematic way. As a firm, we manage about $3 billion. And I think there are plenty of small growth companies out there to invest in. But if too much money comes in all at once, then we have a problem. Three or four months ago it was a real problem because money was coming in quite impressively at $80 or $90 million a month. But it has slowed down a bit. I think it's just human nature. You know, as soon as your favorite mutual fund or asset—whatever it is—starts losing value you start losing your intensity. And right now I'm down 20 percent from last year's highs.

Pilgrim's Investment Criteria

Griffeth: Before we finish, how would you sum up the criteria you use to invest in a company?

Pilgrim: Well, a company has to be growing at rates in excess of 20 percent before we are even interested in it. It has to have some history of consistent accomplishment. We're not interested in one-quarter phenomena or junky companies that are turning around. We are interested in evidence of high quality and sustainable growth that remains above a certain threshold rate. The criteria have to do with profitability, return of equity, clean balance sheets, a clear reason why a company is doing better than most, and we have to believe that it's sustainable. That's what our research tries to determine.

Griffeth: Do you ever fudge it a little bit if you find something that doesn't quite meet the criteria but you really like the company otherwise?

Pilgrim: Oh, yes. The problem with everything I've said is that there are many exceptions. You seldom have all the ingredients in just exactly the right spot. The portfolio is always a set of compromises to some extent, because you can't own just your favorite company. You own a lot of companies in order to be diversified. And they don't all score a 10. There's a whole bunch of sixes and sevens in there, too.

GRACE PINEDA

Birth Date: November 6, 1956

Education: Adelphi University, with degrees in Russian Studies and Psychology; M.B.A. from Fordham University

Hobbies: "Emerging markets cooking"

Alternate Career: "Something art-related"

I *once asked the people at Morningstar to provide me with a list of who they thought the top female mutual fund managers in the country were. Grace Pineda showed up at the top of that list. Pineda is a vice president and senior portfolio manager at Merrill Lynch Asset Management in Princeton, New Jersey, and she oversees $2 billion invested in the world's emerging markets. In fact, one of the funds she manages, the five-year-old Merrill Lynch Developing Capital Markets Fund, is the largest emerging markets fund in the United States. She also manages Merrill's Latin American Fund, which was started in the fall of 1991.*

Both funds have stellar track records. They have consistently trounced the Morgan Stanley Europe, Asia, and Far East (or EAFE) Index by double-digit margins, and year after year they have ranked among the top 5 percent of all foreign stock funds in terms of performance.

But even Pineda will admit that investors shouldn't expect this kind of performance forever, because the road to capitalism for many of the developing countries she invests in can be full of political and economic potholes.

Pineda first started analyzing small, developing countries at Mitchell Hutchins Asset Management in the early 1980s while she was pursuing her MBA at Fordham University. Then when her mentor, Lilia Clemente, left Mitchell Hutchins in 1986 to start Clemente Capital, Pineda followed. She traveled extensively, visiting the countries she was analyzing and investing in. Then in 1989, just as the Berlin Wall was coming down and the whole world was suddenly discovering the investment potential of Eastern Europe, she was hired by Merrill Lynch

Asset Management to manage its brand new Developing Capital Markets Fund.

During our interview, we talked in detail about the criteria she uses to evaluate the countries she invests in, about the tremendous risks people should know about before they invest, and about what shareholders should look for in an emerging markets fund manager.

AUGUST 26, 1994

Diplomat or Money Manager?

Bill Griffeth: You were born in the Philippines, and you've lived in a number of countries, haven't you?

Grace Pineda: Yes, I was born in 1956. In 1957 or 1958 we moved to Paris, because my father was working for the Philippine Foreign Service, which is their version of the State Department. He was assigned to Paris as a diplomat. From Paris we moved to Switzerland and then back to the Philippines and then to the United States in 1966.

Griffeth: What was your first language?

Pineda: That's hard to say. My first language was an amalgamation of French, Tagalog, and English. In fact, when we went back to the Philippines in 1960 or 1961 from Europe, I couldn't speak Tagalog. My cousins couldn't understand me because I would be saying *oui* and *pourquoi*, speaking this mix of French, English, and Tagalog. So I'm not sure what my first language was. It's probably the best time for kids to learn because to them it's just a bunch of words that you put together.

Griffeth: When did you first come to the United States?

Pineda: In 1966 when my father was assigned to New York and Washington.

Griffeth: And then when your parents went back to the Philippines, you decided to stay.

Pineda: Yes. I was already an American citizen by then, simply because I had spent most of my growing years here. I think it's still the land of opportunity, even though that sounds tacky. It is the place where I found a career. When they left I was already at Clemente Capital, and I had already been through Mitchell Hutchins. So I had a lot going on.

I wasn't about to abandon it to go back to the Philippines. When I applied for my citizenship, I had given up on the Philippines. This was during the Marcos era. My original career plans had been to follow in my father's footsteps and work for the Philippine government. That was why I studied Russian and Slavic studies in school because I had hoped to be like my father, assigned to countries like Russia. At that time, the Philippines had just opened its embassy in Moscow, and I wanted to be one of the first people there representing the Philippines. But as a result of the bureaucracy and the usual politicking and and political changes within the Philippine bureaucracy, I couldn't do it. In fact, while I was waiting for the paperwork to go through, I got my MBA and I met Lilia Clemente.

Griffeth: Was that when you were at Mitchell Hutchins?

Pineda: Yes, actually, that was the way it worked out. When I was at Fordham in 1982 Lilia Clemente was independent and she had all sorts of arrangements with Prescott Ball and I guess a couple of other institutions. So she was running some money independently. It was a very small amount, though. It couldn't have been much more than $10 million. But she was on her own, and she needed somebody to work for her part-time to put together spread sheets for her Japanese companies. So that was my first job. I put together company spreadsheets for some of the big ADRs [American Depositary Receipts, which are shares in foreign companies that American investors can purchase directly] like Hitachi, Canon, and Sony. Those were the big obvious names in Japan at the time.

And then Lilia wanted to do bigger things. Paine Webber hired her to do the international component of their first mutual fund, which was a global fund. They were very smart to start with a global fund. It was very forward-thinking back then.

Fortunately for me they wrapped up their talks late in 1982 when I was finishing up my MBA at Fordham. When I got out of school the second week of January 1983, I started working for Lilia at Mitchell Hutchins full time doing research on Japanese companies. Then I gradually took responsibility for more countries like Hong Kong, Singapore, and Malaysia.

Griffeth: How long were you there?

Pineda: I was at Mitchell Hutchins for four years, until 1986.

Griffeth: Were you managing money by the time you left there?

Pineda: No. When Lilia left Mitchell Hutchins and formed Clemente Capital in 1986, I went with her because I thought the opportunities working for a small shop like that would be so much broader than if I had stayed at Mitchell Hutchins. And it sure worked out that way. I kept adding countries to my menu like Thailand, Korea, and Taiwan.

Griffeth: And by adding them to your menu, you mean you traveled to those countries and did research there?

Pineda: Yes. Lilia was a big believer in that. I was visiting Japanese companies the first year I started, even though I wasn't a full analyst. She thought it was very important that she check out all of these companies. I traveled a lot at that time. I would be gone for up to three and a half weeks at a stretch, which I never do now. I make the analysts here [at Merrill Lynch Asset Management] work for me now.

The Fall of the Berlin Wall

Griffeth: When did you come to Merrill Lynch?

Pineda: In 1989. By the time I left Clemente, I was responsible for all our Asian investments, including Japan. That was something like 40 percent of all the assets we ran at Clemente. And I pretty much had full discretion managing those assets. Leo Clemente signed off on all the trades, but they were really my decision.

Then I joined Merrill in 1989 when Arthur Zeikel [the president of Merrill Lynch Asset Management] came up with the idea for the Developing Capital Markets Fund. He liked the idea of developing capitalism. In fact, if you look up the fund's first filing at the SEC, I think it was originally called the Developing Capitalism Fund, which is kind of a tacky name. Arthur actually backed down, which he normally doesn't do.

(Laughter). He backed down and they called it Developing Capital Markets.

They were looking for a manager experienced in the Asian markets. Those were the only real emerging markets at the time. There wasn't much going on in Eastern Europe yet, and there were still too many problems in Latin America.

Griffeth: But then those markets started to open up as a more viable investment for U.S. investors when the Berlin Wall fell, didn't they? I mean that was really the watershed event, wasn't it?

Pineda: Yes, public interest was triggered by the fall of the Berlin Wall and by people like Gorbachev. Here, for the first time, was a charismatic Russian leader who made sense, and he looked good on T.V. It was the first time that I think people really paid attention to the potential for change in a country like Russia.

But the fall of the Berlin Wall was really the confirmation of a trend that was already under way. It was not the beginning. I mean, that was why Arthur Zeikel started the Developing Capital Markets Fund when he did. He already saw a number of other developing countries converting from socialism to capitalism. The Berlin Wall was just a high profile event that brought public attention to that trend.

Value vs. Growth

Griffeth: When you are evaluating companies in the emerging markets, do you consider yourself a value investor or a growth investor?

Pineda: Oh, boy, I hate to have to put a label on it, but I would say that we have to be growth investors if we are investing in developing countries but we do pay attention to value. By saying that, I mean we are not really momentum investors. We do pay attention to valuations in different ways, whether it's a company's price-to-earnings ratio, its price-to-cash ratio, or its market capitalization relative to production capacity. We just try not to pay too much for what we want to buy, whether it is assets or earnings or output.

Griffeth: Is it unfair to try to apply the traditional fundamental analysis we use here in the U.S. to some of these companies and countries?

Pineda: Oh, no, it's perfectly fair. It's just that you might not be able to do it because of a lack of good or timely information about the companies you're interested in. But of course, you should try to apply it because I think we still have the best standards for analysis, and I think it is very important not to pay too much for anything. You have to somehow relate the price you are paying to what you are buying.

Equity Market Lifecycle

Griffeth: Your method of analyzing each emerging market country is based on where you feel it is in what you call the "equity market lifecycle." Let's talk about that. [*NOTE: Refer to Figure 14.1.*]

Pineda: Yes, the further to the left a country is on the lifecycle chart, the less developed its political and economic infrastructure is. In those countries you have to take more of a top down approach to analyzing them. That means looking at things like politics, the rate of economic growth, how accessible the market is (which determines its liquidity), how many institutions there are investing domestically, and how much money those institutions have to invest in their equity markets at all.

The more developed countries are on the right side of this chart. And, as you can see, the most developed of the emerging markets, in our view, are Malaysia and Mexico, which we actually considered an established growth market.

Griffeth: How do you quantify that? How does a country move from preemerging to emerging to established growth market?

Pineda: It is purely our subjective judgment, based on things like how broad the market is, how liquid it is, how high the per capita income is, how many ADRs there are, how much access foreigners have to it, things like that.

Mexico is pretty far up there on the chart. Now some people may have felt it was premature to place it in the established market category before their presidential elections this

Figure 14.1

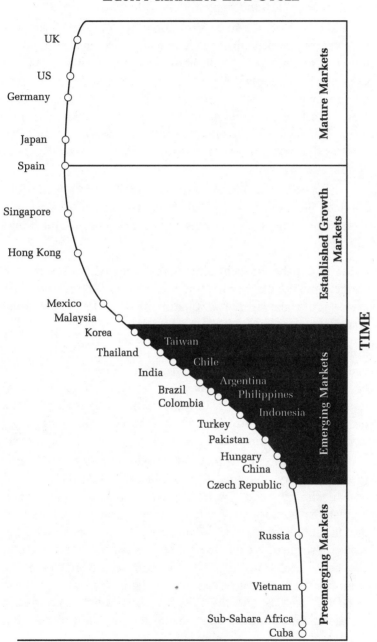

EQUITY MARKETS LIFE CYCLE

year. Their fear was that if the ruling party had lost the election [*which it did not*] it might have caused a reversal in the reforms in Mexico, but I didn't happen to believe that.

But the political issue is very important for what we call the preemerging markets, because you have to be concerned about the government's policy priorities. You have to figure out, for example, if it is going to tighten monetary policy or spend more on the country's infrastructure. You also have to determine whether a foreign company will be allowed to take its profits out of the country. In other words, you have to determine whether the government is friendly to business and business people and investors.

That's why some people were worried about the elections in Mexico. The opposition candidate was talking about restricting foreign investments and raising capital gains taxes, and things like that.

Griffeth: On the far right side of the chart where the mature markets are, it looks like the line is starting to decline. Does that mean you consider the U.K. and the U.S. to be declining markets?

Pineda: No. What you're implying is that there is no way to make money in those markets. And that's obviously not the case, although I don't think there are any more structural improvements to come in the U.S. with the exception of the further internationalization of the markets, allowing more foreign listings in the U.S. stock market.

Now, if, for example, Bill Clinton were to raise capital gains taxes for equity investors, that would verify that there should be a declining trend. Or if they decided to increase market regulations because they felt too much money was going to mutual funds or to derivative products or something, that would also justify a declining trend, because it's a structural change or regulation. All of the countries on the left side of the chart are, for the most part, deregulating their markets, but the trend for the U.S. and the U.K. may be headed more toward re-regulation. I say they "may" be headed in that direction, but I just don't want to make that call.

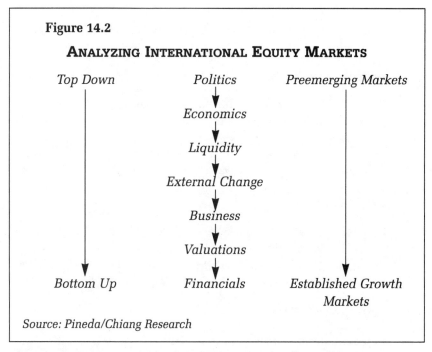

Figure 14.2

ANALYZING INTERNATIONAL EQUITY MARKETS

| Top Down | Politics | Preemerging Markets |

Politics
↓
Economics
↓
Liquidity
↓
External Change
↓
Business
↓
Valuations
↓

| Bottom Up | Financials | Established Growth Markets |

Source: Pineda/Chiang Research

The Criteria for Analyzing Emerging Markets

Griffeth: Let's itemize and explain the specific criteria you use to analyze investment opportunities in a particular country. [*NOTE: Refer to Figure 14.2.*] As you said before, it all depends on how developed the country is, doesn't it?

Pineda: Yes, we use up to seven different criteria to evaluate a country, depending on where it falls on our lifecycle chart. As a country becomes more developed, the things at the bottom of the list matter a lot more. This is the bottom up stuff. Actual valuations and specific business. But in the preemerging countries those count for a lot less. A lot of times because, even though you want to be invested in that country, you don't really have too many stocks to choose from. So you look more at the criteria at or near the top of the list, and those make up the top down approach to investing.

Griffeth: Could you please briefly explain each of the criteria on the list? Let's start at the top with "politics."

Pineda: When you analyze a preemerging country's politics, you simply try to determine the direction the government is headed and its attitude toward business and investing. That's very important.

Griffeth: Economics.

Pineda: You try to determine something as basic as whether a country will experience stable economic growth, or whether it will see a steep decline or a rapid increase that could lead to high inflation. All of this, of course, determines how companies within the country will perform.

Griffeth: Liquidity.

Pineda: Is a particular market accessible to the foreign investor? And is it a market that a large fund can invest in? If it is a market that does not have local institutions investing there, there will be limited liquidity. And that could be a problem.

Griffeth: External change.

Pineda: External change has to do with a surprising political or military development with global implications, like Iraq's invasion of Kuwait. This criterion is in the middle of the list because it tends to affect everyone pretty equally, whether a country is preemerging or established growth.

Griffeth: Business.

Pineda: As a country's political and economic infrastructure develops, you start to focus on various industries within the country. The first question you ask yourself is, "Do I like the business that a particular company is in?" Are prices for its products rising or declining? Is there a lot of capacity in the industry? What is the competitive structure in the business that it is in? Is there a demand for its products?

Griffeth: Valuations.

Pineda: This is when you start measuring individual companies. For example, you measure its stock price relative to some sort of earnings generation potential, whether it's the earnings themselves or the assets that will generate those earnings.

Griffeth: And then the financials.

Pineda: This is where you dig more deeply into how a business accounts for and reports its activities. At this point what you're really trying to do is predict a company's future earnings, going into the next quarter or the next year. The reason you want to do this is because you want to get a leg up on other investors. You want to be able to predict earnings growth before anyone else.

Investing in Hungary

Griffeth: Let's analyze a specific country to see how this all works. How about an emerging market such as Hungary? What do I need to know in order to have enough information to invest in that country?

Pineda: First, you probably should know that the market hasn't done that well since all the euphoria about Europe in 1989–1990, basically since Saddam Hussein invaded Kuwait. Europe and Hungary haven't really done well.

So you should be asking, "What's going to trigger the performance of this market? Why should I be investing there?" And of course, whoever is marketing the Hungarian funds should be pointing to the reforms that have already been occurring over these past few years, the investments that have already been made by the government, the efficiency improvements made by individual companies, and the foreign capital that continues to be attracted by the government.

Griffeth: Is this a country where the infrastructure is still being built to a great extent?

Pineda: Oh, yes. Some of the country's structural problems have been addressed over the past years, and investors can, for the most part, reap profits from that. But going forward they still have a lot of room for improvement, and that would include infrastructure issues such as the actual construction of roads.

Griffeth: So, for example, I would want to perhaps invest in some of the heavy equipment manufacturers there.

Pineda: Yes, and the producers of building materials would be interesting. And for the same reason, you might look at investing in some banks as a way of gaining broad exposure to the rebuilding that is occurring.

I should point out that you are not only looking for confirmation that things have been improving, but that there is more room for improvement and that this improvement will continue. If the improvement is largely completed, then you really aren't talking about an emerging market, and it probably wouldn't be that interesting. There always has to be that room for improvement, whether it's on the political or economic side.

Griffeth: If I do decide to invest in Hungary, how patient should I be with my investment? In other words, how much of a growth rate should I expect from that country and how long should I give it to achieve that growth rate?

◆

"Generally your investment horizon when you go into these countries shouldn't be any shorter than five years . . ."

◆

Pineda: Right. Generally your investment horizon when you go into these countries shouldn't be any shorter than five years because developments and improvements just don't happen over a shorter period. It doesn't happen over six months.

As for the kind of growth you should expect, sustainable growth rates in developing countries—and this is an average number—will be 4 to 5 percent in most cases. In other words, double what you can expect to achieve in a major market like the U.S.

Griffeth: You're talking about a country's growth rate.

Pineda: Yes, and that's real growth. [meaning growth minus inflation]

Griffeth: Fine, but I'm talking about my investment. How quickly should I realistically expect my investment to grow through the years?

Pineda: We don't make projections like that.

Griffeth: But professional investment advisors always tell individuals to set goals for their investments, to develop expectations. So I'm asking what I should expect from this investment before I get in?

Pineda: I think the best way to give a client expectations is to show how similar markets have performed. What you could do is cite the performance of other emerging markets when they were at a stage of development similar to Hungary's. And, in fact, those markets have shown at least a 25 percent per annum return in dollar terms.

Griffeth: And then at the end of five years if my investment hasn't achieved those expectations, do I throw in the towel and sell, or do I give it another five years?

Pineda: You should probably talk to whoever sold you the fund and get an update on your investment. But, you know, being in the fund for five years doesn't really mean you shouldn't be following your investments over the course of those five years. You have to stay in touch with whoever sold you the funds and make sure that your assumptions are still in place.

Emerging Markets in Individual Portfolios

Griffeth: I know it's hard to generalize, but what role do you feel the emerging markets should play in the portfolios of individual investors here in the U.S.?

Pineda: They should only have a role in a portfolio if the investor already has a core portfolio of domestic stocks and then of more mature international companies.

Griffeth: So you feel investors should start their international portfolios with more established foreign markets.

Pineda: Exactly. And not because there is anything wrong with emerging markets but because the client, or the retail investor, might not be ready for the kind of volatility they are going to see in the emerging markets.

And as a mutual fund manager, I feel it is very important to keep shareholders well informed, but there is only so much you can tell them about volatility. If they see a fund run up 30 percent, most likely they are going to say, "Oh, I've got to buy more. This is a great fund. It's done so well." When actually they should probably be holding back and bracing themselves for a drop, because that's just the way things usually work in markets. They go back to some sort of a mean, they don't stay up or keep going up. I think many investors are just not ready for that kind of volatility.

I think emerging markets are great, and if you can get an investor to go into them and understand why they are there and what sort of movements to expect, that's fine because there is nothing wrong with emerging markets.

Visiting the Emerging Markets

Griffeth: When you visit a country what do you do? I've read where you'll do such mundane things as visit a supermarket to see what's being sold. How do you evaluate investments in a country when you are visiting there?

> ◆
>
> "I think emerging markets are great, and if you can get an investor to go into them and understand why they are there and what sort of movements to expect, thats fine."
>
> ◆

Pineda: When you visit a country a lot of times you would have done some research beforehand, so you're not really going there to find out what their inflation rate will be this year from some guy in government. What you do want to see is how much prices are actually rising versus the last time you were there. When you buy a box of Kleenex at some store in Ecuador, you come back six months later to see how much the box of Kleenex now costs. There was a time in Brazil—at least until their recent economic plan—when you just had to come back the same afternoon and you would have probably had to mark up your price about 3 percent.

So it's really to confirm what you are seeing in numbers with what you are seeing in real life. I just want to know what it's like for the local Brazilians, or what it's like for local Ecuadorans buying Kleenex or other things in the grocery store. Visiting a country rounds out the research.

It also gives you a feel for the country and the kind of people who live there. In other words, I want to know if they tend to be easygoing, or if they were put through hardship whether they would rise up and revolt. Or do they tend to be very motivated to make a lot of money? Are they very materialistic? Are wealthy people conservative looking, or do they tend to show off all their wealth? That gives an idea for how consumption-oriented the society is. Do they like borrowing money, or do they like saving it?

And going to a country also keeps your interest up. Some people just read about companies and look at statistics, but that just doesn't cut it for me.

China

Griffeth: I had an interesting letter from a CNBC viewer one time. He had taught school in China for a number of years, and based on his firsthand observations of Chinese society, he felt it was going to take a lot longer for China to become the lucrative market for investments than many on Wall Street would have us believe. In other words, the hope for profits in the foreseeable future was getting ahead of the reality.

Pineda: I agree. But I think the reality is sinking in these days when you see how the markets in Asia have corrected.

There are businesses thriving throughout China, especially in the Guangdong province close to Hong Kong. But as far as stable, sustainable growth that is non-inflationary, that will take a while. I think China's biggest problem right now is inflation. They are working on it, but I don't think they have been very successful. There was something in the *Financial Times* just yesterday about price controls for food, and other things like that. A capitalist doesn't like seeing things such as price controls, but they might be necessary. I don't really know how else they are going to do it.

Griffeth: But U.S. investors have been told that China is the next great frontier for investors. They are told to be patient, but I wonder if expectations aren't too high right now.

Pineda: Actually, I'm very grateful for the corrections we've seen in 1994. All of the Asian funds are down 20 percent year to date, and I think that should bring some of the point home that these markets do have wide swings.

People just got overeuphoric at the end of last year about Asia. They discovered Asia for the first time, and the kind of performances that these funds had last year was very misleading. And that is one of the dangerous things about inexperienced international investors investing in the emerging markets, whether they are institutions or individuals. They were spoiled by good performance over the past year or so, and I guess some thought it was going to continue.

So I'm very glad for the corrections we've had this year, because I think it reduces the possibility for a more drastic correction later on. If you get some of the steam out now, maybe people will say, "Wait a second, my broker told me to buy this because it would keep going up." Maybe next time they will question that broker more closely.

Russia

Griffeth: And what about the people living in a country that is experiencing economic reform? They have to be patient also, don't they? I think of the incident in Russia this summer, when an investment fund that thousands of Russians had put money into turned out to be an illegal pyramid scheme, and a lot of people lost a lot of money.

Pineda: Right, that is an extreme example of something that happens all the time in developing countries.

When you first introduce capitalism into a country, the first people to benefit are business people and brokers. And the gap between the haves and the have nots starts to widen. You certainly have a lot of that in Russia right now.

When I was in Moscow last year we went to a very expensive restaurant. Even by New York standards it was expensive. But there were quite a few local Russians there, and they were very young people talking about trading, investments, privatization vouchers, and matters of that sort. So people in the financial industries are already making a lot of money there. Meanwhile, you have people there who are still living hand to mouth.

That is happening in all of these countries that we are investing in, and it's always the thing that you worry about in the early emerging markets. That's why keeping an eye on a country's politics is so important. How a government responds to the ever widening gap between economic classes determines a country's political direction.

In the case of Russia, I would assume it will result in more regulations of trading or of more disclosure, or perhaps a legal framework of some sort. And I think it is going in that direction.

Banks over here are already starting to look at Russia to set up custodial services, and they are not going to do that until they are very comfortable with the infrastructure that is setup for the delivery of shares, for clarifying ownership of shares, and that sort of thing.

Mexico

Griffeth: Let's talk more about Mexico for a moment. In a long term sense, they are obviously on the road toward major development there. But it has come with a price, namely political jolts like the assassination of the ruling party's candidate for president. [*NOTE: After my interview with Grace Pineda, the Mexican ruling party's secretary general was also assassinated.*] I wonder if we are in for some more market instability in that country if investors start to worry that political reform in Mexico isn't the sure thing some would have us believe it is.

Pineda: Yes, well, there are always bumps in the road, but I don't think those kinds of bumps would cause a reversal of a trend. You might get a decline in the market, just as you get a decline in the market when there is a major strike in a country like Germany.

The important thing to remember in Mexico is the people voted for the reform this time. Like it or not, we are introducing capitalism to Mexico, and they are starting to privatize their largest companies. Once the reforms have gone this far, it is very difficult to turn back. Especially when the people have signed off on it.

Know Your Emerging Market Fund Manager

Griffeth: Right now, there aren't too many emerging market specialists like Grace Pineda out there. But there are a fair number of new foreign stock funds still coming to market. What should an investor look for in a manager, in terms of qualifications? That may sound like a silly question, but realistically the science of evaluating the emerging markets is still, uh, emerging.

Pineda: [Laughing] Yes, well, they probably should find out what the person was doing before he managed the fund. If the guy was a lender at a bank, and he speaks Spanish, and that's why he's running a Latin American fund, you probably wouldn't want that. But if the person running a Latin American fund used to invest pretty actively in Asia, or in some other emerging market, or even in Japan, then that's okay.

And if the person has something in his record that shows that he's a responsible, conservative investor, then I'm comfortable with that. But if a fund company doesn't provide the public with much of a history of their managers because they haven't hired good people, then investors should be made aware of that.

JOHN W. ROGERS JR.

Birth Date: March 31, 1958

Education: Princeton University, B.A. in Economics

Hobbies: Basketball. Jigsaw Puzzles.

Alternate Career: Basketball coach

*J*ohn Rogers is quite a young man to already be considered a pioneer. But he is. He was the first African-American professional employee to be hired by William Blair & Co. after he graduated from Princeton in 1980. And his Ariel Capital Management Inc., which he founded in 1983, is one of the first minority-owned money management firms in the country. His success as a money manager and business man have brought him a number of awards. He was named Mutual Fund Manager of the Year in 1988 by Sylvia Porter's Personal Finance Magazine. The same year, Venture Magazine named him their Entrepreneur of the Year.

Rogers also has quite a pedigree. His father, John Sr., is a presiding judge. And his mother, Jewel Lafontant, was a delegate to the United Nations during the Nixon administration and an Ambassador-At-Large under President Bush.

One of the delicious ironies about the Rogers household is that, while Ariel's company logo is the slow lumbering tortoise (symbolizing the prudent, long-term method of getting rich) Rogers's wife, Desireé, is the director of the Illinois State Lottery, where get-rich-quick dreams are born. John and Desireé have a daughter, Victoria, born in 1990.

During our interview, we discussed Rogers's incredibly hectic work schedule, his value style of investing, socially responsible investing, and the professional hurdles he has faced as an African American.

The Investment Bug Bites

Bill Griffeth: As I understand it, your father got you started in investing.

John Rogers: Yes, he really did. He bought stocks for me every birthday and every Christmas after I was 12 years old. At first it wasn't fun getting an envelope under the tree instead of a toy, but as the years went on and the dividend checks increased it became very much fun to get those envelopes in the mail with my dividend checks.

Griffeth: Do you remember what the first stocks were?

Rogers: They were really conservative. Commonwealth Edison, General Motors, IBM, those kind of things.

> ◆
>
> *". . . I would read the quarterly reports and the annual reports and any information that I could get my hands on about the companies and just cash the checks."*
>
> ◆

Griffeth: What did you do with them?

Rogers: As the quarterly reports would come in, and as I got a little older, I would read the quarterly reports and the annual reports and any information that I could get my hands on about the companies and just cash the checks. He did not allow me to sell anything until I got to be 18.

Griffeth: What was he trying to accomplish?

Rogers: He wanted me to learn about something he thought was important for a young person to know. Especially a young minority person. My father grew up in the Depression (he is 75 years old now), and he just felt that African-American young people really were not being exposed to things they needed to be. And he wanted to make sure that I wasn't left out of that loop.

Griffeth: Did he want you to go into the financial services business?

Rogers: I think he wished I would have become a lawyer like him and my mother and my grandfather.

Griffeth: Why didn't you?

Rogers: I loved the stock market. I really did.

Griffeth: Is it a result of your first exposure from these gifts from your father?

Rogers: I think that's the only place I could have gotten it. By the time I got to college at Princeton he turned the portfolio over to me. I had a broker in Princeton, and I had a broker back in Chicago who was also my Dad's broker. And whenever I had a free moment I was in their offices, whether it was during the summer or during the school year, watching the tape and gathering newsletters and finding new information.

Griffeth: I've read where that broker in Princeton had an enthusiasm for the markets that rubbed off on you.

Rogers: He did. His name is Michael Perkins. He called just the other day with a stock idea for me, so he still stays involved. But you are right, he took me over to the library and showed me where I could find *Value Line* and where I could find other newsletters, and he used to get the O'Neil charts. He was very, very enthusiastic.

Griffeth: So your education at Princeton was helpful, but it was the education you received off-campus that helped determine your career.

Rogers: Yes, it really did.

Griffeth: Why did you pursue the economics degree?

Rogers: I took Soviet politics my freshman year and almost flunked. And I took economics 101, and I got an A. So it just told me I had better stick to what I know best.

Griffeth: You were the captain of the basketball team at Princeton while you were there. Your coach was quoted one time as saying about you, "He always knew what he could and could not do, and he worked hard at doing what he did best."

Rogers: Well that's a lesson that Coach [Pete] Carril really taught me. When I got to Princeton he said, "You don't pass well, and you will never be able to pass well." Now hearing for the first time in your life that you have limits on what you can accomplish is a startling thing at that age, you know. So I learned to work on things that I could do well. I played defense and those kinds of things to make a contribution to the team. You have to work hard on things where you can add value.

Griffeth: Did you use that same lesson in investing?

Rogers: Oh, very, very much so. Sticking to things you do know well. Warren Buffet talks a lot about staying within your circle of competence. That is very, very essential.

Boston Chicken vs. Bob Evans Farms

Griffeth: You are a value-oriented investor. What kind of an investment mind does it take to be a value investor as opposed to, say, a growth investor?

Rogers: I think you have to be a natural contrarian, naturally skeptical. You just don't believe in the status quo on anything. If something's going really well, I'm just always looking for what's going to go wrong. And if something is going really wrong, I'm always looking to see what could go right. To pick stocks the way we do, I think, you have to sort of be that way naturally.

Griffeth: You started Ariel at the beginning of the bull market of the 1980s, in 1983. And much was made of the fact that while many of your peers were going after the momentum-oriented issues of the time, you were still going for the small cap markets. So there is an example right there of your contrarian nature.

Rogers: Exactly. And it's interesting that that's when we performed the best, too. That was the period where the aggressive growth small cap managers were struggling. But we did very well. And then when the aggressive growth managers finally had their day in the sun in the last 3 years, then we did not look as good because we were sticking to our tried and true method of buying things that are out of favor. There are cycles for every strategy.

Griffeth: So your investment style isn't suitable to all business or economic cycles.

Rogers: No, it really isn't. We typically do the worst in periods in which small, aggressive stocks are booming. That's when we don't look so terrific.

Griffeth: And you're willing to accept that? How do you handle those periods? Do you try to do something different in those down cycles?

Rogers: What we try to do is stick to what we do best, because we know that our day will come again. We have to keep reminding ourselves, as well as our clients, that we have a turtle as our logo, that patience wins out in the long run, and the turtle really does win the race at the end.

For example, Bob Evans Farms is our kind of stock while Boston Chicken isn't. Now Boston Chicken went bounding way up to $50.00 when it came public because it is an exciting kind of glamour growth stock. Meanwhile, Bob Evans, day to day, is just serving terrific breakfasts and good sausages to people. And we think in five years you'll make more money owning Bob Evans than you will Boston Chicken, because they [Bob Evans] have proven they are good at what they do.

Griffeth: Are your shareholders willing to accept that? Especially when a Boston Chicken comes to market and has such an incredible performance initially, overshadowing a company like Bob Evans Farms.

Rogers: One thing that I have learned is, and I've learned this in the last three or four years—I've been doing this almost 12—is that there are people who aren't going to understand what we do. They are always going to buy what's exciting and hot, and they are going to be very unhappy with you when you stick to your slow growth mode and patient philosophy. You are going to lose some of those clients, but you are also going to attract strong believers who believe in what you do. And they will be with you forever. They will stick with you through the down cycles, because they understand what you do and agree with it philosophically themselves. So, you end up with some stronger relationships.

Rogers the Entrepreneur

Griffeth: Let me go back to the beginning again for a moment. When you left Princeton you went to work at William Blair, initially to be a broker.

Rogers: Yes.

Griffeth: Did that not suit John Rogers's personality?

Rogers: Not really, because you're being paid per transaction, and I realized pretty quickly that if you really were a good value manager you owned stocks for the long term. (That's why we call our newsletter *The Patient Investor.*) If I were a broker, I would never get paid for buying a stock and holding it forever. In the brokerage business you need to have transactions occurring all the time, and I was actually trying to do the opposite.

And the second reason I didn't stay at Blair is being a broker doesn't give you the opportunity to focus. You really end up with lots of clients who have different needs, and I wanted a chance to really focus on the kinds of stocks I believed in.

Griffeth: How long did it take you to decide to start your own mutual fund?

◆

"Here I was 24-years-old, leaving a good job at a terrific firm to just go into the unknown."

◆

Rogers: It took me about 2 years to really realize that. The great thing about William Blair was they had a money management division and a mutual fund division, and when I saw what they did I realized, hey, this is what I should be doing. But it did take about 2 years for me to come to that conclusion.

Griffeth: Did you find much skepticism about wanting to start a money management firm of your own?

Rogers: I did. Here I was 24-years-old, leaving a good job at a terrific firm to just go into the unknown. Of course my father was the biggest skeptic.

Griffeth: And yet he was one of your original investors.

Rogers: Yes, he gave me a good bit of capital to help me start. So did my mom.

Griffeth: And you had to go back to the well a second time, as I understand it. The company obviously didn't take off in the beginning, and you had to go back for a second infusion of cash.

Rogers: You know the good thing we did during that period was we had regular board meetings, and we kept our shareholders informed on the progress we were making. So it was easier the second time around—even though it was painful to do—to say, "We are out of money." We could show that we had demonstrated steady progress, so people were pretty good about re-upping their commitments to the firm.

Griffeth: You also needed to show a track record. How did you do that?

Rogers: We did that two ways. First, with the newsletter, *The Patient Investor*, we kept track of all the stocks that we recommended each month in each issue. We created a way of showing how those stocks as a portfolio were performing.

And second, we had this partnership that I ran in those early days called The Ariel Fund, and I went to anyone I knew and asked them to put money in. I raised about $500,000 the first 6 months of 1983, and ever since then I've had a real live performance track record that I could point to.

On Being a Mutual Fund Manager

Griffeth: So what are the skills you need to be a successful mutual fund manager?

Rogers: I think the most important thing is discipline. You have to have a very disciplined process of deciding whether or not a company fits into your portfolio. You just can't do it based on how you feel that morning when you wake up. Some broker will call on the phone with a hot tip, and he'll be very persuasive about why I should buy this or look into that. And I can't respond based on some emotion. So I think the most important thing is having a very keen sense of discipline when you are looking at companies and making decisions.

I think the second thing, from a marketing point of view, is to be able to communicate your philosophy clearly and succinctly. Because prospective clients and institutions often have only a few minutes to hear your story. So you have to get it across and make it intuitively obvious why it makes sense. I think people get scared to death when it's too complicated and they can't really get their arms around why it makes sense to invest in a specific strategy.

The third thing I think that has been essential to me all along: I think you have to do an extraordinary amount of reading. I know, for example, when each magazine comes in each week, each month. I do little things like go out to O'Hare Airport on Sunday evenings to get *Time* and *Newsweek* and *U.S. News & World Report.*

Griffeth: Because they hit the airports first.

Rogers: Exactly. Saturday morning I know where I can get the *Barron's* early. And I can read parts of the Sunday papers early on Saturday morning. I'm always trying to make sure that I maximize each day to be able to get as much information as possible.

Every day I go out of the office and do a lot of reading. McDonald's is really my favorite place to go. I just have a Coke over there and spread out all the research reports and new magazines that come in and read them in peace. If I tried to do it at the office I would never get it done with brokers calling and clients calling and the computer screen showing what our stocks are doing.

Griffeth: Just out of curiosity, do you own shares of McDonald's?

Rogers: [laughing] No, I don't. I'll have to buy some! They're one of our clients.

Griffeth: Are you the type who also keeps a stack of prospectuses and annual reports on your night stand beside your bed?

Rogers: No, I read those things during the day or when I go and stop at McDonald's. In the evenings, though, I love to read books. And that's another issue if you're building a business. I love to read books about leadership and how other people have been successful at what they do. I think that's essential. It also helps me become a better stock picker because I can compare success stories I've read to the businesses that I'm evaluating.

That's a lot of what I do when I'm reading: trying to see patterns of behavior that lead to success and patterns of behavior that lead to failure.

On Being African American

Griffeth: At the time you were hired, you were the first African-American professional employee at William Blair & Company. I can see how being African American would open some doors to unique contacts, and I can see how it might work against you. Speak to that issue.

Rogers: I think as the years have gone on it has been helpful, because we've been so unique. If you pick up a *Money* magazine or a *Financial World* you won't see any black faces anywhere. And if you look at ads for mutual funds you don't see any minority faces. But people are interested in diversity these days. I'm on a lot of nonprofit boards, and people are talking about it all the time.

So if they find someone like myself or our firm, and they feel we are competent and bring some diversity to their institution, it's helpful. So I have to say that it's been helpful.

The down side is clearly that there are some people out there who resent the fact that we've been able to accomplish what we have been able to accomplish so far. It's still a struggle everyday. There are certain people who are always going to be skeptical because of your race, or your age, so you sort of have to prove yourself over and over while some of your competition doesn't have to do that. We work very, very hard.

Griffeth: Is it a motivating factor for you, though?

Rogers: Only in that we really don't want to fail now because of what we have created. Sometimes nice things are said about us because we were the first [minority-owned mutual fund] firm. We have set a standard for other firms that have come along. And we've tried to do things in the community to be role models here in Chicago. So it would be horrible to fail now.

You just don't want to be set up as a role model and then fail everyone. So that adds an extra level of pressure, but it also gives us the extra drive to try to do things the best that we can do. To get the best people around us to do the best job possible.

Investing with a Conscience

Griffeth: You're also known as a socially conscious investor. How did that start?

Rogers: Socially responsible investing for me originally revolved around the South African issue. Since we were the first African-American-owned investment company, Howard University was our first institutional client. It was important for us to say that we agreed with the school's leaders on these issues. We wanted to send a powerful signal to South Africa's leadership by not investing in companies that had factories there. And we wanted to encourage corporate America not to have factories over in South Africa.

That's been the real core of socially responsible issues for our firm. And there are some other things that we've done along the way that we think are also important. We think it's important to invest in companies that are doing positive things for the environment. In the long run if you are a good corporate citizen we think you are going to be a more successful business.

> "We wanted to send a powerful signal to South Africa's leadership by not investing in companies that had factories there."

Griffeth: So let me be clear. You found that you needed to be something of a socially responsible investment manager in order to attract the kinds of clients you were after. Or did you bring that to the table to begin with?

Rogers: We brought the South African issue to the table to begin with. That's very clear. We believed in that very strongly. And just getting that first account—the first account that was interested in that issue—just sort of made us focus on that right away.

Griffeth: Of course socially responsible investing is a broad category. Investing in South Africa was the key issue for a time. But then it broadened to nuclear power, to weapons production, to animal testing for certain chemicals and perfumes, and so forth. How far do you take it?

Rogers: For us, we are very much on the conservative end when it comes to this. When we get past South Africa, which is a morally right thing for us to do as an African-American company, the others have really been only things where we could realize that it was going to help us be better investors.

We did not happen to get into animal testing or into some of these other issues that some people did. And we decided we wouldn't invest in nuclear power companies simply because we think in the long run they are not good consistent growth industries. You don't know what's going to happen with the different regulatory bodies making decisions on the future of nuclear power.

When it comes to military armament manufacturers, we felt that with the world becoming more of a peaceful place, with the Soviet Union getting easier to deal with, this was not going to be a good long-term growth business. Future presidents would be closing bases around the United States and therefore defense companies would not be as successful.

We look at those themes from an investment point of view. But from a socially conscious standpoint, we really do care a lot about the quality of the people who run the companies we invest in. We want to be involved with business leaders who attract and retain good people and care about providing a quality product. They don't just want to make a lot of money quickly. And they realize that the way you build a business and make it succeed is to care about your customer.

We think that good returns come from the Sam Waltons of the world who say, "We're going to have a greeter in front of the store, and we are going to make sure that the product is priced effectively and that you have the right product there when you need it." That's why he became so successful. If he had taken shortcuts and forgot about product quality he would not have achieved what he did.

Wal-Mart

Griffeth: Let me play devil's advocate on Wal-Mart. They were charged with being anticompetitive with the way they priced some of their products. The charge was they tried to put smaller competitors out of business in some areas. Does that change your mind about a company like that?

Rogers: Those kinds of things are very important to us. As it happens, we don't own Wal-Mart. It's too big for us. Maybe my Sam Walton analogy pertains more to his early years. But I still think it's valid.

Griffeth: You get my point, though. Obviously not every company can be perfectly clean or doesn't fit all the criteria. Certainly it can get a good reputation for one area where it passes the muster with socially conscious mutual funds. But it might not pass in another area.

Rogers: Right, and what is socially responsible, as you said earlier, to one group is not to another group. It's like the old saying: You know it when you see it.

We have shares in a company, Superior Surgical, that we've owned for quite a long time. We're in the process of selling it now, though, because they have been accused by the government of doing some things with a contract that were not appropriate. When we see that kind of information it raises a huge red flag to us. If they weren't operating their business in a way that was satisfactory to the government regulatory bodies, then it's a major concern of ours.

Griffeth: So as a socially conscious investor, are you trying truly to have an impact by not investing or are you merely trying to invest with a clear conscious?

Rogers: We are doing both, I guess. We want to invest in businesses that we feel comfortable with. At the same time, if we think that we can make a difference by talking to the leadership about developing a more diverse management team, we do that also.

Griffeth: Let me knit-pick a couple more things on the socially conscious issue. I noticed in your bio that you sat on the board of G. Heileman Brewing. I found that rather interesting. You sat on the board of an alcoholic beverage company as a socially conscious investor.

Rogers: Actually I'm no longer on the board, but I did look long and hard at that issue. I don't have a problem with drinking beer from time to time or having a drink from time to time. That's not one of those issues that bothers me at all. But I do get a lot of letters from people, socially responsible investors, whose goals on this issue are different from mine. Gaming is another one where we get major criticism.

Griffeth: When does the criticism start to have an impact? If enough people complain or if there are enough redemptions, does that change your opinion? Or do you stick to your guns?

Rogers: We stick to our guns and do what we believe in and what we're comfortable with.

Money Management vs. Company Management

Griffeth: It seems that every time I call your office you are on an airplane going somewhere. You do an awful lot of traveling don't you?

Rogers: Yes I do. I'm chief executive of our company as well as the co-chief investment officer and portfolio manager of one of our mutual funds. So I really have to wear a lot of hats here. And so sometimes I'm out visiting companies meeting management, other times I'm out seeing institutional clients, and other times I'm out talking to people about our mutual funds. So it really does keep me on the road a lot. And what I've learned to do, which is another important discipline, is to have all of my mail messengered to me during the day wherever I am. So the research that comes here in the morning at 7 A.M. gets on the first plane out to wherever I happen to be. My assistant spends more time gathering information and getting it to me than probably anything else that she does here for me. It's sort of an elaborate process: the messengers meet me at airports, at hotels, in restaurants, at client meetings. I have packages waiting for me here, there, and everywhere.

I think it's extremely important because when I get to a hotel in the evening I can read, when I'm on a plane coming back from California I can read, when I'm in a cab going from meeting to meeting I can read. The joke in the office is that I can't walk by a newsstand anywhere without going in to see if there is any news in there that I need to see.

Griffeth: You left Blair because you wanted to be able to focus and be a stock picker. This doesn't sound too focused to me.

You're all over the place. Do you foresee a time when you would be able to devote more time to managing the fund's portfolio?

Rogers: I should point out that I have a friend from Princeton who joined us two years ago. I played basketball with him on the team. He's our chief operating officer now. So now I don't get involved with personnel issues and the day-to-day details of getting computers up to speed and changing office space and all that kind of thing. I also have another person who does all the regulatory work. As you know this is a heavily regulated industry, and we want to make sure that we do those things exceptionally well. So I'm freed up from those two things, and I'm really left with portfolio management and client service. I think I'll have to continue to do those things my entire career because clients want to talk to me when they are interested in our funds. I don't think there is any way I can really delegate that even though I do have a couple of really good people now who help me with it. And we are going to be interviewing more help on the client services side.

One of the down sides of money management versus mutual funds—we're in both businesses—is that [private account] clients want to see you in person. They want their due diligence. They want to talk to you about why you bought this stock. They want to know what you're thinking about the future and how your organization is evolving, and they don't accept your number two person.

Griffeth: And with mutual funds?

Rogers: With mutual funds I think it is a little bit easier because each individual investor doesn't feel the need to call. I talk to them all the time, but most of them don't try to call me directly.

Mutual Fund Cycles

Griffeth: Is the explosion of cash coming into mutual funds good or bad for the industry?

Rogers: Well I think it's very, very good that people are leaving money in mutual funds more and more and not trying to pick stocks themselves. I think the down side right now, though, is that we're clearly at the height of an extraordinary amount of interest. There are magazines coming out about mutual funds, and people are so excited about it, and there are funds that have been going up 30 percent a year for three or four years in a row. That usually means that there's some kind of correction in the offing sometime.

Griffeth: How do you think it will play itself out, John?

Rogers: I think what you're going to see is a fairly dramatic decline when people realize that stocks go down as well as up. I don't want to be too alarmist, but I do think that when you get to a point where you have so many large companies like Fidelity where everyone's talking to voice mail and computers and the human touch is lost to some degree, it's worrisome.

◆

"I think you'll find that when the markets really do correct it could be a fairly dramatic thing where people are desperate to get out and wash their hands of mutual funds."

◆

So I think you'll find that when the markets really do correct it could be a fairly dramatic thing where people are desperate to get out and wash their hands of mutual funds. It could cause a really severe decline, especially in aggressive growth funds.

Ariel's Future

Griffeth: As we speak, the Ariel Growth Fund is closed to new investors. Do you have plans to reopen at some time?

Rogers: That's something that we'll look at next year. Right now we are comfortable with it being closed. We closed it at $200,000,000 and right now it's about $195,000,000. We don't want to go backwards too much, so it will be under discussion. But I think it will be more like 1995 before we would get around to that.

Griffeth: When you closed Ariel Growth you brought out the Ariel Appreciation Fund. Could you see adding more funds to the family?

Rogers: Right now we really don't. I think that as the years go on if we found some terrific firm that would want to subadvise a fund of ours, that would be something we would look at. We are always going to be a relatively small fund family. We don't want to be all things to all people, but we really believe in having a strong set of beliefs and themes. So it will be a rare occurrence if we found somebody really terrific who would come in and manage another fund for us.

ERIC RYBACK

Birth Date: March 19, 1952

Education: Idaho State University, B.S. in Secondary Education

Hobbies: Fly fishing

Alternate Career: Mountaineering guide and outfitter

*T*he Eric Ryback story is going to make a terrific movie someday. I see Richard Dreyfus playing the young man who—in the late 1970s—leads wealthy people on wilderness trail vacations in Idaho, listening to them talk about the stock market around the campfire. Fast forward to 1992 where the young man—still only 40—takes over an investment company that includes two of the hottest, best-known, and best performing mutual funds in the country.

How Ryback got from point A to point B takes up a portion of the interview for this book. It is a fascinating story full of chance, determination, chutzpah, and good old-fashioned American luck.

In 1992, Ryback bought out his long-time mentor Kurt Lindner and created Ryback Management, which oversees five funds: the Lindner Fund, the Lindner Dividend Fund, the Lindner Bulwark Fund (an asset allocation fund or what Ryback calls a contrarian fund), the Lindner Utility Fund, and the Lindner/Ryback Small Cap Fund.

Personality-wise, Ryback seems more suited to the wilds of Idaho than the high rises of Wall Street. He is a pleasant, self-effacing man with an easy smile and a vocabulary that includes words like "gosh," (which he used twice during our interview). But intellectually, there is no doubt he is cut out for professional money management. His mastery of the fundamental approach to security analysis first developed in 1934 by Benjamin Graham and David Dodd has made him a consistently successful fund manager. Between 1982, when he took over management of Lindner Dividend, and 1994 when I interviewed him for this book, the fund has been among the top 25 percent of all income funds eight separate years, according to Morningstar.

*During our interview, Ryback talked about his very
successful investment philosophy, his Horatio Alger–like success
story, about how the Lindner Dividend Fund was almost shut
down in the early 1980s with only $600,000 in assets, and about
how he corners the market in "sinkers."*

AUGUST 4, 1994

Low Risk and High Return

Bill Griffeth: Your funds are known for providing a higher than average yield with lower than average risk. How do you do that?

Eric Ryback: First we look for things that are higher yielding than what the average is.

Griffeth: But higher yield usually means higher risk.

Ryback: That's correct, but the way we get around that is we are fundamentalist value investors. We look for securities or bonds that are trading at the deep discounts which create those high yields.

Griffeth: What are the criteria that you look at that tell you that you are getting a better yield with the lower risk? What specifically do you look for?

Ryback: Well, we really look at the strength of the company and the only way you can determine that is through the balance sheet. We really scour the balance sheet looking for hidden assets, buildings, or property plant and equipment that's fully depreciated, or large pools of cash. Sometimes a company will have large pools of money, but because of the industry they are in, the banks may be reluctant to do much with them as far as lending. So they have to go out and issue some very attractive pieces of paper.

Griffeth: So you look at strong balance sheets in unloved sectors of the economy. Is that what you are saying?

Ryback: Absolutely. Or companies that are overlooked.

Discovering Undiscovered Companies

Griffeth: I'm always amazed to hear fund managers talk about companies that are overlooked. With all the research on Wall Street, all the mutual funds, all the investors, how in the world can a company be overlooked?

Ryback: Well, you are right. That's a very good question. I would say 12 years ago that there really were overlooked companies. I mean there were lots of them.

And there still are because of all the new issues being brought out. Depending on the market cycle, they can be really hot, then they can become very cold, very unloved, and I think they become overlooked by people who have lost money in them. And what happens to these companies is they fall into a crack and people say, "Yes, I remember that company, I lost money on it." That's how they become really overlooked.

Griffeth: I guess they become unmarketable.

Ryback: Unmarketable, right. We try to get on every brokerage firm's mailing list for IPOs, and we have extensive files on them here. That is one of our fortes, I think. We just file them and go back and take a look at them after about a year. You'd be surprised at the number of issues that have come out, fallen off, and people are not covering them.

Griffeth: You make it sound so easy. Is it? Are there more problem companies than winners when you go for some of these unloved issues? I mean they have to be underfollowed and unloved for some reason.

Ryback: Well, yes, there are a lot of companies out there in that category. But it's also true that brokerage firms want to tout things that are easy to sell. And once a company falls by the wayside or something happens to it and it becomes unloved, there may still be a story there but people don't want to be bothered spending a little time looking into it.

Griffeth: How patient do you have to be with these companies? If they are unloved, what's going to make them loved all of the sudden?

Ryback: Well, their earnings performance. That's where we go back to our fundamental analysis approach. The value approach. We know the value is there. If we can identify a company that's in a turnaround phase where something happened to the company that was temporary, we want to be able to identify that and say yes, this company is really worth more. Often, because they had three bad quarters everybody dumped the stock. It's down and no firm has bothered to pick it up and cover it again. These are the ones we are looking for, where the company picks itself up and we've accumulated stock by then and we ride it up.

Griffeth: I read where you don't make it a habit to talk directly to the company's management.

Ryback: That's correct.

Griffeth: Why?

Ryback: Well, everybody wants to be optimistic about their business. Human nature is to tend to overlook the problems within the company, and they will always want to tell you the good things. Well, once you've been sold the story, then human nature for the buyer is you just want to hear all the good things. You tend to tune out after a while.

The company will say, "We're going to have a good quarter," and they don't come in with a good quarter. So you call them, and they say, "You know, we were going to have a good quarter but we had two production lines that were down for one month out of the quarter and we lost revenue. But we've got them fixed now, and we should come out with a good quarter this next quarter coming up." Well, all of a sudden they don't have another good quarter. You call them again. "Well, gosh, this time Joe was out there and he couldn't get the sales that we were anticipating." So you say, well that's okay, I'll hang in there. Eventually, you figure out that the company really has problems and now you are stuck because you've got higher cost stock and the stock has reacted to these negative earnings. That's why we strictly go by the numbers.

The only way we ever really get involved with a company or call them is when we do own it and we're anticipating something and it doesn't come through and we can't figure out why. Then we'll call them and try to get an answer.

Investing in Sinkers

Griffeth: You often will invest in what could be considered rather eclectic investments, like a sinker. What is that?

Ryback: Let's say a company issues a 10-year bond. After the first five years the company is allowed to start—actually it's mandatory—they have to start repurchasing a certain percentage of those bonds so that by the maturity date all the bonds have been retired.

So after the first five years what is termed "the sinker" starts, where the company has to *sink out*, or buy back X percentage of these bonds. A lot of traditional bond buyers really don't like it. They stay away from them because they say, "I've got a piece of paper that's got a 12 percent coupon on it, and after five years they will start taking it away from me."

I can sympathize with those types of bond buyers, but I look at it differently. I'm here running a portfolio for my shareholders, and I want that sinker—particularly if it's a company I really like—even if interest rates are declining. I will have to cross that bridge when I come to it about trying to replace that coupon, but I have a lot of security knowing that the company is forced to buy back that bond.

Griffeth: It provides you with some liquidity.

Ryback: Yes, and it also provides me with the comfort that after that first five years they've got to start buying it back. And if there is nothing wrong with the company, then I want to buy up as much of it as I possibly can. I want to own the whole issue. That's called cornering the sinker. Ultimately you control it so that in that second five-year period the company has to only make one phone call, and that's to me. And if the bonds are trading at a discount, and they can't buy them back in the open market at a discount, then they are forced to take them off my hands at par. And that, by the way, is one of the key factors in providing the really low beta [or volatility] that our funds have.

Griffeth: You are the Bunker Hunt of the sinker market. [Laughing]

Ryback: [Also laughing] Absolutely, but I like it.

"We Never Have, and We Never Will"

Griffeth: If you are in investments that take some time to realize the kind of return you are after, your investors have to be pretty patient.

Ryback: They are patient, and they are very secure. Knock on wood, the negative redemption days during the history of the fund you could probably count on two hands.

Griffeth: Is that a function of how you market the fund, that people understand going in, that you make it very clear how it works?

Ryback: Absolutely. We don't really market it, it's word of mouth. We don't advertise, but what the press and the public have come to realize is that these are very conservatively run funds and we don't get a lot of mass redemptions forcing me to sell off a portion of the portfolio, which generates higher turnover. A good example is with those sinking bonds. We buy our bonds for yield to maturity so our intent is to hold them to maturity. And therefore we can generate this low turnover rate. Now, last year it did spike up into the 40 percent area, but that was a rare occurrence for that fund and simply a result of interest rates dropping so low that a lot of the companies called their bonds in or redeemed the bonds prematurely to issue a lower coupon.

Griffeth: Given the tremendous number of funds, the competition out there, why don't you market the funds?

Ryback: We've never marketed them. We don't believe in advertising.

Griffeth: You don't believe in advertising your product?

Ryback: That's correct. I've always said, "We never have, and we never will," and people say "Never say never."

I don't know about the "never will," but Kurt [Lindner] was very adamant about performance. And he did not believe in advertising. He believed if you performed, people would invest in the fund, and obviously we are proving that. We haven't grown aggressively. I think we could have if we had tooted our own horn but you can't believe the amount of shareholders I think that would become a little bit disappointed if we did go out and try to start advertising.

Griffeth: Your expense ratio would go up.

Ryback: It certainly would, and we are known for having a low expense ratio and just being very conservative.

Griffeth: But aren't you feeling the heat of the competition these days?

> *"He [Kurt Lindner] believed if you performed, people would invest in the fund, and obviously we are proving that."*

Ryback: That's a good question. I think I'm a little bit more aware of it, although we still kind of work in a vacuum here. We are a little more conscious of our competition, and we are trying to enhance our performance. So in some ways it is good that we've become a little more aware of it.

Yes, I can't deny that it's become quite competitive, and we are capable and ready to compete. The people who will benefit will be the shareholders.

Griffeth: What are you trying to do to improve the performance? Are you changing your investment style?

Ryback: We aren't really changing the style as much as . . . we did everything by hand up until I took over 18 months ago.

Griffeth: There were no computers?

Ryback: No.

Griffeth: You are kidding!? [Laughing]

Ryback: No. [Also laughing] I said, "We have to get into the 20th century before it leaves us," and we've done that now. That's one way we are becoming more competitive. We realize our competition has been able using computers for many years now, running screens, and they've been able to get to things maybe a little bit faster than us, so we've had to compete in that arena.

Man Mountain Ryback

Griffeth: That's amazing! Let's go back to the beginning. Tell me about your mountaineering days

Ryback: Well, I took three long backpacking trips in 1969, 1970, and 1972. I hiked the Appalachian Trail from Maine to Georgia in 1969 and then the Pacific Crest in 1970. (That goes from Canada to Mexico through Washington, Oregon, and California.) And then in 1972 I hiked the Continental Divide, which runs from Canada to Mexico through Montana, Wyoming, Colorado, and New Mexico. And as a result of that I wrote a couple books about the experiences I had on the trips. I only mention that because I had a tremendous drive, I guess, to be in the out-of-doors, and I gained a lot of knowledge. So I felt very comfortable wanting to be an outfitter.

My wife and I were out West guiding people in the mountains. But I realized I had to have something to fall back on. So my parents said, "Well, if you become a teacher you could teach during the school year and you'll have your summers off and you can guide people." And I thought that wouldn't be a bad combination. It would fulfill this love that I had of the out-of-doors.

Well, when I got into the outfitting business, particularly in Idaho, the most successful outfitters were running rafting trips down the rivers. It was harder to sell my product, which was really backpacking, hiking and fly fishing, and such. So from 1976 to 1980 I ran this business, and when we had the slowdown in the economy by 1980 my business had fallen off. The only outfitters who were really surviving had river permits. But they were very expensive and they were on an allocation basis, so I sold the business and my wife and I decided to re-educate ourselves. So we came back to Michigan where I was born and raised.

Griffeth: How did you decide on banking or finance?

Ryback: Well, the customers that I had were somewhat wealthy individuals who could afford these trips, and around the campfires they would discuss buying and selling stocks. And I thought, "That's a pretty neat way to make money."

I should also point out that when I got back to Michigan I took a battery of tests to determine my aptitude. To see if finance was something I should pursue. And, in fact, all the tests led to finance, so I said, "Okay, let me pursue this."

So I answered an ad in the paper about being a security specialist for Ann Arbor Trust Company, and that's where I got my feet wet. First I was hired as a purchase sales specialist. That fancy title meant I settled all the trades that the trust department executed during the day. I matched buys and sells. And then after doing that for about 10 months one of the trust officers who happened to like me said, "How would you like to be my assistant?" So I helped him run the portfolios he was responsible for, and that's where I really got my introduction to fundamental analysis.

My boss turned me on to Ben Graham, and I really absorbed that. I couldn't get enough of fundamental analysis. I read everything I could, and I enrolled in an MBA program at Eastern Michigan University. I read about all the value players. You know, Ben Graham, Warren Buffet, Tweedy Brown. And I also wrote to Kurt Lindner. I wasn't seeking a job, just information about how they traded, how they looked for stocks.

"How Would You Like to Come to Work for Me?"

Griffeth: What was it about fundamental analysis that attracted you?

Ryback: The fact that, by following certain steps, you could value a company and determine its worth. In studying the market I could not understand technical analysis. There were too many unknown factors that could affect what you were trying to determine, like when to buy and when to sell securities. But what appealed to me was the basic approach of determining what value there was in a company. I was fascinated by these fundamental analysts who wrote books. I could read them, I could understand them, and I wanted to emulate that in some way. And so I absorbed everything I could. I wrote to the people who were still alive, who were still actually doing it, such as Warren Buffet and Tweedy Brown. And they wrote me back.

Griffeth: What kind of dialogue were you after?

Ryback: I did research in the library. And I would read articles in magazines or newspapers or other publications. They would either be interviews with them or articles they had written. And I would try to figure out what they were doing, and if I couldn't I would just write them a letter and say, "You said this about this, and could you clarify it for me?"

Some people wrote back and politely said that I was on the right track, but they would not divulge any more information. And one gentleman, Kurt Lindner, picked up the phone and said, "How would you like to come work for me?"

Griffeth: This is without having met you?

Ryback: Without ever having met me. It was just the letter I wrote to him. I was dumfounded. This was on a Friday when he offered me a job, and I said, "I really don't know you and you don't know me and we could be two incompatible people."

And he said, "Well, I thought about that. There is a plane ticket waiting for you to come down this Sunday so that we could discuss this further."

Griffeth: That must have been some letter you wrote! [Laughing]

Ryback: Apparently so! [also laughing] So I talked to my wife and said I'm not going to miss any work. I'll just go down for the day. So I hopped on a plane and went down and talked to him. By the end of that day he offered me a job again.

Griffeth: Were you willing to accept at that point?

Ryback: Well, no, we had a six-month-old child—our first—and my wife was in a master's program for nursing, and so I said, "I'm flattered, but I have to go back and discuss this with my wife." And he sort of understood.

But then I made the mistake of saying, "Well, I'd have to give my current employer two weeks' notice." And he said, "Okay, you can come work for me in two weeks." He had originally wanted me to start that next day.

Griffeth: [Laughter]

Ryback: [Also laughing] You could call him and ask him. This is all true!

So I told him, "Well, let me go back and think about this." And, without getting into too much detail, two weeks later I was working for him.

Griffeth: Oh my!

Ryback: I left my wife and child up in Michigan. I said let's give this about six months and see if it works out. Then we'll make a move.

Getting Started

Griffeth: What did you do to begin with for Kurt?

Ryback: I was a researcher. We had the six-volume set of the S&P corporation records, and he just said, "Go to work and find us some good stocks." [Laughing]

He gave me quite a few words of encouragement. He had said when I was interviewing—well, not interviewing but talking to him on that Sunday—he said I knew as much as somebody who had been in the business for six years. He said, "Let me teach you what I know. If you want to continue your education you can, but please let me teach you what I know first." I never went back to finish the MBA.

So I worked 16 hours a day, six days a week for the first four years just devouring everything I could. I would find an idea that I thought would fit. I would take it into Kurt, he would go over it, take it home and come back the next day with a page full of questions. And that's how I was tutored by this genius.

After the first year I was assisting Kurt and Bob [Lange, Kurt Lindner's co-manager] with the funds. At that time the [Lindner] Dividend Fund had about $600,000 in it, and they were going to shut it down. I begged them not to. So Kurt said, "Okay, you take it."

Griffeth: What year was this?

Ryback: This was in 1983. The fund was so small at the time, we were only pricing it Wednesdays in the paper. [Laughing]

Griffeth: [Also laughing] As opposed to now when you have to have your fund's net asset value turned in each day by 5:30 P.M., or whatever the deadline is. [*NOTE: It's actually 5:45 P.M. now.*]

Ryback: I think the fund only had 22 shareholders. We could practically call them all on the phone.

Griffeth: [Laughing]. And, so you started managing this fund. How did you do at first?

Ryback: Well, it wasn't too difficult. About 85 percent of the fund was in high-yielding common stocks, and we had several takeover candidates, and that really enhanced the performance. But interest rates then were peaking. They were in the mid-teens, and we were afraid the yields were going to start coming down. So Kurt and I got together to devise a formula or a way of determining the intrinsic value of the bond in some of these companies that were issuing high-yield bonds. They eventually, through the courtesy of Drexel and Mike Milken, became junk bonds. So we put our heads together and devised this formula as a way of analyzing companies that had high-yielding bonds.

Griffeth: Is it proprietary? Can you explain it in English?

Ryback: No, I really can't other than to give you some generalities. We really focus very strongly on the balance sheet of a company, and earnings are secondary to it. We buy companies that really aren't earning money or showing a net income to the bottom line at times.

The ideal company has only one bond outstanding. It has a low debt-to-equity ratio, it has other assets that, if sold, could cover the bonds, or it actually has enough cash on the balance sheet to redeem them.

We put this formula together, and we started buying them for the portfolio. And as the fund gained popularity we actually closed the [Lindner Dividend] fund down.

Griffeth: What year was that?

Ryback: It was in early 1984.

Griffeth: Okay. Do you remember how large the fund was at that time?

Ryback: It was probably about a million dollars. Maybe $1.5 million.

Griffeth: Why did you close it down?

Ryback: The Lindner Fund had grown tenfold, because in 1981 it was number one [in its category]. In 1982 it had about $32 million [in assets] and by 1984 it had grown to $320 million, and so we closed the fund down.

So when shareholders called and found out the fund was closed, they said, "Well, do you have any other funds?" And we said, "Yes, we have a dividend fund. It's not the same objective though." And they said, "That doesn't matter. Send me the prospectus." So the dividend fund kind of took off. It started growing in size, and we were forced to put the money to work. So we focused on high-yield bonds, which later became junk bonds.

Griffeth: How did you manage through the tough years for junk bonds around 1989 and 1990?

Ryback: Well, actually the fund had a negative year, but we bought aggressively when junk bonds dropped off. They had quite a negative taint to them by that time.

Griffeth: And here again, your shareholders were understanding of that at the time?

Ryback: It's interesting. I think maybe in 1990 the press had heightened things to the point where it reached hysteria in some cases. And we did get some calls. I would be lying if I said we didn't have some shareholders who were concerned. But I think most of the shareholders didn't realize the junk bonds that we had in the portfolio were yielding 35 percent! Somehow they figured out, "Gosh, I guess that's how we get our high yields."

Griffeth: When did you reopen the Lindner Fund, by the way?

Ryback: Actually, we shut down the dividend fund for about a year [in the mid-1980s], and we opened them both after the crash of 1987. There were a lot of companies selling at deep discounts to their intrinsic value, and we bought aggressively because we had high cash positions.

Griffeth: You had enough money coming in when you opened them?

Ryback: Oh, money was pouring in. It was like the dam burst. They had been waiting for 3, 3-1/2, almost 4 years [for the Lindner Fund to reopen].

Ryback Management

Griffeth: Who first broached the subject of Eric Ryback taking over Lindner Management?

Ryback: Kurt was of the mind-set that he was never going to sell. But a combination of things came together: He had been in the business for over 40 years, the assets had grown to billions of dollars, and there was his multiple sclerosis. He had been diagnosed with the disease in 1981. So he finally started indicating that he was going to sell.

Griffeth: And he decided you should be the buyer, or how did that work?

Ryback: No, it really came down to who could get the money. Who could come up with the money. And I was able to jump that hurdle.

Griffeth: Where did you find the money?

Ryback: Ultimately, I did not find it in the banks, because there is no collateral in this business. So I ended up going to a longtime friend of about 20 years who fortunately was blessed with a lot of money within his family after his father sold their business. He and I are now partners.

Griffeth: So you bought Kurt out, and now suddenly you are the boss.

Ryback: Yes.

Griffeth: Tell me about that.

Ryback: Well, they were very exciting times. You know, Bob and Larry Callahan—who manages our Bulwark Fund—and I had many ideas. Kurt was obviously reluctant to expand the business by creating new funds. That was a result of his MS and being very content with just having the two funds. So we had quite a large wish list, and as soon as we consummated the deal I got into gear and started fulfilling those wishes immediately.

Griffeth: Like?

Ryback: As I said, we were still doing things by hand, and I realized that in order to become competitive, in order to fulfill our dreams of creating additional funds, that we would have to modernize our facilities. So I took over the last one-third of the floor that we're on here, computerized everything, and we are now our own transfer agent, too. So we did everything to enhance the shareholder services. We gave them an 800 number, for example.

On the management side I hired additional researchers, and we created three funds that we wanted to do desperately: a utility fund, a small cap fund, and a contrarian fund. And now we are just ready to launch a money market fund. You know, people wanted a way to be out of the market but still be very close to the funds.

Griffeth: So you've become a full menu company.

Ryback: Yes, and I did that in 18 months.

Griffeth: My goodness.

Ryback: It's been a very long, rough 18 months. I am happy to say that of the three new funds we have, two of them are doing an outstanding job. One of them, the utility fund, is number one in the country [in its category] since its inception.

Griffeth: When was that?

Ryback: It started October of 1993.

Griffeth: Right at the top [of the market for utility stocks].

Ryback: Right at the top. But, you know what, the [Dow Jones] Utility Index is down like 24 percent, and we are up just about 1 percent.

Griffeth: And how did you do that?

Ryback: Actually, it was an offshoot of the Lindner Fund's forte over the years. The success of that fund was its ability to buy and sell utilities very successfully.

During the late 1970s and 1980s, you could make a lot of money in utilities. We were able to identify particularly when they had all their nuclear problems and all the construction problems. We knew how to figure out how to analyze the cash flow of a utility and know when to buy them.

So we created this utility fund, but we wanted to be different. People perceive utilities as being rather boring, and we decided to redefine "utility," and we went worldwide. We included anything a consumer would pay for monthly or quarterly or annually. That covered services you don't necessarily need, but if you want them you are going to have to pay for them. Like cable TV and telephones, which most people have anyway.

But then we expanded further by going after companies that provide services to utility companies. Gas and oil transmission pipelines, companies that manufacture products for utilities such as telephones, cables, wires, whatever magic black boxes you need to hook up a cable to a telephone line, and so on.

So we just decided that if a certain utility segment was doing well then why not buy the companies that are going to provide them with the product they need to sell to their customers. And so that's what really separated that fund from most traditional utility funds.

Griffeth: This is an awful lot of expansion in a short period of time, Eric. How do you keep the expense ratio down?

Ryback: Well, Kurt taught me that. He was a CPA, and he ran a very, very tight ship. And I guess working with the man for almost 13 years I absorbed that. We watch every penny.

Mutual Fund Explosion

Griffeth: What do you think of the explosion of the mutual fund industry? I mean, you thought the dam broke in 1987, but my goodness, right now Lindner Dividend and the Lindner Fund each have over $1.5 billion in assets.

Ryback: Well, I'm very pleased for the industry. And I'm pleased for the people in the country who have a conduit to achieving a higher savings rate. Gosh, I want that myself.

Griffeth: All right, but have we achieved sort of a critical mass here where any new funds coming on board actually reduce the overall quality of the industry by diluting the total product?

Ryback: It's funny that you should ask that, because we have people in here who are actually doing a study for us about that same question.

Griffeth: The purpose being?

Ryback: Well, we just want to get an idea of how the Lindner Funds fit into this mutual fund business. I'm having it done just for my benefit to figure out where I want to take these funds in the future.

Griffeth: In other words, so many companies likes yours are rushing to bring a variety of funds to market. But are you perhaps suggesting you are going to have to find a niche in the industry, eventually?

◆

"What we think is going to happen is you are going to see a consolidation over the next three years where funds will start acquiring funds."

◆

Ryback: Well, I created the family of funds because the shareholders were asking for it. In other words, the fund industry forced my hand to do it, although we've been wanting to create these funds for several years. Kurt would tell you that.

Griffeth: But are you able to maintain the same quality you had with just the two funds? I mean you can only do so much.

Ryback: That's correct. I've hired people. As I said before, Larry Callahan is the portfolio manager for the Bulwark Fund. And I'm hiring other people to help. I can't do it all, that's for sure.

But, to answer your question, I don't think you are going to see many more new funds created. What we think is going to happen is you are going to see a consolidation over the next three years where funds will start acquiring funds. I mean, you are seeing this a little bit now, but I think you will see this become more prevalent over the next few years.

Griffeth: What's the downside, though? I mean, it seems that the industry runs in cycles of booms and busts. What's the next bust going to look like?

Ryback: Well, the last bust was the result of the 1973–1974 bear market where people were frustrated and eventually bailed out, and it was kind of a snowball effect.

Is that going to happen again? It could. We are definitely much larger now, so it could be worse. But I don't think so. I think consumers are better educated about how mutual funds work. Now if rates continue to go higher, you will see some exodus at some point. I don't know if it will be a mass exodus, but there will be a certain group of investors who will say, "Hey, I can get 12 percent from 30-year bonds. I'm very comfortable with that. I don't need the mutual fund any longer."

But I don't think we're going to see a disaster.

A. GARY SHILLING

Birth Date: May 25, 1937

Education: A.B. in physics from Amherst College (Magna Cum Laude, Phi Beta Kappa) M.A. and Ph.D. in Economics from Stanford University

Hobbies: Beekeeping

Alternate Career: Physicist

*T*he first thing you should know about Gary Shilling is that he doesn't manage a mutual fund. His economic consulting firm, A. Gary Shilling & Co., based in Springfield, NJ, manages private accounts for high net-worth individuals, plus a couple of limited partnerships. The first, Thematic Investment Partners, is a $50 million fund that closed to new investors in March of 1994. So a second L.P., Thematic Futures Fund was opened. The minimum investment required is $250,000. Shilling also writes a column for Forbes Magazine.

So why is Gary Shilling included in a book about mutual fund managers? He's here for two reasons: First, his limited partnerships are good examples of mutual funds' distant cousins, the hedge funds, which employ a freewheeling, no-holds-barred, very risky style of trading that sometimes turns a very smart profit. (Witness the whopping 148 percent Thematic Investment Partners returned to shareholders in 1993).

Shilling is also included in this book because of his rather unusual investment philosophy and methodology. Like Richard Hoey, the manager of the Dreyfus Growth & Income fund (see page 133), Shilling is an economist. But unlike so many fund managers who employ the so-called bottom up approach of filling a portfolio on a stock-by-stock basis, Shilling is a top-down kind of investor. In other words, he identifies broad economic, political, and even meteorological themes and then searches for investments that will benefit from them. And his style is unique, to say the least. I mean, who else do you know who invested in natural gas here in the United States because of a volcanic eruption that occurred halfway around the world in the Philippines?

To be sure, Shilling's investment style is unorthodox and risky. But, to date, it has been successful for him and his shareholders.

During our interview, Shilling and I discussed his freewheeling investment style, about why he doesn't place much value in the generally rosy forecasts from Wall St. economists (even though he used to be one), and about why he believes finding the economic glass half-empty is more profitable than finding it half-full.

JULY 19, 1994

Shilling's Early Days

Bill Griffeth: You didn't originally plan to be an economist.

Gary Shilling: That's correct. I was going to be a physicist, but then I had an attack of common sense my senior year [in college] and realized I didn't really want to be a research physicist.

Griffeth: That was a heck of a time to determine that.

Shilling: Yes it was. As a matter of fact, I had only one undergraduate course in economics, but I still had all the math that goes with physics. At that time Stanford was one of the first to pursue what's now the trend of graduate education in economics which is very quantitative. So I actually got through all the [undergraduate] course work without the economics but I had all the math and the guys who had all the economics hadn't taken any math and they had to go back and start taking calculus. It was amazing.

Griffeth: When did the economics bug bite you?

Shilling: During my senior year. I took a year off between my junior and senior year. I had an opportunity to do some traveling. A friend of mine's father had a fleet of oil tankers and I was sort of kicking around the world, just sort of getting from one place to another on the tanker and getting off and seeing the sites.

Griffeth: You weren't working on it?

Shilling: Well, I was technically a junior officer but it meant that I was playing bridge with the captains and writing their letters in English. They were all Italian crews. Liberian flags. Anyway, it was an opportunity to kind of think things through, and I came back and said, well, physics is fine and I was really dumb at the time. Physics was the toughest major at Amherst and so I was interested in taking all challenges, which was absolutely insane but as I say, I had an attack of common sense and decided that enough was enough of that.

Griffeth: So what was your first job out of college?

Shilling: After graduate school I went to work for Standard Oil in New Jersey (now Exxon) as an economist analyzing and forecasting the U.S. and Canadian economies. That was 1963–1967. Then I went with Merrill Lynch as their first economist. I set up their economics department, but I made a strategic blunder in that I forecast—correctly as it turns out—the 1969–1970 recession. Now that wasn't exactly being bullish on America, to use a Merrill Lynch term, so one Donald T. Regan (who was running the firm) [and who later became Treasury Secretary under Ronald Reagan] and I had a difference of opinion, which obviously he won. So I took my entire staff, left Merrill Lynch, and ended up at White Weld, another Wall Street firm, with no idea that in 1978 Merrill Lynch would buy White Weld.

Griffeth: Oh my goodness.

Shilling: So the story on Wall Street, which was absolutely correct, was that Shilling was the only guy fired twice by Don Regan. [laughing] So I decided to reduce the odds of that and set up my own firm in 1978 and, by golly, I haven't been fired by Don Regan since!

Griffeth: How difficult was it to hang out your own shingle?

Shilling: It really wasn't that difficult because we had developed within White Weld sort of an economic forecasting business working with financial institutions who were obviously interested in the economic outlook and how that affected the markets. I mean that's what Wall Street economists pretty much do.

Griffeth: So you were able to take your clientele with you?

Shilling: Yes. And it worked out very well, but let me just say in brief that starting a new business is tough enough. I mean, you arrive your first day at the office and your first instinct is boy, now I realize how much time I spent previously getting from here to there around the structure of the firm and you say, "Hallelujah, I don't have to worry about that anymore." But 37 seconds later you say, "Yes, but there's nobody to call up to order the typewriters and figure out which color the drapes are going to be." But we were lucky in that we already had business on the books, and, boy, revenues cover a multitude of mistakes.

Griffeth: Every time.

Shilling: I really sympathize with people who start with an idea but with no revenues and they have to do the selling while they're trying to run the business. At least we had a leg up on that.

Shilling on Wall Street Economists

Griffeth: Let me go back for a second. You alluded to what you felt the job of a Wall Street economist is. Do you want to add to that?

Shilling: I think generally Wall Street economists had been trying to forecast the economy in a macro sense for a general audience and how it affected interest rates, stock markets, etc. I think the job changed a great deal 10 or 15 years ago. The change was led by Citibank, which had a huge economics department. They had over 100 professionals at one point, and they turned out a magnificent newsletter.

But then they subjected that department to the profit test. They started to charge money for the newsletter, and I think they went from, I don't know, something like a 300,000 mailing list down to 10,000 overnight. What they discovered was that people weren't really willing to pay an awful lot for economics, and that sort of changed the whole character of the field. I think economists now have largely been dispersed, or specialized. For example, they'll have someone work with the government trading desk trying to outguess the Fed, or they'll have somebody working on the future of agricultural commodity prices.

My approach, I think, was a little different. I recognize the fact that GNP, or GDP, doesn't trade on any exchange that I'm aware of. In other words, an awful lot of what economists talk about is wonderful among themselves, but is it relevant to the rest of the world.

Griffeth: There's not much practical application to it.

Shilling: Not much application, yes. So what I've always concentrated on (and this is one of two very fundamental principles that I've followed for a long, long time) is trying not just to get the best forecast on GDP, but instead trying to find the significant but undiscounted aspects of the economy where the surprises are. Because that's where the opportunities are. Finding things the markets have not fully discounted. Or, in terms of corporations, seeing situations that their business plans haven't taken into account.

In other words, it isn't the rehashing of the consensus that adds any value. It's finding things the consensus has missed or hasn't fully discounted.

Griffeth: And this, you feel, makes you a better money manager.

Shilling: Well it's essential with money management. It's a principle that I've long held, because I just didn't see how you add any value otherwise. It's essential in money management, in my view, because I think markets are very efficient and they do discount what's generally known and there's no free lunch. There are just not any ways you can invest with low risk with something that's got above average returns indefinitely. You've got to find the glitches. Where's the stuff that people haven't fully understood, or where they've just got the wrong forecast.

Dr. Doom & Gloom

Griffeth: I've known you more than ten years and—correct me if I'm wrong—in all that time you've been pretty bearish on the economy. But yet you personally are a pretty upbeat kind of a guy. Is that because it's more profitable, shall we say, to be able to find the problems with the economy than to find what's good about it?

Shilling: Yes, that's a very good observation, Bill. There are a couple of things that can be said about that. First, most people by nature are optimistic, and they are paid to be optimistic. I got fired for being negative, and I'm not the only one who has. As you know there is a whole string of Wall Street people who have been shown the door for being negative.

A second feature is that markets tend to go down quicker than they go up. So what you're saying is if you can find the problems you are probably adding more value because there are fewer people looking for them and they're probably going to have more dramatic results.

But I think aside from that the thing over the last decade that has driven me more than anything was my realization going back over ten years ago, that we were entering this period of greed and glitz. I've been a student of the long wave, the 50-odd-year Kondratiev Wave, and what it looked liked to me in the early 1980s was that we were entering a period very much like the 1920s with a lot of excesses that ultimately came to grief. The 1990s resemble the 1930s in terms of working off excesses and multi excess debt problems and financial difficulties and so on. That was the script.

◆

". . . human nature changes extremely slowly over time, if at all."

◆

And, by the way, that's sort of the second principle that I use in not only the economic forecasting but the portfolio management: a very strong belief that human nature changes extremely slowly over time, if at all. That means people will react to similar circumstances in similar ways. In other words, history is relevant. Now that doesn't make forecasting or money management sciences. They're arts, in my view, because the trick is finding the right piece of history that applies.

So I think patterns have developed over the last ten years where I think we've been in this down phase. I won't bore you on the Kondratiev details . . .

The Kondratiev Wave

Griffeth: If you don't, I'm going to have to write a footnote explaining it. And I think it is important. So, could you explain the Kondratiev Wave please?

Shilling: Well, this is a cycle that was first identified in the 1920s by a Russian economist, Nicholai Kondratiev. Interestingly enough, he was studying long patterns in France, Germany, the UK and to a lesser extent the U.S. And, as a matter of fact, he correctly forecasted that the capitalist world was going to be in for big trouble in the 1930s. But he made a strategic blunder as a Soviet. He suggested it would survive. So he spent the rest of his career in Siberia. He shows up in Solszhenitsyn's book, *The Gulag Archipelago*, by the way.

Anyway, he identified a 50-odd-year cycle. People date it variously between 50 and 60 years. But it starts with an upswing which, in the period I've been talking about, started right after World War II and lasted until the early 1970s. It is a period when new technologies are driving the economy at a very rapid rate. In this case, the new technologies were the huge postwar expansion in construction because of the lack of it in the 1930s and the war years, the highway expansion which was a very big driver of the economy, and of course during the cold war it was all the military spending.

Then that cycle, that first phase, tends to end with a big inventory blowoff, which is what happened in the early to mid-1970s when the feeling was the shortages would last forever. So you had this huge inventory buildup.

We were lucky enough to correctly pinpoint that. I was looking back historically and found a parallel for it. It wasn't in the post [World War II] period but in what happened after World War I when price and wage controls came off. In 1919 there was an unbelievable doubling of wholesale prices and everybody was ordering all the inventories in anticipation of still higher prices. And then that collapsed in the sharpest recession on record in 1920–1921.

I was talking to a friend at that time [in the 1970s] and I told him what I found as a parallel and he said, "Oh, that's the Kondratiev Wave." I said, "Who?" I had never heard of it.

In any event, that inventory blowoff is the second phase. Then the third phase is the 1980s (and before that the 1920s). A period of greed and glitz. Everybody's having a wonderful time, huge borrowing, big spending. The economy is basically slipping and the technologies that were driving it earlier are starting to peter out, but everybody's having such a good time they don't realize it.

And then the final phase: the 1930s were a good example, and before that there was a decade in the 1880s and 1890s and one in the 1830s and 1840s. And now we have the 1990s, which is kind of "the morning after." It's a period of working down the excesses of the 1980s. In this case, we're working down too much debt, too many people on payrolls, too much real estate. And the driving forces earlier are pretty much absent. The consumer no longer has the cash he had in the first couple of decades after the war, the defense spending is unwinding, and so on.

Griffeth: But our hangover here in the 1990s is not as severe as it was in the 1930s, is it?

Shilling: No.

Griffeth: Is that because the speculation in the 1980s wasn't as extreme as it was in the 1920s?

Shilling: It's a tough question, Bill. The thing is, if you look at the three previous Kondratiev Wave depressions—the 1830s and 1840s (which by the way were called the "Hungry '40s"), the 1880s and 1890s, and the 1930s—the 1930s were far and away the worst. But I think it's a very, very difficult question to say why it was so much worse than the two in the 19th century. It's very difficult to talk about things that happened in the 19th century, because that's so far back that it's hard to put together precise parallels. People do react to similar circumstances in similar ways, but it's tough to carry the parallel too precisely.

Griffeth: Let's move on.

Shilling: One final note, if I may. There are usually two wars within a Kondratiev Wave. One is a very popular war, and that occurs at an economic bottom. At the beginning of the current cycle I'm talking about, we had World War II, and in the cycle before that we had the Spanish American War and in the cycle before that the Mexican War. These are wars that everybody is very cautious about at first, because you've just come through a decade of real contraction and so you take on somebody like the

Mexicans or the Spanish, whom you beat easily, and it turns out to be a very popular war.

And then at the economic peak, when everybody's feeling like they can take on the cosmos, you bite off too much and get into a very unpopular war. And that was the Civil War, World War I, and Vietnam. I guess that means we're going to take on somebody "tough" like Grenada about the end of this decade.

Griffeth: I don't know. Wouldn't the Gulf War qualify as a popular war with an easy-to-beat enemy?

Shilling: Well, that's an interesting point. As a matter of fact, I did one of my *Forbes'* columns on that at the time. My conclusion was that it was about six or eight years too early.

Why Shilling Manages Money

Griffeth: All right. Now let's go on. When did you decide to start managing money?

Shilling: I decided that in the late 1980s. We were looking for ways to diversify. The problem with economic consulting—at least the way we practice it—is we provide written material, we keep in touch by phone, and we meet with them in their shop one on one. They almost always want to talk to the head guy. Whether that makes any sense or not is debatable, but they do. And what it meant was each new client was another two to four visits a year by me in their shop each year. And I was already spending year in and year out—literally—over half the working days on the road.

So we were looking for ways to diversify that would get some leverage, and one of the ways seemed to be money management. So what we did was to develop the idea of using our economic themes as the approach. And this goes back to what I described as sort of the first principle that I feel is important: If markets are efficient and discount what's commonly known then if you want to consistently beat the averages you've got to have some niche, some area where you've got a bit more understanding than most people. And if we have that at all it's obviously in the area of the economic themes. In other words, for us to go out and say we're going to be technicians or market timers or finders of undervalued stocks or a lot of other things, we just have no edge. We'd be playing in the other guy's sandbox. I want to play in my sandbox where I might have a little bit of an advantage.

Griffeth: The kind of sandbox you decided to put together, though, is private placement money.

Shilling: Well, yes, That was really, to a great deal, a matter of expediency. We never had any experience in managing money, and it takes a lot of courage and maybe a bit of faith for somebody to put money with somebody whose never had any experience.

> *"I want to play in my sandbox where I might have a little bit of an advantage."*

We really wanted to raise money to start a mutual fund. But when you've had no experience it is obviously pretty tough. It's very expensive with all the regulatory issues, for example. So we just basically looked to clients and friends who had some degree of blind faith in what we were doing to raise the money. And our initial vehicle was the Thematic Investment Partners, a limited partnership.

Griffeth: And how has it done since you started?

Shilling: It's actually done pretty well. I have our track record here somewhere. Here it is. We started on April 1, 1990, and in 1990 we were up 26 percent. In 1991 we were down 3 percent. In 1992 we were up 27 percent, (this is after all the fees). And in 1993 we were up 148 percent.

Griffeth: Not bad. So is the tail going to wag the dog? In other words, will the economic consulting become secondary to the money management part of the business?

Shilling: Let me sort of introduce a note of philosophy on that. I hope not, because I think one of the great mistakes on Wall Street is, somebody has a little success at something and they assume they know everything there is to know in the world. And they go off and triple their staff and do all these other things, and the next thing you know they fall flat on their face. I'm very conscious of that and very anxious to avoid that very common mistake.

I think one of the things that would signal that we've gone wrong in the head is if we were to junk the economic consulting firm and concentrate on the money management. We've got a nice steady business in economic consulting. It pays the rent. And if the money management continues to grow, fine. It just becomes a bigger part of the business. But it's not going to become our only concern, because of the fact that our roots are in finding economic themes.

Volcanoes and Natural Gas

Griffeth: Let's talk about how you identify the themes and then find the actual investments in stocks or commodities that fit those themes. And let me start with a specific example of a theme you used in the past: the eruption of the volcano, Mt. Pinatubo.

Shilling: All right. Now Mt. Pinatubo in the Philippines sent out a giant eruption in June of 1991. And I happened to remember some historical data about some of the volcanoes that had blown up in those latitudes earlier. There was one that blew up in, I believe, 1816 in Indonesia. It had created magnificent sunsets in the northern hemisphere with all the ash and aerosol it spread northward.

Now I did a senior thesis on something called geostrophic flow and coriolis force, which have to do with the rotation of the earth as hot air moves north from the equator toward the poles. It shifts west from the northern hemisphere and east from the southern hemisphere. It's why, for example, if water were flowing down a sink perfectly it would go counterclockwise in the northern hemisphere and clockwise in the southern hemisphere. It's also why hurricanes turn counterclockwise.

Let me just say that as a result of this I had a vague—not much more than a vague—understanding of volcanoes. At least I had the curiosity. So when I started to see some write-ups by meteorologists about what had happened after some of these previous volcanoes had erupted in that latitude, I was curious.

I mean, with this one [that erupted in Indonesia in 1816], the next summer in New England they had what they called the year without a summer. It snowed in July in Connecticut, and there were massive crop failures and so on.

So [after Mt. Pinatubo erupted] we looked around and said, okay, what does that mean? Well, if you get colder weather in the northern hemisphere it means that people are going to burn more energy, and natural gas looked like a prime candidate particularly since there hadn't been a lot of drilling of natural gas because prices had been depressed.

Griffeth: Did you buy natural gas companies?

Shilling: We did buy some natural gas stocks as well, right. Our predilection is to go the quickest, most direct, purest play on a theme. And in the case of the weather if we decide natural gas prices are going up, buying natural gas futures is the purest play.

We bought natural gas stocks for our accounts that we consider to be more conservative, because sometimes the natural gas price is not translated one for one into the price action of a stock. Obviously it depends on any regulatory problems they have or the fact that it may not be a pure gas company.

I mean, we were negative on oil at the same time. And when you get some of these companies that are involved in both gas and oil, the two things work against each other.

It brings us back to the idea that our strength is in picking themes. The worst thing we do is pick stocks.

Picking Stocks

Griffeth: When it comes to finding a stock that fits one of your themes, how much—and what kind of—research do you do?

Shilling: You've got two issues to deal with. One is the timing. Now nobody has come up with the right name for the way we run money. I guess some would call us a hedge fund, but goodness gracious, the term doesn't really describe what we do. We're not really hedging, we're speculating more properly.

But the point is that a lot of money that is run this way is run systematically or technically. In other words, the computer gives you an analysis of patterns and when one bell rings you buy and when two bells ring you sell.

In our case, when we have a theme we don't know when the thing is going to come to fruition. Timing is very, very difficult and you know, I can tell myself and anybody else who'll listen, markets can remain irrational a lot longer than we can remain solvent. We can have a wonderful theme, and maybe it's right but it may be a month, it may be two months, it may be two years before the market appreciates it. So that's one problem.

The other problem is the one that you're talking about. How do you then pick the vehicle, particularly where it's a theme that relates to stocks. Now natural gas companies are reasonably pure as this goes, but another theme that we've been very big on is the idea of productivity improvement in this country. First in manufacturing a decade ago, now in the much larger service sector. We think this is something that is going to be with us for the next decade or more. So we've been very interested in companies that help others improve their productivity by cutting costs, and it can be high tech, low tech, no tech, telecommunications, office automation, all these kinds of things.

I mean, boy, it's pretty tough. Because, for example, work stations seem like a very, very logical candidate to fulfill this theme. You know, they are much more high powered than PCs, they help people design new products, they have tremendous accounting capability, etc., etc. But within the workstation group, you have Sun [Microsystems] and Hewlett-Packard, and they're killing each other with competition. They have been for years. Sun comes out with a new machine and you say, hallelujah. And then two months later Hewlett-Packard comes out with one for half the price and twice the speed, and Sun's stock takes a nose dive. Sometimes finding the vehicle is very tough.

Griffeth: How do you solve that problem?

Shilling: [laughing] With great frustration!

Griffeth: [also laughing] That's a whole book!

Shilling: Yes, that's a whole book. I mean, it is very, very difficult.

Griffeth: Well, do you find yourself then having to do what could be considered traditional stock market analysis and research? Do you have to visit the companies?

Shilling: What we do is we will go to our various street brokers and we'll say, here's an area we're interested in. Give us your top three picks. Now the broker may say, "I don't like any of them." So I'll say, "Don't worry about that. If you had to buy three of them, which three would you buy?" And then we'll do our own research. But we don't have a cast of thousands here in the office doing it.

So what it means, usually, is we'll pick a basket—maybe four, five, or six stocks—to represent the theme, and we let the markets sort of winnow out the winners from the losers. Then we add to our positions in the winners and kick out the losers.

The End of Inflation

Griffeth: Does another theme come to mind that you've used that we could highlight as an example of how you've translated from the broad picture to a specific kind of an investment?

Shilling: Yes, it's a sort of a super theme which has led to many themes below it. It is this whole idea of the unwinding of inflation. You know, the first book I wrote in 1982 was entitled *Is Inflation Ending? Are You Ready?* In the book I answered those questions.

With the first question, I said yes it is ending, but with the second question I said no, you're not ready because you're up to your eyeballs in tangible assets and you don't have enough financial assets. The tangibles, of course, are the winners in inflation. And when inflation unwinds, the financial assets—stocks, bonds, etc.—are the winners.

And that led me very logically to be very bullish on bonds. So one theme was a bull market in bonds here [in the U.S.]. The second theme was being long bonds in Europe. And the third one was being negative on commodity prices, particularly things like copper and oil which are produced by financially weak countries. A lot of them depend entirely on either copper or oil for their foreign exchange earnings. So what happens is as the price goes down they don't cut back supply to avoid losing money. If anything, they increase production to get the same amount of foreign exchange to service their debts. So as the price goes lower they produce more, and the more they produce the lower the price goes. It's a lovely vicious circle.

This also led us to being bullish on the stocks, because as inflation comes down, so do interest rates. And that is generally good for stocks.

Griffeth: And you believe that this dis-inflation theme will be in effect for the rest of the decade?

Shilling: Yes, although I think in the intermediate term it's completed or reversed because right now I think we're in this very typical end of the business cycle phase where the Federal Reserve, rightly or wrongly, has decided that there is a clear threat of inflation. And so it has been raising interest rates.

Now historically, a Fed tightening has resulted in a flatter or inverted yield curve which leads to a recession. So right now we're in a period where we will see a further rise in long rates, a monstrous increase in short rates, and a bear market in stocks leading into recession. And we probably don't know how long it will take. Historically it has taken four months to four years! But I rather suspect it [the recession] will be in 1995.

So that causes us to employ an almost diametrically opposite investment strategy while this is going on. But it doesn't change the long-term trends. As a matter of fact, the recession enhances the deflation case.

What Color Is That Moon?

Griffeth: We've talked about how your economic forecasts have affected your investments. What about the other way around? Now that you manage money, has it impacted the way you forecast the economy?

Shilling: Oh, I think it has. It is of immense help, for example, with our clients who are professional investors or financial institutions. You know, an economist will come in and say, "Interest rates are going up." Well, hey, that's about as handy as a pocket in your underwear for a money manager. But to say which rates—short rates, long rates—and to be able to say where you should be on the yield curve, and over what time frame, that's all very helpful.

So I go in there now, and I'm talking shop with these guys. We don't just give them some vague pronouncement. It's amazing that some of these guys don't look upon us as competitors. One of the first things they'll say to me now is, "What are you doing with your portfolio?" even though we can do a lot more things than they can, in terms of being short or long futures, and so on.

But it takes me back to what I said earlier. I think one of the very important things to finding success in this business—and this goes for whether your are a money manager or an economic forecaster—is you've got to feel comfortable being out of the consensus. I think there are very few independent economic forecasts made, and a lot of [money] managers like to be with the big cap growth stocks or where it's nice and safe and conventional and well accepted. But that's not where the opportunities are.

> ◆
> "... you've got to feel comfortable being out of the consensus."
> ◆

If all you do in making a forecast or constructing a portfolio is call up all your buddies and find out what they are doing, you're not doing your job. You know, someone will call up dear old Joe because he's a smart guy. And it turns out Joe got it from Louie who got it from Sam who got it from Bill who got it from you. I mean you end up listening to yourself!

By nature, I just tend to challenge people. I'll go to a party, or I'm in some other social environment, and I'm an embarrassment to my wife. Somebody may say, "Wonderful yellow moon tonight." And I'll say, "Are you sure it isn't green?"

Somebody who feels uncomfortable being in the consensus feels much more challenged by seeing where the consensus is going to be wrong. And I've managed to stumble into trades where there was some value by being that way.

The Dastardly Dollar

Griffeth: One more thing. We've discussed the themes that worked for you, investment wise. Give me an example of one that didn't.

Shilling: Oh! [laughing] The dollar! The dollar! The dollar! I've argued for the last couple of years that the dollar should be strong because although the U.S. has got problems, it's the best of a bad lot. You know, in the kingdom of the blind the one-eyed man is king.

It has just been such a frustrating mess. We made some money in some currencies last year and gave it all back in others that went up, down, and sideways. I mean, we were short the yen and that worked out, and we were short the D-Mark and that was a problem. Luckily this year we've been largely out of currencies.

Griffeth: So does the money manager in you scold the economist in you for making a lousy forecast on the dollar?

Shilling: Yes, the money manager says, "I don't know what you're talking about, Shilling the economist, but boy, I can't afford to be in this game. You're losing money for me."

Griffeth: At what point do you throw in the towel? I mean, economically the theme may still be valid, but the investment just hasn't worked out.

Shilling: Well, what we do, we have a discipline that basically says that we don't want to lose more than 1 percent of the portfolio on a given position. When that happens, we just say, "Hey, we've got to stand aside." It doesn't mean we've got to stay out forever, but it means we've got to stand aside and see what's happening with this thing. We'll either wait for the markets to come around, or we'll simply throw out the theme. But we're not going to sit there and take a battering forever.

HEIKO THIEME

Birth Date: September 16, 1943

Education: Law Degree from University of Hamburg, Ph.D. from University of Edinburgh

Hobbies: Magic, chess, running, skiing, tennis

Alternate Career: Preacher or lawyer

*I*f you accept my premise that a mutual fund master's personality, philosophy, and vision are strong enough to shape his or her fund, then Heiko Thieme certainly belongs in this book, even though he is a relative newcomer to the fund industry. Thieme is a fast-talking showman who doesn't mind telling you he manages one of the riskiest mutual funds in the country.*

He took over the tiny, beleaguered American Heritage Fund in 1990. Within two years the aggressive growth fund's assets had grown from roughly $1 million to $100 million, and with great fanfare he took it from worst to first in terms of performance. By 1994, the fund had grown to $125 million, and Thieme had started a companion growth stock fund called the American Heritage Growth Fund.

Thieme's storied foray into mutual funds has not been without its share of controversy. In 1993, he found himself in the middle of a nasty battle between Spectrum Information Technologies, a tiny telecommunications firm in Long Island, New York, that possessed some potentially very lucrative patents, and former Apple chairman John Sculley, who was Spectrum's chairman for all of four months before he quit. Thieme had taken a sizable position in the company, and he found himself privately and publicly mediating the dispute. Eventually, Sculley left the company, and various members of Spectrum management found themselves the object of a federal investigation involving violations of securities regulations.

Heiko Thieme was born in Germany during World War II. He comes from a family of doctors and lawyers. But, being the rebel that he is, he decided on a career in finance. In the fall of 1968, he drove around the United States in a 1959 station wagon he bought for $100, and slept on a 24-cent air mattress that, as he tells it, usually ran out of air around 4:30 each morning. He then did some postgraduate work in law at U.C. Berkeley in 1970–1971, at the height of the anti-war demonstrations. That was when he fell in love with a country that allows its people to speak their minds.

Heiko certainly loves to speak his mind, too. On a number of issues. The interview you are about to read represents roughly 25 percent of our total conversation for this book. He is a highly intelligent man whose mind is constantly juggling several thoughts at once. He is a frequent guest and panel member on CNBC who is given to making bold forecasts about the economy and the markets. He is, as we say in the business, "good TV."

Whether Thieme can continue his early, and rather spectacular, success with his funds remains to be seen. But he is certainly off to a great start.

During the interview for this book, Thieme described his rather complicated investment philosophy, he discussed the lessons he learned from getting involved in the Spectrum controversy (and why he would do it again!), and he also discussed his refusal to sell his position in IBM even as it fell from the 80s to the 40s.

JUNE 29, 1994

Taking Over the American Heritage Fund

Bill Griffeth: I remember interviewing you several times on FNN in the 1980s when you were an analyst for Deutsche Bank. Then suddenly one day I was interviewing Heiko Thieme, the chairman of the American Heritage Fund.

Heiko Thieme: Correct.

Griffeth: How did that happen?

Thieme: I came across the American Heritage Fund through a colleague of mine from Deutsche Bank who was on the board of the fund. Here was a fund which was totally dilapidated. It had less than a million dollars in assets and an appalling track record. As a matter of fact, it was the worst in five years and the second worst in ten years. They asked if I would like to acquire the management company. Now acquiring a management company means, basically, you make a presentation to the board, then they might elect you as the chairman of the company, and then you obviously have to get the shareholders to agree with you.

So what I did in order to acquire the fund, I made a presentation to the board and they basically wanted to sell because the existing partners in the fund realized this was a bottomless pit. If you run a half-million-dollar fund, it costs you $50,000 or $75,000 at least, up to $100,000 or more to run the fund, the legal costs and everything else. Now if you have assets of $500,000 and you get a management fee of less than $5,000 a year, you make a very, very difficult living spending $100 in order to make $10.

The fund had over 3,000 shareholders in it, but it was basically a fund which had no meaning whatsoever. It was smaller than a pocket account. But the fund was registered and every newspaper still listed it. My attraction was twofold: A) the name was great, American Heritage. If I built the fund on my own with that name people could have called me arrogant and said, well, why would you, as a Kraut, call it American Heritage Fund. How dare you? B) I also liked that it was the worst performing fund. I could tell myself, look, even if I finish as the worst I could always just say it was impossible to turn around. So I felt my downside was very, very limited.

Griffeth: Let's spend a moment on the history of this fund. I was surprised to find it was started in 1952 and that it remained so small and had such a dreary record. Its expense ratio was also astronomical, I noticed.

Thieme: 13 percent.

Griffeth: I saw where it was 20 percent in 1986.

Thieme: Yes. Yes.

Griffeth: How in the world did this fund stay in business?

Thieme: Well, in the beginning I guess you had a group of brokers selling this fund who felt they could put their private customers in and make some nice returns. But because it was a small load fund, it had a very high expense ratio and that worked against it. When you have more than a 10 percent expense ratio, or let's use the 20 percent you saw, even if you produce 25 percent a year in a bull market you are only up 5 percent at the end of the day.

Griffeth: So you took it over in 19 . . .

Thieme: I started in February of 1990 with assets of around one million dollars because people had invested money in anticipation of my coming in and, I think I was up 5 or 6 percent by June or July. So I held my own, but it was nothing to write home about.

Griffeth: Did you change the fund's prospectus?

Thieme: No, I kept the same prospectus. I liked it because it gave me a lot of latitude.

Griffeth: Yes, I read it. It allows you to do a lot of things.

Thieme: Correct. I can go short, use leverage.

Griffeth: And when you came in, did you sell whatever was in the portfolio?

Thieme: I did not. And that was a mistake. Today what I would do if I took over a fund, I would sell everything without even seeing it. Just give me the cash.

I manage individual accounts, and the worst thing that happens is when a new account comes in and the client says, "Look, I bought this stock. What do you think?" I say, "Well, it's not our favorite but since you already have it, don't worry about it." Then the damn thing goes down 50 percent, and who is to blame? The money manager, even though I did not buy it. So my view would be: everything out and then build your own portfolio if you really want to see what you can do.

Griffeth: You did not have much time before your first baptism by fire: the invasion of Kuwait.

Thieme: Yes. The invasion of Kuwait I did not anticipate, and secondly I totally underestimated the impact of it. I thought it would be a very short-lived affair. The fund really went down. It was down 30 percent by October 11th [of 1990] when we reached the bottom of the short bear market which started in the middle of July lasting until the 10th of October.

So I had taken over the worst performing fund, held my own the first few months, and then all those gains were absolutely wiped out. It seemed to be the history of the fund I couldn't escape from, and it was a pretty miserable situation.

Griffeth: When did the fund start to take off?

Thieme: The fund started to take off when I was leveraged coming into the Gulf War. I was fully leveraged, and the fund took off in the first quarter supported by the blue chips we had and by some special situations. We were up 56 percent in the first quarter.

Griffeth: Of 1991.

Thieme: That was 1991. And, therefore, 13 months after I had taken over I suddenly had the best performing fund in the country, and now the pressure was on me.

I checked with Mike Lipper [the president of Lipper Analytical Services, which tracks mutual funds]. Mike is a very kind person, I really like him a lot. He said, "Look, what I would do in your case, you are extraordinarily lucky, why don't you protect yourself, sell everything and go out and enjoy it." It was a very tempting thought from a pro. I did not take it because I felt I would cheat my investors who had come into an aggressive growth fund. And just to protect my turf, that's not what investors wanted me to do, I thought. So I stayed fully invested and maneuvered myself in and out. We lost a couple of points in the second quarter then made up some, were up 22 percent or so in the third quarter, then we finished up 96 percent in 1991, being number three of all mutual funds, you know, in the country and being number one in our segment of the small funds. A spectacular return, but it was still done with relatively small amounts, because at that time we had a little over $5 million with everything told.

Thieme's Investment Style

Griffeth: It's pretty easy to be a nimble trader with that small a fund.

Thieme: Well the thing is, if you have $100,000 you can still lose money and possibly be just as bad off as if you had $100 million.

I think there's a point where it is very difficult to over-achieve if you have a fund the size of a Magellan Fund. I must say it is a tremendous achievement to see what the Magellan Fund has done, given the size. But I think to say when you have a small portfolio it is easier to outperform, it's not necessarily so because you are also just as exposed. There is no way of knowing which stocks will go up or down.

Griffeth: You have been quoted as saying that you prefer holding a stock for maybe six months to a year, hoping for a 50 to 60 percent gain, and then you get out.

Thieme: Ideally, I would like to go into a company, let's say it's a $5 stock that I think will be worth $50 by the end of the decade, and hold it until it's $50. However, having said that, you and I know stocks don't go up in a linear progression. They fluctuate. So if this $5 stock moves in the first six months to $10, and my price target is $50 in five years, I will possibly sell some or all of the stock and come back when the it drops back. So I use the daily fluctuations of the market. And I trade with 5 to 10 percent of our fund's assets daily in order to keep current with the market field.

> "... my strategy is built on four pillars ... John Templeton, ... Peter Lynch, Warren Buffet, and George Soros."

Griffeth: You day trade with some of the money in the fund?

Thieme: Yes. Like today, I used $2 or $3 million, which is 2 or 3 percent of fund, to day trade. We covered all our shorts last Friday, and we were net long in our trading positions. Then on Monday we closed out all our positions, because we felt 50 points was enough. Then yesterday we tried a couple of shorts and a couple of longs. We were 75 percent successful. We are not talking about big money. In the end, you make maybe $40,000 to $50,000, maybe $100,000. And we also have occasional losses.

Griffeth: Describe your investment strategy.

Thieme: Actually, my strategy is built on four pillars. The four pillars are four people I associate myself with. A couple of them I know personally. There's John Templeton, there's Peter Lynch, Warren Buffet, and George Soros. Why do I pick these four?

John Templeton has done a tremendous service to our industry because he showed people that investment is a long-term process, and equities are the investment of choice. I do not have a single doubt about that theory. Equities are number one over time. There are very few occasions, like the mid-1980s, when interest rate instruments rival equities with yields of more than 10 percent. When that happens, they give you the same return on a secure basis that stocks offer you on a risk basis. Maybe 10 percent. That, by the way, is the annual return you've gotten from equities over the past 65 years. That's the reward for taking the risk. Fixed income has given you around 5 percent a year for the last 65 years and cash has given you about 3 or 4 percent.

Templeton also says investments should be global. I agree. I think that when you look at investments today you should look at the world at large. We are up to 30 percent invested overseas in Heritage Funds.

By the way, I disagree with John Templeton on at least one issue. He feels that the 1990s will be inflationary. I think the 1990s will not be an inflationary decade. I think that's where he is clearly wrong. He sees a strong pick up, and I don't.

But I like his enthusiasm. I think he's a role model for all of us who are in the money management business.

Griffeth: Peter Lynch.

Thieme: Peter Lynch kicks tires. And I like his attitude. He's not a showoff. Peter Lynch has a concept that I fully agree with. He says, "I invest for the next three to five years, and please do not come to me if you have a shorter time span."

If I had to put it in a nutshell, what do I buy? Whatever I've told you so far, ultimately you only buy a price because if you have a great company, a great management, a great product, a great future, that's all in the price. My business can be described as a business to identify bargains. Now that is important because sometimes you find bargains in a lesser quality product.

But you should not be blindsided by just the price, because sometimes there may be hidden problems [with a company]. But it is the price, ultimately, which gives me the final reason why I buy something.

Then my third investment pillar is Warren Buffet. He strikes bargains. Warren Buffet is a person who says, "If I identify something which is attractive, how can I get it cheaper than everybody else gets it?" When he bought the Salomon Brothers' preferred that paid him 14 or 15 percent, he could care less if the stock went from 28 to 18. Because he got paid while he was waiting.

So what we are doing is focusing on what the [American Heritage] fund can do with private placements, too. [*NOTE: Private placements of stock are purchased by high net worth individuals, investment funds, or insurance companies through special arrangements with the company issuing the stock. The shares do not have to be registered with the SEC the way publicly traded shares do. Normally, a private placement restricts the buyer from selling the stock for a specific period of time. But in the meantime, the shares will often pay an attractive dividend to compensate.*] That, by the way, led to a critical article about us in the *Wall Street Journal*.

Griffeth: Well, part of the criticism about buying the restricted securities is the liquidity factor. Plus, placing a value on those shares [in order to calculate the fund's net asset value] is sort of a gray area.

Thieme: That's correct.

Griffeth: So you end up placing some of your shareholder's money at an even higher risk.

Thieme: Normally what we do is, we value a company's shares at the price we paid for it even if the stock trades above that price. When it is fully registered and fully tradable, only then will we mark the stock up to the tradable price.

Why do I buy private stock for the fund? If I can buy something that is worth $5 and pay $4 for it, I already have a 25 percent profit. Is that guaranteed? No, because the stock could come down. But what I already have, I have an advantage over the market. I'm already in at a lower level.

So I see nothing wrong with identifying companies that need money, and make a deal with them that cuts out the broker or the investment banker. I don't think there is anything wrong because actually the largest of my responsibilities is to really look out for the interest of the shareholder.

The problem, which you alluded to, is when you are possibly locked in for a year or two. You can say it's dormant money. But I accept that.

Griffeth: How much do you restrict the fund to private placements?

Thieme: Well, we can use up to 15 percent [of the fund's assets]. Originally, we were restricted to 10 [percent], but since the end of [1993] we've moved that up to 15 percent, because our private placements have given us extraordinary success.

Griffeth: All right. While we're at it, let's talk about your fourth pillar.

Thieme: The fourth pillar is George Soros. George is always a speculator and with 5 to 10 percent of funds being invested, of course, I speculate, which I call the trading aspect.

So there's trading, private placement, special investment, kick tires with a long-term vision, equities as the superior choice of investment. That summarizes my strategy. A strategy which borrows from prominent people. That's why people say, "The guy is an eclectic investor."

"I am flexible and I question myself every single day about my overall philosophy."

Griffeth: Some portfolio managers, when they have a highly quantified investment philosophy and the market goes against them . . . If, for example, a value investor finds value and the market still does not realize the value in those securities and they continue to go down for whatever reason, the value-oriented portfolio manager will tell me that he or she will patiently hang on to those securities and wait it through. What you seem to be saying is that you will get out of the shares and go wherever the market is realizing value. And then you will come back to your original value stocks when the market discovers them. You try to be a pretty nimble trader, don't you?

Thieme: Absolutely. I am flexible and I question myself every single day about my overall philosophy. We have the highest turnover of any mutual fund, and I believe it will continue to be the case. But I should also point out that, even with all the trading we do, 75 or 85 percent of my portfolio will be untouched. I will hold those positions for five years, and then actively trade with a small amount of the fund.

Griffeth: I would think that increases the capital gains your shareholders have to pay.

Thieme: You are right on that. But I take the view that if a $10 stock goes to $20 and I take a profit and then it falls back to $10, the shareholder is better off to be taxed on the $10 profit than to see the stock move up to $20 and then back to $10. He has a nontaxable zero performance.

Griffeth: As your asset base grows in the fund, would you imagine you would become less of a trader?

Thieme: I would like to close the fund when it goes to $250 million, minimum, with $350 million as more of a target. My style is perhaps not the most suitable for open-end, no-load funds, because you always have to anticipate what the cash flow will be. You have to watch what people take in and take out. At the moment, we've had net redemptions [in other words, more money is leaving the fund than is being invested] so I always have to anticipate with my cash reserves how many people will come out and how many people will come in, which makes it very difficult. That is a third dimension [to fund management beyond buying and selling stocks] over which you have no control. People come in when you least need it, and people get out when you least want it

Sticking with IBM

Griffeth: Let me ask you about IBM. You have obviously appeared a number of times on CNBC, and here in the early 1990s you mentioned a number of times that you were still bullish on IBM and that you were still buying shares even as the stock fell from the low 80s to the high 40s.

Thieme: Correct. We first bought our current position at 82.

Griffeth: I may be misreading the situation, but how much of your seemingly steadfast support of IBM was simply your professional pride not allowing you to publicly admit that you were wrong.

Thieme: Excellent question. I think it will be difficult for me to say no pride at all. I think if you go deep, deep down, I hate to be wrong. But it is much easier to say you are wrong as a strategist than when you have invested the money.

Let's take IBM, because it's a first-class question for me. First, a very quick background: we traded IBM a couple of times successfully. This goes a couple of years back when it was trading between 80 and 100. And then when the stock was down to 82 we bought some more. And then IBM made the break, which I did not anticipate.

Griffeth: The dividend was cut, among other things.

Thieme: Yes. So I said, okay, maybe it's just going to the low 70s so let's buy some more. But I had a very small position at that point. What I did not tell people is we only bought 1,000 shares then. It was not a big position. We were in it, we liked it, and I wanted to accumulate on weakness, but I was not giving up.

Here, your pride argument may have been part of it, but what was more important to me was that this stock should have been more than $100. I realized the difficulties, but I said, "Look, this company conceptually speaking, is a winner, it's big, it will survive. It's parallel to Citicorp, which I also started buying from the low 20s all the way down to 8-1/2."

So IBM we bought systematically and here comes my strategy, which I think is worth noting. When you buy a stock and you are wrong there is a school of thought that says, "Just cut your losses." They say the first loss is the best. I say, wait a minute. When you buy a company and the stock goes down 10 percent, do you believe that circumstances have changed enough to cause the stock to drop 10 percent?

"Oh, the market is always right," they say. Well, I dispute that notion. The market only reflects investor sentiments, and my function is to sometimes go against the sentiment and find bargains.

Then the argument is well, find something else. But who's to say the next stock I buy will not go down 10 percent as well? And if I do it five times, I'm down 50 percent.

So I say to people, sure you can analyze 2,000 companies, but if you focus on one you will learn how the company trades and you will understand why it's down.

On IBM at the moment we have 45,000 shares and we have traded back and forth between 50 and 60. Having new money [come into the fund] enabled me to actually buy more and I showed an average price below $50. So when the stock moved up to about 50, although I started at 82, we were already making money.

The lesson for the reader is the following—this is my biggest, possibly the biggest message I can give—stick to your guns, don't change midstream. You are more likely to create more losses by wavering midstream because then things look hopeless and at the end of the day you say, oh my God, had I known, if I had just held on a little more. On the other hand, there is a little footnote to it: don't get too stubborn.

> ◆
> "... I am on record as saying that I believe IBM will hit $176 before the end of the decade."
> ◆

Now, I am on record as saying that I believe IBM will hit $176 before the end of the decade. And I don't mind mentioning that part of the reason I say that is for publicity. Because if I mention IBM will go to $80 or $90, that is not a spectacular call. Everybody forgets about it. Instead, I want to be remembered for that sentence, and I want to be held accountable to it, within reason. You could say that IBM would see a new all-time high before the decade is over. Its previous high was in August 1987 when it was 175 and a fraction. So therefore, I say the stock will be at $176 by the end of the decade.

You may say, Heiko, where is the analysis in this? I call it vision. I am not an analyst who pushes a pencil on this one, but I don't find it totally inconceivable looking at the past of the company, when I go back 15 or 20 years, that it will not return to its old highs.

Lessons About Spectrum

Griffeth: Let's talk for a moment about any lessons you may have learned from your involvement with Spectrum Information Technologies. You found yourself in the rather unprecedented position, as a fund manager and shareholder, of mediating a dispute between the company and its chairman, John Sculley. What was the idea behind becoming so involved?

Thieme: The idea was to enhance value, because when I buy stocks I would like obviously to buy a company because the price is right and because I believe there is a future. If I have now involved myself in the company and I find myself in a situation where a company needs help, I think a money manager should offer his help.

I was actually asked by some parties if I would like to run the company. I said, look, I know my limitations, that's crazy, and it wouldn't work. I would never do that, because I would not be the right person for it. I have been asked to become a board member, and I also declined. I have a conflict of interest, because I want to maintain the flexibility [to be able to sell a stock]. When you have a stock which is badly beaten, when you become an insider you cannot sell unless the news is out and so forth.

But it doesn't matter with Spectrum, because the stock is so cheap I will under no circumstances sell it. There comes maybe my stubbornness and pride again. But look, I bought a stock at 7 and the stock's at 3 or 4, and I believe the stock is worth 10 or 12 or 15, rightly or wrongly. If I believe this, I would be an idiot to sell now and not admit that I ever owned the stock just to save face.

Griffeth: But looking back now, I mean, Sculley is long gone, [company president] Peter Caserta is gone, at one point some staff members were taken out of Spectrum's headquarters in handcuffs, and the stock is still trading between $1 and $2. Would you do it again? Would you have participated as heavily with Spectrum knowing how it was going to turn out?

Thieme: Well, it's an impossible question. Obviously, if I had known that Sculley would resign . . .

Griffeth: Would you just sell your shares next time?

Thieme: No, I would not sell.

Griffeth: Or would become as involved as you were with Spectrum?

Thieme: Yes, even more so. I have gotten involved in so many companies, helping them to restructure. I think this is one reason people can find the justification to invest with me. Because here is a money manager who actually does get involved when needed. I don't seek the involvement, but if the investment goes wrong I would do everything to mend it, because I think it is wrong to walk away. If IBM goes down, well, then I can always sell it. But why sell when you think the stock is at the low? I think that is very poor judgment.

> ◆
> "Should a money manager get involved in a company? In my view, yes."
> ◆

I think my involvement with this company [Spectrum] is a vital, vital chapter in my career. Should a money manager get involved in a company? In my view, yes. I don't want to be only a parasite who purely trades on price. I mentioned it earlier to you, money managers can be very creative and can help companies. I think they should lend their expertise to the company if they have some, thereby creating value for their own shareholders and the outsiders. I think that serves the system, so I find it a very, very important issue.

Griffeth: Okay.

Thieme: I find it actually sad somehow that the SEC prevents us [fund managers] from sitting on corporate boards. I think there are various cases now where I am very tempted to go on the board of the company, and I would accept the risk if my share-holders would allow me to.

Griffeth: But you understand the SEC, or the Investment Company Institute's reasons for not wanting a fund manager to sit on the board of a company they are invested in, because of the conflict of interest possibilities.

Thieme: But this is where the SEC forces us indirectly to put a trading mentality in us rather than saying we would like you guys to think long term.

I realize [when you are a member of a company's board] that even if you have a bad news item you can't sell your position until the news is out. But if you believe in the company and your fund already has whatever position you're going to take, why not help the company to meet its target? Why waste an intelligent brain in lending advice?

The company comes up and says, look, we have the following product, what do you think? If I can help persuade them that this is not a good investment for this and that reason, I think I've done myself and somebody else a service rather than letting the company make the wrong decision.

What Next for Thieme?

Griffeth: You are obviously still a very restless fellow, curious about a lot of things.

Thieme: Absolutely.

Griffeth: Looking back on your career after you've retired, will the American Heritage Fund and the growth fund have been just a phase of that career, or do you see this as sort of a culmination of what you have been building to, to allow you to implement many of your creative ideas through these funds?

Thieme: I think the latter one, definitely, and I think for me it is the next level of what I would like to do. Being 50 years old, what I would like to do in the next 10 or 20 years is to help build companies, to get involved in the companies. I would like to run the portfolio and various funds of a billion dollars where I would segment between the blue chips and the midsized companies that are unknown and unrecognized. In other words, from the venture capital side, not on the same fund, but in different groups, catering to different people, to use my entire talent in managing money and creating value.

My real ambition is to take significant positions that would cause my fund to be up 100 percent. Now you can call that an ego trip, you can call it the magical trip, but if you don't have ambition you should not be in this business.

In an aggressive growth fund what I try to achieve is 15 to 25 percent a year, even though we are down so far this year. We are managing 15 percent [average return per year] since I have run the fund, so I have shown through the ups and downs that this is a feasible target. But it requires hard work, diligence, stubbornness, vision but most important, luck. You are in your position because you are a great human being, but you are also lucky. And I am where I am because I am also lucky.

RALPH WANGER

Birth Date: June 21, 1934

Education: Massachusetts Institute of Technology, B.S. and M.S. in Industrial Management

Hobbies: Bridge, golf, hiking

Alternate Career: Computer programmer

*R*alph Wanger has been called the king of the small cap funds. For almost a quarter of a century, his Acorn Fund has consistently been successful in finding small companies with better than average growth rates. An initial investment of $10,000 in the fund when it was created in 1970 would have grown to around $320,000 by the middle of 1994, according to Lipper Analytical Services.*

Wanger has also been called the court jester of the mutual fund world. And it's true. Beneath his quiet, seemingly shy exterior is a very funny man with an incredibly dry wit. The reports he writes to his shareholders, which often have nothing to do with the stock market, are known for their humor and their insight.

For example, in his report to shareholders dated June 30, 1986, he revealed the secrets of writing a report that people will want to read. Here is an excerpt:

"If your own writing is still stuck at the high school junior level, you have two things that will help. One is to practice writing conscientiously, just as you would do practice questions for a CFA [Chartered Financial Analyst] exam. This means a lot of time and work, so it is impractical. The second method is a shortcut: plagiarism. You ought not to take another analyst's work, but you can use quotations to brighten up your own sludge pile of dreary prose.

"To use quotes, you first need a pile of them, so start a file called 'Quotes,' and when you see a good one, put it in the file. When you use a quote, it is nice to use it correctly, but many people do use quotations out of context, which is fair, or change a few words, which isn't fair, but who is to know?

319

"The last rule on quotes is to tell who said it. If you can't remember who said it, the rule is: say it was John Maynard Keynes if it is about money, and Mark Twain if it is not.

"Have I left you with the impression that style is more important than substance? Good. It is, if you are trying to get to the top of our profession. Every analyst makes some good forecasts and some bad forecasts, but wit gets remembered, and so a well written report is more likely to get the reader to take action than a dull report is. "The world is full of accurate, boring, underpaid drudges."[1]

Wanger learned to manage money from his longtime mentor, the wealthy entrepreneur Irving Harris. In 1970, Harris Associates created the Acorn Fund, which was designed to invest in small companies with a high growth potential, and Wanger was tapped to manage it. It grew from $7 million in 1970 to roughly $2 billion in 1994. (It has been closed to new investors since 1990.)

In the fall of 1992, the Acorn International Fund was introduced. Incredibly, it was closed to new investors 18 months later with $1.3 billion in assets.

I called Wanger at his summer home in Aspen, Colorado. He had only recently celebrated his 60th birthday, and various members of his staff had congregated there to plot the future course of newly formed Wanger Asset Management LP. He hinted to me that the new company would create some new mutual funds, but SEC regulations prohibited him from saying specifically what kinds of funds they would be.

During our interview, Wanger talked about his penchant for investing in companies involved in transforming technologies that change the way we live, about "the brother-in-law problem" that led to the creation of the Acorn Fund, about how to successfully invest money overseas, and what it would take to convince him to open the Acorn Fund and the Acorn International Fund to new investors.

---

1. J.M. Keynes, "Mark Twain's Cambridge Year."

AUGUST 12, 1994

"You're Fired!"

Bill Griffeth: Tell me about your first job.

Ralph Wanger: I was supposed to be in charge of installing a computer in Indianapolis for Lane Bryant Mail Order down there. They were trying to computerize it, and that was very confusing because after about six months I kind of learned what the job was and what the capabilities of that machine were. I did two calculations as to how fast the machine could run, and it turned out the machine wasn't going to be powerful enough to do the job. So I went to the boss and I said, "Boss, assuming we do the job correctly, we are going to run into capacity constraints in the rush, in the busy seasons. I don't think this machine can handle it." And he said, "Well, then you are fired." I never did figure out exactly how A led to B! [Laughing]

Griffeth: [Also laughing] They shot the messenger.

Wanger: Yes. But that conversation got me into the finance business in Chicago. Irving Harris, who had actually been responsible for helping me get the job in Indianapolis said, "Well, then fine, I'll give you a job here." And I said, "Great, what do we do?" [Laughing]

I didn't care. That was back around 1960 when business wasn't so good. The idea that the world owed every college graduate a job had not yet become completely powerful doctrine.

Griffeth: How did you meet Irving Harris?

Wanger: Well, actually I grew up with his children in Highland Park, Illinois. Our houses were about three blocks away, and I guess he knew me when I was a kid. Actually, the first time I worked for him was when I caddied for him.

Griffeth: And he got you the computer job?

Wanger: Yes. I had been through graduate school, and I actually had a job at an insurance company in Chicago. I was a smart kid in high school, and Irving's theory was to hire smart kids and figure out something for them to do. Or, if they were really smart they would figure out something to do themselves.

Griffeth: So what did you do for Harris after you were fired from the computer job?

Wanger: Well I started out as basically a security analyst. Irving made a lot of money in business. He and his brother built the Toni Home Permanent business, and they sold it to Gillette, I think, for $14 million cash in 1949. That, of course, was real big money in those days. And he turned out to be a vigorous and intelligent investor at the start of the greatest bull market in history. So he took a large fortune and made it larger.

Small Companies

Griffeth: Did you know anything about security analysis?

Wanger: No. [Laughing] I had been to college and had taken a couple of courses in finance, but I didn't know anything. Why should you know anything about security analysis when you're a kid? But it was something that I turned out to be good at and much better at than computer stuff.

Griffeth: When did you become interested in investing in small companies?

Wanger: Irving liked small companies. He was entrepreneurial in his outlook, and he thought small companies were more interesting, and he could talk to people in the businesses more easily, especially in those days. They sold a lot cheaper than big companies, so there was more value to them.

Griffeth: Did you just help manage Harris's money, or were you also managing other people's money?

Wanger: Irving had joined a brokerage firm in New York. Those were the days of fixed commissions, and he figured after a while that he was generating enough commissions that it made sense for him to be a member or a broker and recapture his own commissions.

And then various friends and relatives had come to him and said, "Irving, you are a smart man and you are a good investor. Why don't you run some of my money?" So we started to get a little bit into the investment counseling business. We had three guys and a trader and a secretary. It was a pretty compact branch.

Griffeth: When you were with Harris, did you subscribe to any investment philosophy you could quantify? For example, were you a value investor or a growth investor?

Wanger: We didn't know about that stuff in those days. [Laughing]

Griffeth: [Also laughing] How would you describe it?

Wanger: Well, I would just say we did lots of relatively small company stuff. And we made a lot of money in the airline stocks in that era, around 1965. That was probably our best group.

Transforming Technologies

Griffeth: What attracted you at that time?

Wanger: Well, actually, that's a very good example of a basic technological change really causing dramatic changes in the industry, because that was when the jets came in. I remember the jets just started showing up around 1958, 1957. They were mainly for long haul specialty flights. But as they came into the U.S. market they suddenly figured out that these things made flying nicer. And people were going to fly more because the speeds were higher, the planes were larger and it really made the airline business a dramatically different business.

So it was just a jet engine that transformed the transportation industry in a very profound way. And Delta and Northwest, all these companies suddenly grew dramatically.

Griffeth: Who did you make your money on? Was it the manufacturers or the airlines themselves?

Wanger: We basically bought the airline stocks. The first stock I bought for myself was Capital Airlines and the first security I ever made 500 points on was an airline security.

Griffeth: Was that Capital?

Wanger: No, it was a National Airline convertible bond. I didn't have very many of them, but I bought at 300 and sold at 800. So I was very proud I made 500 points on something. I thought that was neat.

Griffeth: Did you find very much success early on, or did you find it difficult?

Wanger: Well, the problem was I got lucky the first time. [Laughing] I got hooked.

Griffeth: [Also laughing] You made money on the first horse race you bet on.

Wanger: Yes, which is always a danger. I remember the company. It was a fastener company that made specialty nuts and bolts in Morton Grove, Illinois.

Griffeth: Do you remember the name of the company?

Wanger: H.M. Harper.

Griffeth: That seems to be a theme with you. I read another interview where you pointed out that you liked to go for high-tech companies that produce service-oriented products. Is that a fertile place to find growth?

Wanger: The airline example was a good case of a transforming technology. The jet engine was a terrific invention, and General Electric and Pratt & Whitney and Rolls Royce, I suppose, made reasonable money making jet engines. But we didn't try to buy any of those companies partly because they had a lot of other businesses, and the jet engine was only going to be a part of it.

Griffeth: They weren't a pure play.

Wanger: Yes, so they would only benefit to a certain extent. And for every dollar the jet engine manufacturer made, probably the airline made more. And the airline customers turned out to be the big beneficiary.

A good reason the western United States grew rapidly in the last 40 years was the jet plane. It made travel very practical. You know, it was always easy to go from New York to Philadelphia and suddenly going to San Francisco or Phoenix became just as easy. So the concept of a transforming technology is that the big money is downstream.

The thing that changed Aspen, I suppose, was the railroad. It showed up here in 1887. And it obviously transformed the United States in very dramatic ways. The guys who made steam locomotives and railroad cars made some money, but you may not be able to name the major makers of locomotives, because they barely exist today. They do as divisions of some bigger companies.

Griffeth: So you invest in companies that profit at the point where technology finds its way to the public.

Wanger: As you go downstream the dollars spread out. Now you probably can name the railroads that made a lot of money buying the steam locomotives and using them to build the railroad industry. You probably remember the Union Pacific and the Santa Fe and the Great Northern and the Pennsylvania and all the other tremendous railroads. They were great for a while. I suspect that 70 years ago if you asked anybody who was in the securities industry what the best-run company in the United States was, Pennsylvania Railroad would have gotten most of the votes.

> *"The railroads made some good money. But the people who made even bigger money were the people along the right of way . . ."*

The railroads made some good money. But the people who made even bigger money were the people along the right of way who could use the railroad to develop mines and factories and farms and cities. So the guys who owned the silver mine here in Aspen saw the value of their mine at practically nothing before the railroad showed up, because they couldn't ship the ore out on a practical basis without the railroad. But as soon as the railroad showed up the mines became economically profitable, the city grew, and the people who had owned land and built stores made a lot of money.

Griffeth: Can you think of another example of an industry where you found success because it fit this same scenario?

Wanger: The most obvious and largest and most long lasting trend of this is, of course, the whole idea of electronics, computers, communications, and information processing of all sorts. Here your transforming technology is really the semiconductor. It made computers practical, it made telephones much cheaper. All of the things you didn't have in your house 10 years ago that you can't get along without today. Things like your cellular phone, your fax machine, your PC, your E-mail, and your phone mail.

Griffeth: But using your investment method, you wouldn't purchase shares in the semiconductor makers.

Wanger: Well, until a few years ago I would guess the amount of money made by the American semiconductor industry was zero. There were many companies that made some money, but there were many companies that went out of business and made no money at all. Now everybody remembers how well Intel and Motorola have done, but they've forgotten about the Fairchilds and dozens of others who started bravely and failed. Some of them took a lot of money down with them.

Griffeth: But you would have done pretty well if you had gotten into Intel early on.

Wanger: Intel was the exception. But when you think about the amount of money that Intel has made, I think you would easily find that Intel's customers made more. The people who are making real money on it are people like you. The reason you are in business is because of cable TV. That is a new technology which has enabled people to sell blue jeans and pantyhose to millions that they couldn't have reached otherwise. And it needed electronics to make it possible. And we've made a whole lot more money owning cable TV stocks than we ever would have owning semiconductor stocks.

The Brother-in-Law Problem

Griffeth: Let's talk about the beginning of the Acorn Fund.

Wanger: We decided in 1970 we wanted to start a mutual fund. It was not suppose to be anything big. At that point, investment counseling firms started little mutual funds basically to solve the brother-in-law problem. [Laughing]

Griffeth: The brother-in-law problem?

Wanger: Yes. You know, a money management firm would get a nice $3 million account in from an important businessman. They would be very glad to get it. And then, of course, the businessman would say, "My brother-in-law Harold has $40,000 dollars. What are you going to do for him?" That was always a very difficult question to answer. But once you started the mutual fund it became a cinch. You have a terrific fund Harold can put his money into, and everything will be great. So it really solved the brother-in-law problem. The fund was an adjunct that was running along with everything else we were doing.

Griffeth: You were the manager of the fund to begin with?

Wanger: Yes, I was the manager of the fund to begin with, and I didn't know how to do that. We just ran it as another account, put a bunch of little companies into it, and we did fine in 1970 and 1971. In 1972 it got to be a pain in the ass because the big stocks did well and the small stocks we owned didn't. Then in 1973 and 1974, of course, the wheels fell off. I was a good manager and only lost half the fund's money.

Griffeth: [Laughing] Were you starting to rethink this mutual fund concept then?

Wanger: There were discussions about whether it should be kept going or not at that point, because we were back to where we had started. I think we were just hovering around the break-even point. So there was a real question about whether it made sense to spend any time on it, or not.

Griffeth: How much money did you start with in the fund? Do you remember?

Wanger: It was $7 million. So it was a big start.

Griffeth: Yes, it was. Did brother-in-law Harold bail out in 1973, 1974?

Wanger: No. It wasn't a redemption issue. It was a capital loss issue. The fund lost 25 percent in 1973 and 25 percent in 1974, rounding off. And this was rather better than average. It was a very, very long disgusting market, and a lot of people decided that they were much better off working in their uncle's shoe store after those couple of years. It was very, very depressing.

Griffeth: Plenty of managers will tell me now that they saw that period as a buying opportunity. Did you?

Wanger: No. We were looking at it as a survival opportunity. [Laughing] The big question then was what we could do to keep from being fired.

When the market turned, though, we had some cash at that point. But we didn't spend it so damn fast. Nineteen Seventy-five, 1976 and 1977 were very good years, and that put us back in business. Seventy-six actually was our best relative performance year ever. That was the year we suddenly realized we had a mutual fund that was important.

Griffeth: Was there a temptation during the down years to go with the groups who were doing well at the time? You mentioned that the blue chips outperformed your small caps in 1972, for example.

Wanger: We didn't change our style, because the blue chips were obviously very overpriced in 1972, so we knew enough not to buy them. What we weren't smart enough to realize was that when the big stocks fall they take the little stocks down with them.

Wanger Asset Management

Griffeth: Tell me about your new organization today. I would imagine you have researchers and analysts now. Describe the decision making process that goes into putting a stock in the portfolio.

Wanger: We are trying to get it decentralized so I don't have to do anything anymore. We have a domestic team and an international team.

Griffeth: How many on each team?

Wanger: About five. But there are a few cases where the research overlaps. We have one guy doing health care stocks, for example. And it turns out an Israeli drug company is more like an American drug company than it is like an Israeli tire company.

We have another guy doing energy stocks, and it's the same thing. A guy drilling for oil and gas in Guatemala still has the same problems as somebody doing it in Louisiana.

Griffeth: So they bring the ideas to you or to the committee for your stamp of approval, or how does it work?

Wanger: Chuck McQuaid is basically the director of research, and he certainly leads the domestic team. Leah Zell supervises the international team. But we try to divide responsibilities on a regional or a geographical basis because of the cost of going to see companies.

I'm not sure how it is all going to work out, but one advantage is that everybody talks to each other. Let's say we have a computer company in Norway. We have a lot of conversations with the domestic electronics guys, there is a lot of very useful interplay, and it also allows us to improve investing in both areas by knowing the international competition. There are a lot of companies, and a lot of analysts look only at U.S. companies. They forget there is some guy in Hong Kong or Sweden who is going to be a major competitive factor. And if you leave them out you don't get it right.

Griffeth: Does a stock ever go into one of the portfolios over your objection? Or do they all have to have your approval?

Wanger: I bless everything as it goes by. I'll try to make some suggestions on things to look at, and I'll suggest some additional questions as cross checks people can make. So I try to be a strategist and make sure they have allocations in the right areas. And I still follow a bunch of companies myself, so I have everybody doing a little of everything.

Time Machine Investing

Griffeth: Let's talk about your international fund. You opened it and it took off right away, and then you had to close it to new investors right away. It's very symptomatic of the explosive growth in the industry right now, isn't it?

Wanger: Yes, that's exactly right. When we started it off, if anybody had told me after a year of being in business we'd have $300 million I would have been thrilled. In fact, after a year we had $900 million, and after a year and a half we had $1.4 billion. That was just remarkable.

Griffeth: That is astounding.

Wanger: Yes, it is a definitely holy cow kind of event.

Griffeth: Does it thrill you or scare you?

Wanger: Depends on which day it is. On payday it's kind of a thrill! [Laughing] Obviously that kind of enthusiasm is a high point [for the markets]. However, I don't think international investing is going to go away.

I think for a very long time international investing was a very, very negligible part of investing. I think institutions and individuals had about 5 percent of their money outside the United States, and for a long while that was right.

In 1960 the United States was the only real country. Every place else was not as nice. Every place else was poor and badly run, and the United States had the only real currency and the only real industry, and the rest of the world was second rate. If you tried to say that today, you'd be looked at as a loony.

The United States is still a great country, and in many respects it is the greatest country. But nobody would say the Japanese can't make a car, or the Italians can't make a suit, or the Brazilians can't make a pair of shoes that is better and cheaper than we could do here.

Griffeth: Are you able to apply the same investment philosophy in these developing countries as you did in the 1960s in the United States?

Wanger: It still works. To a certain extent, you can do some time machine investing. Cultures and peoples have some interesting differences which you have to know about, but they are also very much the same. Everybody needs food, and everybody would like to have better food. I can't think of any country in the world that, as it gets rich, doesn't eat more meat and protein foods and less bread and rice. I can't think of anybody who doesn't prefer a large, clean, air conditioned house to a small, dirty, uncomfortable house. Everybody would like to have nicer clothing. Everybody wants to have a pair of Reeboks and eat at

McDonald's once in a while, and everybody wants to take a vacation once in a while. So demand for food and shelter and clothing and entertainment are pretty constant all over the world.

In most places something like an American standard is the desired standard. There are some places where that is logical and some cases where it isn't. American houses are very nice houses. Whether American rock music is the best kind of music, I don't know. If McDonald's is the best kind of food there is, I don't know. I was talking to a Chinese-American who had just taken his family to Beijing for the first time, and he said, "Okay, we are going to go out and eat. There are all these marvelous restaurants I've talked to you about all my life." And the kids said, "Let's go to MacDonalds." It's like home.

Anyway, there are certain patterns that repeat, and if you can find some places down the time line a little bit you can make some predictions. You know that China and India and the Philippines are going to put a lot more telephones in over the next decade. So who is going to build those telephones, and how much money are they going to make? You have to start doing the detail work after you know what the trend is.

It also enables you to invest in international markets on a long time scale, which is helpful because most of these markets are no different from how our market used to be. You go back over the first 150 years of the U.S. stock market. Everything was speculation and manipulation and short-term trading, and the idea of buying some stock and holding onto it forever was not the desire. The abuses that happened in the market were frequent and significant and unpunished. So the fact that the same sort of thing may happen in Kuala Lumpur today is . . .

Griffeth: . . . not surprising.

Wanger: . . . certainly regrettable, but not surprising. It took a long time to develop the idea of shareholder rights and investor communication and all these sorts of things.

Griffeth: Do you find that American shareholders have the patience to wait for the value you find overseas to be realized?

Wanger: Yes, much more than the locals. The locals are still dominated by short-term traders whose goal is buy it at 85 and sell it at 92. You can't outtrade the locals.

Griffeth: By "locals," you mean the local investors in those countries.

Wanger: If you decide you know a whole lot about soybeans and you decide to trade soybeans every day, after a couple of years chances are you will have discovered that you have transferred wealth from yourself to a bunch of floor traders in Chicago. [Laughing] And I think if I tried to trade stocks in Hong Kong—on the same basis that the local traders do, you know—the folks who run them up and run them down—if I tried to beat them at their game, I'd lose.

Griffeth: So how *do* you beat them?

Wanger: The only way you can do it is to take a different time span. You can get nailed for a couple percent by front running or bad execution or just thin markets going in and out. But if you hold the stocks for ten years, the first 2 percent nick doesn't kill you. So you try to identify long-term trends and take more of a buy and hold attitude, and that means what happens in the daily activity over there is not as crucial.

> *"I don't mean to imply that we will have a smooth, calm progression until the whole world is one large Scottsdale."*

Griffeth: You are quite right that there is this Americanization, if you will, occurring in various developing countries around the world. But I wonder if that will reverse itself at some point, if there will be a backlash. I think about the troubles they had in Russia in 1994 with this investment fund that turned out to be a pyramid scheme. Some might lay that to the excesses of the free markets. I wonder, though, if some developing countries will become disenchanted with the American system?

Wanger: I don't mean to imply that we will have a smooth, calm progression until the whole world is one large Scottsdale.

Griffeth: But your point is, the way to overcome some of the volatility is to take the longer term view. I just wonder if it is as easy as that in reality. Is the development truly inevitable?

Wanger: Certainly you have to watch. Sometimes things go very wrong, or they get way overdone. And when that happens, sometimes it's time to bail out. But you should have in mind in a long-term viewpoint even though you are going to review everything from time to time. It doesn't mean you buy and go to sleep, but you also don't buy stocks for the purpose of trading.

I mean, any stock has the potential of being sold either because things get very good or things get very bad. You still have to react to what the world hands you. In 1993 lots of markets went up 100 percent, and some of them came down 50 percent this year [in 1994]. You got very volatile action, and it's rather nice to try not to buy at the high and sell at the low every time.

Information Superhighway's First Road Kill

Griffeth: What seminal trends do you see now that will still hold five to ten years from now?

Wanger: Transforming technologies in electronics may change a little bit once in a while, but I don't think they're going away in any big hurry.

Griffeth: Will the Information Superhighway be fully paved by then?

Wanger: If the government keeps its hand off it, it will. [Laughing] I have no idea why they are trying to mess with it. The most the government should do is try to help people set standards so you have interfaces that are consistent. They should say how wide each lane should be and what the speed limit ought to be, but then they should let other people decide where to build the highway and what to build it out of.

It's already changing lots and lots of businesses. I had a meeting with some people from Encyclopedia Britannica a few months ago. They realize they are in a whole different business. [Laughing]

Griffeth: [Also Laughing] Yes, they are!

Wanger: Whether they are going to survive is very, very unclear.

Griffeth: The encyclopedia man is going door to door selling CD-ROMs now, isn't he?

Wanger: It used to be the guy sold the encyclopedia for a lot of money, and he delivered 300 pounds of books. The books were kind of imposing. You could put them up there on the shelf and tell your friends, "Hey, man, I bought all these expensive and difficult books. I am therefore cultured and educated. I will have culture and education in my home, and there are the books to prove it!"

Now you can't tell them that, because the whole encyclopedia is on one or two CDs! [Laughing] You've got a whole different business. The idea of making revisions and selling everybody a revised edition suddenly becomes trivial. Five years from now you should be able to update your encyclopedia for $12. They will send you a new disk.

Griffeth: Would encyclopedias be a good investment even though the price of the product comes down?

Wanger: It may well not. As you know, Britannica is not a public company, but I think they are pretty screwed up. It is an example of how they are likely to be the first road kill on the Information Superhighway.

Yet Another Sailing Analogy

Griffeth: Let me focus on you for a second. You are known for your dry wit. Does that get you through the rough spots when your funds are down? I mean, 1994 has not exactly been the kindest year to the Acorn Fund.

Wanger: Well, so far it has just been a flat year.

Griffeth: But my point is, are you able to sleep nights when you've got these rough periods, or does your sense of humor carry you through?

Wanger: This is not a rough period.

Griffeth: Well, it's certainly not 1973–1974.

Wanger: I've seen rough periods. This has actually been a fine year. Everything has been fairly flat, and it has enabled us to work on systems and personnel and infrastructure and do all sorts of constructive things. I think it has been, from our business's point of view, a very useful, dynamic year.

Up to now, the performance statistics are very boring, but that's not the idea of the game. Basically, when the market is going down it's not because you are stupid, and when the market is going up it's not because you are smart.

One of my partners occasionally does sailboat racing. He can get out on one day where the wind is blowing 15 knots, and he can't even put up all his sails. He may go around the course in half an hour and he may beat the number two boat by 50 yards. Then he gets another day when the wind is almost calm, and in two hours he can gain one boat length on the guy next to him. You just have to sail the conditions.

It's the same thing in the market. You just have to adapt to what is going on, but don't assume it has anything to do with your own abilities in either direction.

A 500-Pound Squirrel

Griffeth: All non-shareholders of the Acorn Fund and of Acorn International want to know when you are going to share the wealth again. Do you have any plans to open them up at some point? Or will you start a new fund?

Wanger: We are looking at new product ideas.

Griffeth: But do you have plans to reopen the other two funds?

Wanger: Not at the moment.

Griffeth: What would it take to change your mind?

Wanger: Either unwarranted greed [Laughing] or a change in format where we decided to buy bigger companies. If you are trying to do a small stock fund where a big position is three or four or five million dollars, you can't do that with a $10 billion fund. It just ends up being like an index fund, or it might give a satisfactory performance but it's going to be almost unsteerable.

Our logo is the squirrel. Now a one-pound squirrel is a very successful, alert, active animal. A 500-pound squirrel would not be! If he tried to jump from limb to limb, it would be quite a different effect! [Laughing]

Griffeth: [Also laughing] Yes, it would. You won't at some point have to rethink the logo and go with an oak tree or something? Acorns become oaks, you know.

Wanger: Well, that's true. The lucky ones do. If we wanted to do that, I think I'd probably start with a different fund that was going to be a bigger company fund. We are a private partnership, so we're not under pressure to be enormous.

Griffeth: You are not in danger of being acquired?

Wanger: We won't be acquired if we don't want to be! I'm sitting here in Colorado where I see Berger selling out. Janus sold out. I'm sure we have a salable firm, but we're not in any hurry to do it.

A CONVERSATION WITH PETER LYNCH

Birth Date:
January 19, 1944

Education:
B.S. from Boston College,
M.B.A. from Wharton School
of Finance at the University
of Pennsylvania

Hobbies: Golf

Alternate Career:
"Gee, I've never thought
about it. I guess whatever
I did would have to have
something to do with
investing. That's what
I love to do."

*I*f you don't know who Peter Lynch is, you should. Peter is probably the most successful mutual fund manager of all time. He is certainly the most famous. And for good reason. A dollar invested in the Fidelity Magellan Fund when he took over the reins in 1977 had grown to an eye-opening $28 by the time he quit the fund just 13 years later in 1990. And, as if that weren't impressive enough, he accomplished it with a fund that grew from $200 million in 1977 to $14 billion by 1990.[1]

How did he do it? Very simple: one stock at a time. In fact, Lynch is quite open about his deceptively simple investment method. His two bestselling books, One Up on Wall Street (published by Simon & Schuster in 1989) and Beating The Street (which Simon & Schuster published in 1993) are incredibly easy reads that very clearly delineate

---

1. Of course, by 1994 Magellan had grown to more than $35 billion, and somehow current manager Jeff Vinik had continued to produce a very creditable return to the fund's shareholders. But that story is best left for another book. One Fidelity Magellan fund manager per book is enough.

his simple, kick the tires method of finding cheap stocks, which has been emulated by a number of other mutual fund managers.

Notice that I used the word "simple" three times in the previous paragraph. That's because Lynch likes to keep everything simple. As he wrote in One Up on Wall Street:

"Getting the story on a company is a lot easier if you understand the basic business. That's why I'd rather invest in panty hose than in communications satellites, or in motel chains than in fiber optics. The simpler it is, the better I like it."

Peter Lynch in retirement is probably busier than he was when he was running Magellan. Certainly he spends more time with his wife and three daughters. But he also manages money for a dozen different charities, and he still maintains an office at Fidelity where he acts as a mentor to a number of the young fund managers.

I called Peter at his office at Fidelity on a Friday morning. During our hour-long conversation, we were interrupted a number of times as he wrapped up business that had come up during a just completed trip to Europe. And he was busy preparing for a much-anticipated vacation in Hawaii with his family. Like I said, he may be retired, but he certainly hasn't slowed down.

During our conversation, he briefly outlined how individuals can outinvest professional money managers. We also discussed what's good and bad about the mutual fund industry today, how much you do and don't need to know about a mutual fund manager before you invest, why the huge Magellan Fund is not closed to new investors, and whether he will ever manage another mutual fund.

AUGUST 26, 1994

Lynch, the Legend

Bill Griffeth: It is obvious that a number of fund managers—and some of them are in this book—use you as a benchmark. When people define success in the mutual fund industry, they think of Peter Lynch. So, how does it feel to be a legend?

Peter Lynch: It's a surprise. You know, basically you just work as hard as you can. It's helpful to work for a great company and have a lot of resources and when you finish your 13 years, and somebody says "that was great," it's good to hear. You don't think of it while you are doing it.

Griffeth: Not everyone returned what you did over those 13 years, either.

Lynch: A lot of people have great records, but they make it all the first three years. Then they do sort of mediocre for ten. If you had three terrific years when you were small and then ten average years you would still be number one for the 13 years. But who actually made the money? The first three years you might have had a few thousand shareholders, and then when all the other people got in they did mediocre.

What was notable was the last five years I ran Magellan, it was the biggest fund in the world. It beat 99 percent of all funds the last five years and that's when I had a million shareholders. So I think that's one fact that impresses these people, these peers. Fact number two is that it never had a down year in 13 years. And number three is every year it beat the average fund, and that's hard to do when you have a big fund.

Some funds, the reason they become number one is they are terrific in good years and they do mediocre in bad years so they more than make up for the good years. Even in the most difficult of those 13 years, Magellan did better than the average fund. There were some tough years—1987, 1983 I can't remember all the years—but there were some that were kind of tough. In every year Magellan beat the average of general equity funds. So it's hard to do well in good years, and then when the market turns the other way still beat the average fund.

Griffeth: Are you as impressed when you look back?

Lynch: I'm just saying I'm more impressed by Joe DeMaggio's record of 56 games in a row of getting a hit, or all the home runs Babe Ruth hit during his career than by some player's short-term batting average.

If you are in the top quartile every year, for ten years, you'll probably be number one. If you made it to the top half every year you'd probably be number one. Part of the reason I was able to do that was because I was diversified.

I've always thought Magellan was miscategorized. They call it a growth fund, but I never, ever had over half the fund in growth stocks. I mean, I would own cyclicals. I'd own electric utilities. I would own some special situations, turnarounds. I was always looking in every part of the market. If all you buy is growth companies, there may be several years where every company in that field happens to be overpriced and you have to buy the best ones even though you don't really think they are attractive. They just happen to be the best of 300 growth companies. Then you have two or three mediocre years because you are dealing in a universe of overpriced stocks.

I would love to buy a great growth company at five times earnings with a great balance sheet. If I'd found enough of those I would have had my whole portfolio, but I didn't seem to find those. So I think that's one reason that the fund was always fresh and did well. It was very flexible.

Why Not Close Magellan?

Griffeth: I'm not asking you to second guess [Fidelity chairman] Ned Johnson, but why isn't Magellan closed [to new investors]? It has $35 billion in assets. I mean, it's huge . . .

Lynch: Well, people said we should close it when it got to be a billion. They said we should close it when got to be $2 billion, and then when it got to be $5 billion.

Griffeth: But is it unfair to expect Jeff Vinik to continue the kind of performance you had with that large a fund?

Lynch: When my fund got to be very big I said, "If I can beat the market by two or three percent a year I'm doing a real service to the public." The public, in general, hasn't come close to even matching the market on their own. If they buy an index fund, by definition, they'll match the index.

Jeff Vinik and Morris Smith [Lynch's immediate successor as the manager of Magellan, who left after a couple of years] more than beat the market by two or three percent a year, and they are doing people a real service. They are doing a service to the one out of every 100 Americans [who own shares in Magellan].

So if people hadn't invested in Magellan the last three years, the last five years, or the last ten years, they would have invested somewhere else and they would have done worse. Some would have done better but I mean, in general, the average fund hasn't done as well as Magellan in the last ten years, and I think it will continue to do better than the average fund in the next five.

Mutual Funds vs. Individual Stocks

Griffeth: Your great message has always been that individuals have the ability to successfully pick stocks for themselves. Your line is, "Buy what you know and know what you buy." It seems to run counter, though, to encouraging people to invest in mutual funds. I mean, the idea behind a mutual fund is to allow professionals to invest on your behalf.

Lynch: That's a good point. There are some people who simply don't have the patience, the energy or they are just not willing to do the fundamental research. I'm talking about looking to see if the company has no debt.

◆

"There is a company behind every stock. And if you are not willing to follow the company, I don't think you should be investing on your own."

◆

You know, you do a balance sheet check. If you made it through fifth grade math you could handle this. This is not difficult stuff. If you look at the left side of the balance sheet and you see a bunch of cash and you look at the right side and there's no debt, you're over. You know this company. You are not worried about insolvency. The company is strong. That's a check you should always do. But many people aren't willing to do that. And if they are not willing to do the work, they are not going to be very good investors. I mean, stocks are not lottery tickets. There is a company behind every stock. And if you are not willing to follow the company, I don't think you should be investing on your own.

Griffeth: Is it fair, then, to say that the mutual fund is for the lazy investor?

Lynch: Well, there are some people who are just simply too busy. Or they may have the tendency to only chase after what is hot. You know, the thing of the future right now is biotechnology. Five years ago the thing of the future was disc drives, and before that the thing of the future was semiconductors, and before that it was plastics. They read somewhere that this is going to be fast growing and they put money there without first checking it out, and their experience is usually very poor.

In my book *Beating The Street*, I had 40 or 50 pages on mutual fund investing. And I mentioned that in the 1980s, there were something like 6,000 or 8,000 investment clubs. These are people who are not professional investors. They have full time jobs. They are investing relatively small amounts of money. And yet, 62 percent of these investment clubs beat the market in the 1980s. And that's when only 25 percent of professionals beat the market. That put them in the top 20 percent of all professionals.

Why did they do well? First of all, they didn't predict the market, they stayed fully invested. They were fully invested at the bottom, and they were fully invested at the top. But they did well because they stayed invested. Number two, they bought companies. During their meetings, they would stand in front of their peers and talk about these companies. They did some research, and they beat the market.

When the public buys a refrigerator or an automobile, or when they buy a round trip air ticket to Europe they do some work. Yet, they'll put $20,000 in some stock they don't know a thing about in 12 minutes and wonder why they do poorly. That doesn't happen in these investment clubs.

Remember 1990? Here was a classic period. To me 1990 was much scarier than 1987. In 1990 you had the banking system very shaky, I'm talking seriously shaky. You had a full-scale recession, people's friends were being laid off, their spouses might have been laid off. Business was poor.

You'd call the company and they would say, "Our business has really slowed down." We were sending 500,000 troops to the Middle East, and we were about to fight the fourth largest army in the world according to the newspaper. The market had a big correction, went from like 3,000 to what 2,200, 2,300 [on the Dow Jones Industrial Average]. Is that the point in time when people cash in their chips, or do they say, "Now's the time to buy more." That was a much scarier period than 1987. In

1987 the market dropped real fast and stocks went from 50 to 30, but the companies didn't change. You'd call a company and they would say, "Business is terrific." You weren't worried about a major war, or you weren't worried about Citicorp or Chase or Manufacturers Hanover closing its doors. There were very serious people [in 1990] saying that this or that bank was going to go under over the weekend. I know people who are not radicals or crazies who took $10,000 out in cash and put it in a drawer at home.

Griffeth: I remember.

Lynch: It was a scary period.

Griffeth: Yes, I had the same experience with some people.

Lynch: So what does the public do in an environment like that? Is that the time when they tend to go to the bank and take half their life savings and buy mutual funds? Probably not. They tend to do it when they read on the cover of *Time* magazine about a major bull market. When the economy is doing well and everybody is doing well. The people who have timed the market by reading the newspaper haven't had a good performance.

How to Choose a Mutual Fund

Griffeth: What exactly do investors need to know about a particular fund—and about its manager before they invest?

Lynch: Well, first of all I think they have to know what type of fund they are buying. They should know whether a fund is a capital appreciation fund, or a fund that just buys quality growth stocks, or emerging growth companies. Or is it a fund that only invests in overseas stocks, or does it invest in just emerging markets?

And, by the way, you haven't diversified if you buy nine emerging growth funds. I think people should diversify by discipline where maybe they have a couple of value funds, maybe a couple of emerging growth funds, and they might have a couple of emerging market funds. Or they could buy three index funds. They could buy an index fund of mid cap stocks, they could buy one of the Russell 2000, and they could buy one that just invests in the S&P 500 for larger companies.

Griffeth: And choose funds based on what? Purely on their track record?

Lynch: Well, not only the track record. The first exercise you do is you say, "How do I want to divide my money? I feel very good, I'm very confident about small emerging companies. They're over the hump, they're profitable, they are doing well, and I think over the next 10, 20 years that they should do a lot better than the S&P 500." Then you go out and search for which are the best funds in that category.

Maybe people want to buy a balanced fund that invests some in bonds and some in quality blue chips. Or Putnam, for example, has a fund called Dividend Growth. It just invests in companies that have raised their dividend something like five years in a row.

You can get whatever information you need at the library. You can get it through your broker, or you can get it from *Barron's*, from *Forbes*, from *Money* magazine. You can get it from Morningstar, Lipper, Value Line, there are a lot of services. You can go to your broker and use their Value Line or their Morningstar. They're free.

Choosing a Fund Manager

Griffeth: What you can't get, though, most times is the background of the fund manager. How much do you realistically need to know about the fund manager you are investing with?

Lynch: Well, it's very important if this person is operating out of a small operation, or he is a one-person operator working out of his office in—you name it—Vermont, or Flagstaff, Arizona. That's different than a Jeff Vinik or a Morris Smith or Peter Lynch working at Fidelity with 35 analysts and 20 other portfolio managers. Every one of those 55 individuals are all doing research, all calling companies, you know, in some ways you are investing in this team of people all doing homework, we share ideas. If you are investing in a one-person place, you'd better know a lot about that person.

Griffeth: So, for example, Eric Ryback with Lindner is not exactly a one-man operation, but Ryback Management is certainly smaller than a Fidelity. You're saying I should focus on who Eric Ryback is because of that.

Lynch: And if you notice that he's suddenly gone, he's hit by a truck or whatever, pay attention to who they trot out of that organization to run it.

You know, at Fidelity, besides Magellan, we have this fund called Destiny Fund that's had a brilliant record. We have this fund called Puritan Fund that's had a great record. Equity Income Fund, Equity Fund II. I hate to say we're sort of like the New York Yankees were in the 1920s and 1930s and the Boston Celtics were in the 1960s.

> *". . . we're sort of like the New York Yankees were in the 1920s and 1930s and the Boston Celtics were in the 1960s."*

Griffeth: I agree. But do I need to know as much about the people managing those funds as I need to know about Eric Ryback at Lindner?

Lynch: You need to know much more about the person running the fund pretty much by himself.

At Fidelity we interview like 500 people a year. We narrow it down to something like 20, and we hire like five or six. Last summer we interviewed 500 people to have four summer students. So we hire outstanding people every year, and then we watch them and we give them real jobs. It's not academic. They follow chemicals, they follow the airlines, they follow insurance. So it's not surprising that if you hire five or six outstanding people every year, and if you watch them for two or three years, that you come up with good fund managers. It's not an accident.

"Bottom Down" Investing

Griffeth: Today there are so many different disciplines among fund managers when it comes to choosing stocks. I think of value versus growth, top down versus bottom up. In your first book, *One Up on Wall Street*, you seem to say that this kind of quantifiable methodology really puts managers at a disadvantage.

Lynch: Right. I think the absolute key to making money in the stock market, and this is why individuals can do well, is you've got to just look at companies. I call it bottom down. The heck with this bottom up approach. You just look at companies, and if you look at 10 companies you will find one that is surprisingly good. If you look at 20 you'll find two. If you look at 100 you'll find 10. The person who turns over the most rocks wins the game. That's the essence of research. And you don't have to be a professional to do it.

And the advantage individuals have is that they work in the paper industry, they're an automobile dealer. Let's say you're a Buick dealer or a Honda dealer or whatever. If you saw Chrysler bringing out the minivan and then you saw Chrysler with the Jeep and you saw people packing into the showroom, and you could look to see that they had lots of cash, you could make ten times on your money if you invested. If you worked in that industry you were a fool not to invest in Chrysler.

Then you could have seen Ford bring out the Taurus/Sable. When they brought the Taurus/Sable it was a big hit. You made over six or seven times your money in Ford. So maybe once or twice every decade an auto dealer ought to be able to make a lot of money. Over a lifetime, how many times do you need to triple your money to get a lot of money?

What if you are in retailing? You would have seen Blockbuster, you would have seen Toys R Us, you would have seen The Limited. Ten years after Wal-Mart went public you could have bought the stock and still made 30 times your money.

And then there are some companies that become mature like a Sears or a JC Penney or a Tandy. Those are great growth companies, but eventually there were 6,000 Radio Shacks in every city. Then they had to do something different. In fact, those are now turnarounds. (I happen to like Sears and Tandy now as turnarounds.) But clearly, when Sears had a store in every single market and there were 17 Radio Shacks in every market you had to say, "Where can they go?"

There are thousands and thousands of companies and there are some you are going to know a lot more about, you could lecture on them. And you don't need to have an MBA or an accounting degree. And that's where people should be investing, rather than in Microsoft if they don't know anything about software. The tendency is to forget there is a company behind every stock. These are not lottery tickets.

So that's what people can do. They see a trend way before the so-called professional does. The pros are out buying biotechnology stocks or offshore oil drilling stocks they know nothing about. That's stupid. People have fabulous information, and they don't realize how valuable it is. When a company goes from doing terrible to mediocre to fair to good to excellent, the stock goes up. That's all there is to it. They see that process.

Griffeth: But to be fair to some of the professionals, some of them—with their computers and their number crunching and their top down or their bottom up approaches—have done pretty well.

Lynch: Oh, yes. You can do both things. I'm just saying that individuals are occasionally going to find a really good stock they know something about in their own local company or in their industry.

> ——— ◆ ———
> *"When a company goes from doing terrible to mediocre to fair to good to excellent, the stock goes up. That's all there is to it."*
> ——— ◆ ———

Griffeth: But fund managers have to keep track of, what, 2,000, 3,000 companies.

Lynch: More like 10,000 companies.

Griffeth: Okay . . .

Lynch: There have been 1,200 companies come public in the last two years alone.

Griffeth: So there is less intuition and more numbers crunching then that has to come into play for the professional, right?

Lynch: Well, let's say there are 200 companies that are savings and loans. If you talk to one of them you learn a little about the other 199. You keep popping in, and you talk to one energy service company and they say, "Well, business is really picking up." So you say, "Maybe I ought to look at the other 125 public energy services companies, because business has been terrible for 12 years." So I mean, there aren't 10,000 industries. Maybe there are 150 different industries.

There are people who just use quantitative analysis, and they do fine with their funds. The 20th Century Group, for example, has a good record just using a lot of quantitative stuff. We [Fidelity] had this fund called Stock Selector that Brad Lewis has run. He's had a great record every year, and he is very quantitative-oriented.

I'm not discounting fund managers who use quantitative methods. I think some people have done very well with it. I just think of it [stock selection] as more of a process where if you look at enough stocks, when the day is over and you've found some good ones you'll do fine. You know, you just take stock 106 and sell it and stock 182 and you replace it with the ones you found today. Keep your fund fresh.

Too Many Mutual Funds?

Griffeth: As we speak, Peter, there are more than 5,000 mutual funds out there. Is there room for that many funds in the world?

Lynch: Oh, sure. As a percentage of household assets, if you look at the amount invested in stocks directly and into mutual funds, it is still lower than it was 30 years ago. The public sort of peaked in the mid-1960s with their direct and indirect exposure to the stock market and then it declined, I think, for almost 20 years. The 1972–1973 bear market was the final capper, and people said, "That's it. I hate stocks." And they tuned out.

◆

"As a percentage of household assets, if you look at the amount invested in stocks directly and into mutual funds, it is still lower than it was 30 years ago."

◆

Also, you had a boom in real estate. Real estate looked a lot more attractive and people were pretty smart when housing was doing better. They said, "It's better to buy a second house or put an addition on my house."

I think people should have money invested in a house, I think that's a good asset. And they should have money invested in common stocks, you know, either directly or through mutual funds. I think those are two ways to invest money, and I think people realize that there is room for both. Recently they have been putting more and more money into the stock market, primarily through mutual funds, not directly. But as a percent of household assets it is nowhere near a record level.

I think people are saying, "Social Security is not going to be the answer for me when I retire," and we've gone from this situation when people didn't have to worry about their pension. It used to be it was a defined benefit. When you retired you either got one half of your last year's salary, or three quarters, and you knew exactly what you were going to get. Now, you have defined contribution plans. And some people have no pension plans. So they really have to say to themselves, "I've got to start saving now." And, of course, the beauty of individual retirement accounts is that they compound tax free. That's a huge plus. The numbers become amazingly large when you don't have to pay taxes for the next 30 years.

Griffeth: But all that new money has obviously caused tremendous competition among fund companies. The big ones are buying the small ones, for example.

Lynch: Yes, and all these brokerage firms are waking up and saying, "Wait a second, we ought to have our own mutual funds," because when you manage mutual funds you don't have to worry about someone calling up to do a trade. It's a nice little business to have these management fees recurring every day, every month. For a long time, the brokerage firms were always selling someone else's product. Now the Merrill Lynches and the Paine Webbers and the Shearsons, and the Smith Barneys you know, the big wire houses, they're building up money management. And they have become a major factor.

And then you have the banks saying, "Wait a second, we should have a line of mutual funds, too." And insurance companies are doing the same thing.

In the old days, the mutual fund industry basically was the mutual funds themselves sold through either brokers or part-time broker-dealers who might have been full-time school teachers with a broker-dealer license.

Now you have brokerage companies that are big time with their own line of mutual funds. You have insurance companies and you have banks. Every financial group now has decided they want to have a product. It's not just the old line Putnams and Fidelities and Dreyfuses. It's a whole broader audience of people with mutual funds.

Are Mutual Funds Dangerous?

Griffeth: There is a book about mutual funds making the rounds right now. The basic premise is that with this kind of growth, and with all the banks and brokerage firms jumping on the bandwagon, it is ultimately unhealthy because of the silly things fund managers do to try to increase their returns just a bit more. The derivatives used to excess by various money market funds in 1993 and 1994 are a good example.

Lynch: It sounds like garbage to me.

Griffeth: But is the industry growing too fast? And isn't that why some funds got themselves into trouble by overleveraging?

Lynch: The problem is, for example, when it comes to what people thought were simple run-of-the-mill income funds, they should have been wondering why they were doing so much better than normal. You know, there had to be some reason. There is no free lunch in the money market area. And the fact that some of these funds had to be bailed out by their parent companies doesn't mean the world is going to end. If a fund does poorly, you get the results every week and people either stop putting new money in or they redeem [their shares]. That's just how it works.

If all fund managers start doing zany things, first of all, there are rules like you can't overleverage. You can only put 5 percent in one stock. You can only put 25 percent in one industry, you can't go on margin. I mean, there are rules to prevent people from going cuckoo. There are a lot of regulations to prevent that.

Griffeth: So mutual funds are not becoming a dangerous place to invest.

Lynch: No. Now, you have to be careful how you define the word dangerous. If the stock market goes down, equity mutual funds are going to go down.

I have always reminded people that when I ran Magellan the fund went up 28 fold in those 13 years. But nine times the market went down in those 13 years, and nine times my fund went down.

I think people think that when the market goes down and their funds go down, there is something wrong. And that is not the case at all.

Griffeth: The excesses I'm talking about, though, have less to do with the way a fund is managed and more to do with the way it is marketed.

Lynch: I would agree with that. If people are buying funds on the basis that over the next two or three years this fund is going to go up 40 percent because the last three years it went up 40 percent, that's crazy. No one knows what the fund is going to do the next two or three years.

So far, we have completed 93 years in this century, and in that time, 50 times the market has declined 10 percent or more. I don't mean we had 50 down years but 50 declines of 10 percent or more. So about once every two years you have a 10 percent decline. Of the 50 declines, 15 have been 25 percent or more. So once every six years the market has a 25 percent decline. And when that happens funds are going to go down. People have to understand that.

Griffeth: Do they, though?

Lynch: I think so. You've seen examples where they understood. We had 1987, we had 1990, we had this year's [1994s] correction. Some funds have done poorly, you know, and yet people haven't taken a walk. There was one day, what year was it, 1991? The market fell 200 points in one day, and the next day the public was in buying. It declined in 1990 and the public didn't cash in. Sure, some people left, but in reality they didn't cash in all their chips. In 1987 the people who were on margin, you know, they got cleaned out. They learned a lesson.

"You Can't Sort of Run a Fund"

Griffeth: Do you miss managing a fund?

Lynch: Oh, yes, oh, yes. I loved every minute of it. I worked for the best company in the world, I got paid extremely well, and we had free coffee. [laughing] And I could call any company in the country, or the world, and I could visit it. No one said, "You can't visit California, you can't visit an electric utility." You know, at Fidelity you have total freedom.

Griffeth: You are still a young man, though. Any chance you'll get back into it?

Lynch: No way. No way. No.

Griffeth: Why?

Lynch: Well, you can't have three kids and a wife and do outside things and still manage a fund. I'm involved in about 10 or 12 different charities. You can't work 85 hours a week and do the charity work, too. When I was managing Magellan, I'd leave for the office at 6:00 A.M. six days a week, and I would travel 12–13 days a month. That doesn't work with a wife and three children. Plus, until I was 30 I was involved in no charities. Zip. So that's what I want to do now.

You can't sort of run a fund. You can't say, "Well, I'll sort of work 40 hours, and I'll just beat the market by 2 or 3 percent." You don't beat the market by 2 or 3 percent by sort of working. You have to break your butt to beat the market by 2 or 3 percent.

Postscript

We have a nightly ritual in the Griffeth household. Before our two children go to bed, my wife and I read a book or two (or three) to them. (I realize that part of the attraction for them is that it delays the time when they actually have to go to bed, but I'm happy to say that they both seem to be genuinely attracted to books.) Like all children, they become attached to one or two favorites that must be read over and over, night after night, until none of us can stand to look at the books again for awhile.

One such book in the summer of 1994, when I was putting *The Mutual Fund Masters* together, was called *Seven Blind Mice* (Philomel Books). It is a wonderfully illustrated book based on the ancient Indian fable about the blind men who converge on an elephant from different sides and argue about what they have stumbled upon. In the case of this particular book, it involves seven blind mice of different colors, each of whom takes a turn trying to identify what they have encountered. The blue mouse, for example, is convinced that the tail he is climbing is nothing but a rope, while the orange mouse—who is clutching the elephant's waving ear—is sure he has discovered a giant fan. And so on.

You, no doubt, see where I am going with this. I am not, however, about to suggest that the money managers in this book are blind. But there is a valid analogy here. It occurred to me more than once, as I listened to each manager discuss his or her investment philosophy in detail, that they were, in fact, describing different parts of the same elephant. And the important thing to remember is none of them would have us believe that they could actually see the whole animal. Instead, their job was simply to successfully identify the part to which they had been assigned.

If there is a single truth to be taken from *The Mutual Fund Masters*, it is that there is no single correct answer when it comes to investing. Success and failure are relative. The mutual fund managers who invest their shareholders' money based on broad economic themes, are just as successful as those who fill their portfolios stock by stock. And the managers who move a portion of their assets to cash when they fear a market decline, generally do just as well as the managers who remain fully invested through bull and bear markets. (I am not suggesting, by the way, that all fund managers consistently make money for their shareholders. The mutual fund business is like any other highly competitive service industry. Those who don't get the job done eventually go out of business.)

◆
> *"My point is, don't try to find the most successful mutual fund that was ever created. It doesn't exist."*
◆

My point is, don't try to find *the most successful mutual fund that was ever created*. It doesn't exist. Some funds may run longer hot streaks than others, but all funds have their periodic dry spells. That is simply a fact of life in the investment world.

The key to successfully investing in mutual funds is first deciding which part of the elephant you are comfortable with, and then finding a fund manager who agrees with you. In other words, buy shares in funds that own the stocks and bonds you would have purchased if you had invested the money yourself. It really is that simple.

Mutual funds are a wonderful way to accumulate capital over time for a variety of purposes. As long as shareholders realize they won't get rich in a hurry investing in mutual funds, and as long as fund managers don't take unnecessary chances with shareholders' capital, the mutual fund industry will have served its purpose.